Praise for *The Long Shot*

'*The Long Shot* is a gripping account of the UK Vaccine Taskforce's response to the pandemic by a remarkable, determined, thoughtful and practical individual who was at the heart of the critical decisions that had to be made. I spoke with her frequently throughout 2020 as we battled logistical headwinds and the media storms in development of the Oxford vaccine and was always better for our chats, absorbing the positive energy that she emanates and benefiting from her wisdom. Her clarity of thought and action in such a dark and turbulent time is a seam running through the book, and I know for certain that her efforts saved many lives. But I have to disagree with the title, because the book shows that it really wasn't such a "long shot" with Kate at the helm.'

Professor Sir Andrew Pollard,
Director of the Oxford Vaccine Group
at the University of Oxford

'Fast-paced and very compelling… The Vaccine Taskforce will always be remembered as British science at its very best.'

Sir Jonathan Symonds,
Chairman of GSK

'An excellent read…capturing the exceptional pace and energy of everyone involved in discovering and producing effective therapies against Covid-19. All in all, this is a book I will treasure.'

Sir Mene Pangalos,
Executive Vice President of AstraZeneca

The Long Shot

The Inside Story of the Race
to Vaccinate Britain

KATE BINGHAM
AND TIM HAMES

ONEWORLD

A Oneworld Book

First published in Great Britain, the Republic of Ireland and
Australia by Oneworld Publications, 2022
Reprinted twice 2022

ISBN 978-0-86154-564-3
eISBN 978-0-86154-565-0

Typeset by Geethik Technologies
Printed and bound in Great Britain by Clays Ltd, Elcograf S.p.A.

Oneworld Publications
10 Bloomsbury Street
London WC1B 3SR
England

Stay up to date with the latest books,
special offers, and exclusive content from
Oneworld with our newsletter

Sign up on our website
oneworld-publications.com

Kate would like to dedicate this book to Jesse for his constant encouragement and love.

Tim would like to dedicate this book to Julia for exactly the same reasons.

To Ian Armitage for the original idea for this book and his inspirational backing for it throughout.

The proceeds from this book are being divided equally between two fantastic charitable institutions.

Kate has chosen the New Model Institute for Technology and Engineering (NMITE) in Hereford. This new university breaks the mould of current engineering higher education with a curriculum that places its emphasis on learning by doing and working in teams. It also has a real focus on women.

Tim has selected Kindred², a charitable foundation that concentrates on advocacy, education and development in the very earliest years of life.

CONTENTS

AUTHORS' NOTE

This is a volume with two authors but one voice. It has been a joint enterprise throughout, which started when Tim was encouraged to write a book about the Vaccine Taskforce and he asked Kate whether she would be willing to co-operate with him. We are equally responsible for the content. We did, though, have to make a decision about whether it should be written in the first-person or the third-person. As so much of this story is about what Kate thought, observed and did, it seemed to make sense to write the words with her as the sole narrator. We hope that you the reader will agree.

Kate Bingham and Tim Hames

PROLOGUE

Early May 2020. Over the previous few months, a lethal new coronavirus had leapt beyond its original Chinese borders. In the course of an ever-more-anxious March, the disease had pushed British hospitals to breaking point and swept through care homes. The whole country now languished in lockdown. So, like everyone who could, I ran all my work from home, in my case a cottage near Hay-on-Wye.

That afternoon I faced a diary clash. Two online meetings, both compulsory, both running at exactly the same time. One meeting involved my proper job: the one I was paid to do. I work in biotech venture capital, a real-world version of the TV show *Dragons' Den*. Investors trust me and my team with their money, which we then deploy to build up the most promising biotech companies we can find. If those companies do well, and if their new drugs work, then all of those involved – including, vitally, the patients – do well too.

But I'd also been roped into something else.

Years ago, I'd worked with Sir Patrick Vallance when he led the Research and Development team at GlaxoSmithKline, a behemoth of a pharmaceutical company. He and I had worked to set up biotech companies to create new drugs for pain, hearing loss and dementia. Patrick was now the Government Chief Scientific

Adviser and, in response to the pandemic, had set up a Vaccine Taskforce, or VTF. He had been catapulted from relative anonymity and was now never off the nation's screens.

Patrick wanted the VTF to be supported by an 'Expert Advisory Group', and duly assembled impressive figures from the worlds of science and pharmaceuticals. But still it lacked someone with an in-depth knowledge of the smaller but intensely innovative biotech sector. Patrick asked me to help supply just that biotech perspective, and I'd jumped on board. That May afternoon, our Advisory Group was due another regular catch-up.

One afternoon. Two meetings at the same time. Both essential.

There's no good way to manage these things. I had two computer screens set up – in my son's bedroom, now my office – and switched headsets from one to the other, doing a poor job in each meeting.

As I was performing this impossible juggling act, in came a text message from Matt Hancock, the Health Secretary: 'Can we talk?' Somewhat grumpily, I reminded him that I was in a meeting – the Expert Advisory Group one – that he was meant to be in himself. If he wanted to talk, he could do it there, or immediately afterwards.

As soon as everyone clicked 'leave', Matt called.

'Kate, the Prime Minister would like you to accept the position of VTF Chair. What do you think?'

What did I think?!

I thought: after thirty years in the industry I've come to know a hell of a lot about biotech and drug discovery and development. But very little about vaccines.

I thought: I already have a job. One I like and am good at. It's also a job that makes a real contribution to the world.

I thought: investors and team members rely on me. I can't just stroll away from existing commitments. I face urgent duties elsewhere – ones I'm contractually obliged to deliver.

I thought: I have a husband and family. Any deeper into the world of the pandemic and my life will be swallowed up. Did I really want that?

And also: I knew that, to put it brutally simply, vaccines *mostly don't work*. Drug and vaccine discovery is hard in all circumstances. But drug discovery at breakneck speed for a never-before-seen virus amid an international crisis? Was this asking the impossible? And something I *did* know about viruses: they mutate. Although scientists had already started developing early vaccines, it was perfectly plausible that those vaccines, by the time they were ready, would prove impotent against newly emerging strains of Covid.

I felt I was being asked to take responsibility for a huge amount of government expenditure that would, most likely, prove completely wasted. The longest of all long shots.

Once I got off the call I swore so loudly and insistently that my husband Jesse and daughter Nell came running to see what was wrong.

On the phone I'd told Matt that I'd think about it, that I needed twenty-four hours, but I was already heading in one direction. Yes, it was an interesting idea. Also, of course, it was flattering. But although the country certainly needed a Vaccine Taskforce, surely I wasn't the right person to lead it. I was already thinking how to refuse gracefully. I was rehearsing how to say 'No'.

But what tragedy was unfolding? It was the crisis that had changed all of our lives. It had emerged from nowhere and spread everywhere. Infections and deaths were mounting inexorably. The pandemic had ruptured economic activity more than any recession. It had triggered restrictions on personal freedom that would once have been unimaginable. It placed the Prime Minister himself on the edge of his life in an intensive care unit.

On that sunny May afternoon, the disease did not look easy to kill, or even tame.

I didn't refuse. I took the job.

What followed was an incredible seven months, a roller coaster from joy to sorrow, anxiety to relief and back again, as we fought the disease and the grim timetable of Covid deaths and sickness. I saw how some people and some institutions rose to extraordinary heights in that battle. I saw extraordinary scientists, extraordinary dedication and, in some cases, rapid and imaginative responses to new challenges. But I also saw how some institutions failed the test, did not reform, caried on a blinkered 'business as usual' approach, as the world around them was stricken by disaster.

I'm a practical person. A scientist and a businesswoman. I'm interested in outcomes, not processes, and I call things as I see them.

This is that story.

1

TASKFORCE WANTED

'This pandemic won't go far beyond China. And by the summer we will have forgotten all about it – it will be a self-limiting disease just like SARS and MERS.'

It was Saturday 11 January 2020. I had just flown twelve hours into San Francisco to attend an annual healthcare investor conference and was feeling knackered. As so often in that city, it was gloomy and rainy, torrential storms forecast. I had brought extra shoes so I had dry ones to change into, as well as a big raincoat – umbrellas aren't my thing. I dumped my bags in the bland beige and white Hyatt hotel room.

Exercise is the best way to get adjusted to a new time zone, and I had pre-booked a 5 p.m. spinning class at SoulCycle. After all, you can't go to sleep on a spin bike. So I changed, grabbed my water bottle and ran down the street to the class, trying to forget it was one o'clock in the morning back home.

The changing room chat afterwards was all about an unknown respiratory virus causing pneumonia in Wuhan. No one felt especially troubled by the early reports. Many so-called experts said they had seen it all before. Their view was that most viruses like this, despite devastating consequences locally, fizzled out before they caused any major problems in the West.

That complacency would come back to bite us all. In fact, plenty of warning shots had been fired over the past two decades. SARS, or Severe Acute Respiratory Syndrome, caused a minor pandemic in 2002–3. That coronavirus originated in China and killed 744 people across five countries before it was contained – causing death in ten per cent of those infected. A bird flu called H5N1, related to the 1918–19 flu pandemic, was identified in Vietnam in 2005. This novel virus killed about sixty per cent of those infected but was contained by global culling and stricter management of poultry farms. Swine flu followed, then came Middle East Respiratory Syndrome (MERS) and of course Ebola. But none of these outbreaks was widespread. Human to human transmission was limited. The idea of a global public health crisis remained the stuff of apocalyptic fiction.

Very few people had any sense at that time of what might be about to happen. Insufficient caution bordered on institutional complacency. The UK's pandemic plans turned out to be based on a false premise. Around the world, governments had treated a global pandemic as no more than a theoretical possibility, highly unlikely ever to happen.

By spring 2022, internationally, there had been more than 470 million infections with over 6 million deaths (while total excess mortality exceeded 21 million by one estimate). And even as I write, the pandemic is still rampant in many countries, especially the very poorest which have been unable to buy and distribute vaccines to protect their populations.

As a result, society had to endure an unparalleled transformation. Individual liberties were sacrificed in wave after wave of lockdowns and other forms of restrictions. Unprecedented measures were imposed to fight the spread of the new coronavirus. Economies were shuttered. Schools closed. Hospitals, care homes and NHS staff reached breaking point under the strain of events. Pop-up 'battle-field' hospitals were built to absorb the overflow of patients. The most vulnerable had to shield indoors, hiding themselves away from family and friends.

In the UK, thousands of elderly hospital patients with Covid-19 were discharged into care homes with catastrophic consequences.

Newspaper headlines stated bluntly 'Life Put on Hold'.

The Prime Minister, Boris Johnson, said normal life would stop for up to a year, as that was the only way to save a quarter of a million lives. There didn't seem to be any way out. Once the virus really took hold, there was no strategy in place to resist.

In time it would become clear that mass vaccination was the only credible solution, but no vaccines then existed. In the first days of 2020, no one could imagine the challenges we would face.

★

The early weeks of each year have a familiar pattern for me, my senior colleagues at work and our sector. Every year tens of thousands of healthcare specialists, including the team at my venture capital firm, SV Health Investors or just 'SV', make an annual pilgrimage to California. In my venture capital world, it's the moment to meet the latest hot biotech companies, pharmaceutical giants, investors, entrepreneurs, scientists, clinicians and other venture capitalists. We wanted to invest in promising new technologies and build exciting new businesses. We wanted to sell. We met in hotel bedrooms converted into tiny meeting rooms to hear the latest pitch. We crammed into ballrooms for presentations. Everyone was doing deals.

My job is to make money for my backers by investing in the most successful high-growth biotech companies. I spend my time finding or building ambitious teams who are developing great science and then I'll invest in their companies to help develop life-saving medicines. By investing and building new businesses, I want to get those medicines safely and securely approved and get them out to doctors to transform the lives of patients.

Years ago, when my children were starting to take an interest in what I actually did, they thought at first that I made drugs in a lab. Although it was obviously much more glamorous to be the inventive scientist who discovers magic cures for deadly diseases, I had to admit that my job was more prosaic. My work did not involve wearing a white coat and filling test tubes, but rather investing money in others to discover and develop new drugs. They were astonished to hear that over ninety per cent of drugs that enter clinical trials will fail.

'So why do something so risky?' they asked.

Developing new drugs is not for the faint-hearted. However, on those rare occasions when the drugs work, no achievement can compare. We provide hope where previously there had been none.

The San Francisco conference was the craziest week of the year. I had been coming for nearly thirty years and every year it grew more manic. On 11 January 2020, the day China released Covid-19's genetic sequence to the WHO, my day as usual started with 6 a.m. meetings. I was so crammed all day and through dinner – with endless discussions about drugs, patients and new companies with sparkling technologies – that I didn't pay attention to the reports of the unknown 'pneumonia'. This was the week to get out and hustle.

Even SoulCycle doesn't start before 6 a.m., so in order to stay sane I would get up at 4 a.m. – 12 noon UK time – to go running round the extremely steep streets of Nob Hill in the dark. Podcasts were my friend.

I had no inkling that my year would be entirely dominated by the need to combat a coronavirus causing severe acute respiratory disease in Asia.

★

Back home in the UK, a degree of professional indifference prevailed. It took the better part of the first ten weeks or so of 2020 for scientists and then policymakers to appreciate the sheer enormity of what loomed over the horizon. The coming storm took a long time to recognise. Virtually nobody in government saw the danger quickly or recognised that the entire world was about to be upended by a public health emergency without parallel in a century. But there was one person who did.

That was Sir Patrick Vallance, whose actions in early 2020 would prove critical. No one had developed a successful vaccine for a coronavirus before, but Patrick was determined that we would do it now. We all knew the odds – history is littered with failed vaccines and long-drawn-out clinical trials – but we had to try. And we had to do things differently.

Without Patrick, there would have been no Vaccine Taskforce. But it took him a while to find the right model.

Patrick had a distinguished career before entering government service. He had grown up in Cornwall and had come to the capital as a teenager to study medicine at St George's, within the University of London, for his Bachelor of Science, followed by a Bachelor of Medicine and Doctorate of Medicine.

He taught at St George's Hospital Medical School between 1986 and 1995. After that, and at a relatively young age, he became a professor at UCL Medical School, adding the title and responsibilities of Head of Medicine in 2002. He was an instinctive reformer with an interest in how medicine was delivered as well as how it was developed. In a piece entitled 'A post-take ward round' for the *Journal of the Royal Society of Medicine* in 2005, he asserted that the 'reinvention of doctors, nurses, therapists and social workers seems like an important task in medicine.' Almost twenty years later, it still is.

Patrick was set to reach the very highest peaks of academic medicine. In 2006, however, to the surprise of his colleagues and contemporaries – and quite possibly himself – he agreed to leave the ivory tower for the very different challenge of becoming Head of Drug Discovery at GlaxoSmithKline (GSK). He had moved to a huge corporate institution and the heart of the pharmaceutical industry itself. By 2010 his role had expanded: now he was Head of Drug

Discovery and Development. In 2012 he was settled in place as Head of Research and Development.

I had first met Patrick at the fancy GSK HQ in Brentford in 2006. I was keen that he should be up to speed on the range of companies we were building at SV, with the hope that GSK might be interested in partnering with our little biotech firms or even buying these new companies and their novel medicines. Given that two-thirds of all diseases are either not treated adequately or not treated at all, we started to speak regularly about GSK's priorities. We would share views on where we saw the next breakthroughs in science and medicine to help patients live longer, better lives.

A couple of years later, Patrick was developing his vision for increased entrepreneurialism in drug discovery at GSK. He turned to venture capital for lessons on risk-taking investment and management in biotech drug discovery. I got the call.

As I biked over to GSK's London offices in Berkeley Square, I wondered whether Patrick was really serious about change and whether I could help.

I tend to arrive at work meetings a bit early so I can cool down from my ride and swap my fleece for a proper work jacket. But Patrick was down in a flash when I entered the lobby.

'I'm so pleased you came. I want you to help drive this change in pharma mindset in R&D [research and development] to be more nimble, like biotech. Come up to my office and we can chat before we start.'

Patrick's office was at least two floors up a grand staircase. Far from cooling down, I got hotter. The meeting was excellent. GSK scientists had designed some incredibly clever experiments to create models of diseases in the lab so they could test their new precision medicine approaches. I was dead impressed by recent data for their new way to treat severe autoimmune diseases. With most new drugs failing, we discussed how to manage risks and losses.

In 2010 GSK announced it was abandoning some areas of neuroscience research to cut costs and improve research productivity. I called Patrick to see whether there were any opportunities for SV to set up and finance new spin-out companies based on GSK neuroscience teams and assets. There were. We created and funded two companies to treat pain, age-related hearing loss, schizophrenia and epilepsy.

With Patrick's support, GSK was one of six major pharmaceutical investors in the Dementia Discovery Fund. This fund exists to finance new medicines to treat, delay and even cure Alzheimer's disease and other forms of dementia. SV was appointed fund manager as part of a competitive process.

All this meant Patrick was well acquainted with my work at SV in creating new companies, building teams and developing ambitious pipelines of novel medicines.

Patrick's time at GSK was fundamental to the vaccination approach that the UK Government took as the Covid-19 crisis exploded. His experience gave him an understanding of how pharmaceutical companies work and taught him to be sensitive both to their strengths and weaknesses. He was well known for his advocacy of open innovation. Patrick understood how the best results often came when university research, biotech and pharmaceutical corporations worked co-operatively.

Patrick could easily have remained at the helm of GSK's R&D work and ensured himself an unusually comfortable retirement. He did not do so. More than a decade at GSK turned out to be a prelude to the most astonishing period of his career and, perhaps, his life. Not that this was obvious when he put his name forward to be Government Chief Scientific Adviser (GCSA) in 2017 and chose to take a substantial salary cut.

The GCSA has a splendid title and serves as the personal adviser on science and technology to the Prime Minister and the Cabinet. Of late, the GCSA also chairs the Scientific Advisory Group on Emergencies, or SAGE; that acronym moved from near-obscurity to almost universal name recognition in 2020.

The position might sound grand, but the reality was that Sir Patrick (as he became in the New Year's Honours List 2019) had no managerial control over the many other chief scientific advisers in Whitehall, had a minimal budget and was obliged to rely on persuasion, not power, to exercise authority. In his new position, he became close friends and allies with Professor Chris Whitty, the Chief Medical Officer for England.

Neither man anticipated what was about to hit them in January 2020. Nor did SAGE members.

SAGE is a surprising entity in many respects. It is not a standing committee within Whitehall. It meets only infrequently, responding to events. It had been called into action once in 2014 (because of the Ebola outbreak), once in 2015 (triggered by the severe Nepal earthquake) and again in 2016 (in response to the Zika outbreak).

The sole example before 2020 of SAGE meeting on a domestic matter occurred in the form of a short teleconference held on 6 August 2019. After days of heavy rain, the dam wall supporting the Toddbrook Reservoir was damaged, threatening homes in Whaley Bridge, Derbyshire. SAGE had to determine at what point it would be safe for local residents to return to their homes. This was the first time that Patrick found himself exercising this part of his GCSA responsibilities.

Both SAGE and its subcommittees would meet many, many times in the early weeks of the pandemic. They seemed to have an excessively large and unwieldy number of members – over eighty at one count. The identity of the members and meeting minutes were initially kept confidential, which meant it was difficult for the public to know who was providing the expert advice to government, and key policy decisions remained opaque.

Responding to the pandemic: the early days

Alarm bells were ringing ever more loudly and urgently in the expert community. The first time I saw evidence of a UK vaccination strategy – even before any Covid-19 cases were recorded in the

UK – was in a memo of a non-SAGE meeting run by Patrick on 27 January 2020. As Chair, Patrick raised the issue of vaccination with Chris Whitty, Jonathan Van-Tam and Jenny Harries, figures then unknown to the public, on what they would do as the virus spread from China. This brainstorming recommended that the UK had to prepare not merely for the arrival of a few cases but potentially for high levels of sickness and death.

Patrick drove the discussion to consider options for vaccination. He was expecting to be formally asked for his assessment on this by Matt Hancock, then Secretary of State for Health and Social Care at the Department of Health, who was rapidly coming to terms with what might be the worst-case scenario. Hancock's department was quickly revising its existing pandemic plans, which had been based on influenza. It was also deciding what emergency legislation might be required. An early political decision had to be made on the weight to be placed on vaccination.

Patrick was clear that developing effective vaccines might be the only means of containing the virus. Vaccines were likely to be the best and most practical way to build protective population immunity to limit the death toll and minimise severe disease. He knew it was important not to overestimate what could be delivered. There was no chance at all that a vaccine could be found in time for the expected peak of the epidemic, estimated at about three months from the outbreak beginning to take hold. And worse still, it was possible that the virus could become endemic globally – and we would not replicate the successes of containing SARS and MERS.

With his long-standing interest and expertise in vaccine technology, Patrick could be more visionary than others. In his early months in the post, he had stopped Whitehall from making an expensive investment in old-style vaccine development involving literally millions of reconstituted chicken eggs – the historic and slow means by which viruses were grown to be turned into vaccines. Instead, he pushed Whitehall to explore more modern vaccine manufacturing options.

Patrick recognised that novel messenger RNA (mRNA) technology could be the fastest way to develop a pandemic vaccine, even though this approach was unproven and the UK had no mRNA manufacturing capacity. He thought it was worth considering an investment in UK mRNA production facilities as the cost could be relatively low and this capability could be important for long-term resilience.

In January 2020, Patrick wanted to engage with those working in experimental vaccine fields and issue a rapid open call to fund new solutions, so as to embrace all vaccine approaches. These vaccine applications would be quickly peer-reviewed and funded. He also recommended starting immediate conversations with the Medicines and Healthcare products Regulatory Agency (MHRA), about how to accelerate the assessment of new vaccines.

Exactly how this would all occur was, understandably, still somewhat sketchy. Insofar as there was institutional 'ownership' of the initiative at this time, it lay inside the Department of Health. Patrick's primary concern was that various critical institutions – the National Institute for Health and Care Research (NIHR – in effect the research arm of the NHS), UK Research and Innovation (the main government research funding body) and the Wellcome Trust (the largest non-government backer of scientific research in the UK) – were 'joined up' and that funding for new vaccines would not fall through the cracks or lose out if attention was diverted elsewhere.

His concerns increased as January turned into February and the data made clear that the virus was spreading exponentially. Those concerns grew stronger as February became March. All the data indicated that the virus was already likely to be in the UK, and at a substantial if unquantified magnitude.

Patrick kept asking officials in the Department of Health what was happening with vaccine policy. Despite their assurances that 'they were on it' and all was well, Patrick noted: 'I was not convinced by the answers that I was getting. We weren't dealing with annual flu infections but something far more serious.'

The blunt truth was that the Department of Health's expertise and plans in the vaccine field were too narrow and constrained. Their influenza models offered little insight into the consequences of asymptomatic transmission with a virus about which we knew very little. A more contagious and more lethal disease hadn't been contemplated.

Worse, Patrick was far from confident that the necessary technical knowledge existed within government to identify and assess new vaccines and formats. While senior officials had outside experts for scientific and clinical advice, they did not have equivalent advisers for pharmaceutical manufacturing and distribution.

His time at GSK had taught him that discovery of a new drug or vaccine was only the very first step in an enormously challenging process that ultimately demanded large-scale clinical trials, complex scale-up and bulk manufacture, plus a robust distribution network to ensure prompt delivery.

The birth of the VTF

Patrick started to take a more focused and personal interest in securing potentially life-saving vaccines. He pressed the Prime Minister on the creation of a dedicated capability to focus on vaccine procurement, development and manufacture. The PM was excited but careful not to demonstrate this publicly. Patrick became convinced that vaccine preparatory work needed to be liberated from the Department of Health, which was massively overstretched on issues ranging from PPE (personal protective equipment) shortages to insufficient testing. Dominic Cummings, the Prime Minister's controversial advisor, would later condemn the Department of Health in early 2020 as a 'smoking ruin'. Although a figure prone to dramatic description, he was not necessarily mistaken in this case.

Where could the vaccines effort be embedded instead? Nothing would happen without a department to act as host. Fate intervened.

For historical reasons, the Prime Minister and Cabinet are the primary 'employer' of the Government Chief Scientific Adviser. However, the position is actually paid for by the Department for Business, Energy and Industrial Strategy (BEIS). This meant that Patrick had an institutional set of ties with civil servants in that corner of Whitehall. Patrick used BEIS as the base in which to establish a nascent Vaccine Taskforce, or VTF.

But he needed an imaginative figure who could create a new unit. Someone who could shake the trees in BEIS and help set up the VTF. He asked a very punchy BEIS civil servant, Alexandra (Alex) Jones, to start by finding a team of officials dedicated to vaccine procurement and manufacturing within Whitehall.

By chance, I had worked with Alex and John Kingman, the first Chair of UKRI, the government body that provides funding for UK research and innovation, in 2019. We were interviewing new non-executive directors for UKRI and I had spent a day with them both in a glass room overlooking the Thames. I remember that Alex arrived very promptly and brought the meeting to order in her no-nonsense manner. Although our nominees were never in fact appointed, Alex was quick to respond to my evening emails explaining how she was managing the process and the challenges she was facing. I could see why Patrick asked her to lead this initiative.

By March 2020 a small internal Covid-19 vaccine team was coming together. But Alex's tiny band of officials had little expertise in the pharmaceutical industry or knowledge of recent advances in vaccine development. On their own, they were unlikely to slay the Covid-19 Leviathan. They would need skills that lay beyond the confines of Whitehall.

Wanted: vaccine experts

The next move by Patrick was to secure a VTF External Advisory Board to assist him and the small team in BEIS. He wanted a combination of people of deep expertise and experience from industry, academia, regulators and the funders of medical research. Its terms of reference made a bold statement of intent:

> The key objective of the Vaccines Taskforce as set out in the spec-
> ification is: The UK must be in a position to vaccinate the right
> proportion of the population as soon as possible after a vaccine is
> available. To the extent it is complementary to that primary objec-
> tive, we must ensure longer-term UK vaccine capability and capac-
> ity for clinical and industrial benefit.

Such was the obvious urgency of the situation, combined with Patrick's wide array of contacts, that he had no trouble assembling a great group of people willing to give their time to the Vaccine Taskforce External Advisory Board, with himself as Chair.

The names were highly impressive. They included the Oxford duo of Sarah Gilbert, Professor of Vaccinology at the Jenner Institute and Nuffield Department of Clinical Medicine, and Andrew Pollard, Professor of Paediatric Infection and Immunity at Oxford. Professor Robin Shattock, Head of Mucosal Infection and Immunity at the Department of Medicine, Imperial College, London, also had a seat at the table. So did luminaries such as Sir Jeremy Farrar, Director of the Wellcome Trust, Richard Hatchett, Chief Executive at the Coalition for Epidemic Preparedness Innovations (CEPI), Sir John Bell, UK Life Sciences Champion appointed by the Prime Minister and Regius Professor at Oxford University, and June Raine, Chief Executive at the Medicines and Healthcare products Regulatory Agency (MHRA).

In the world of science and medicine this was a rock-star list. But no less important, as it proved, were the less celebrated experts brought in to offer industrial perspectives and expertise. Sir Mene Pangalos, Executive Vice President of BioPharmaceuticals R&D at AstraZeneca, came with decades of experience in drug and anti-body discovery and development. Ian McCubbin was, in effect, the acting representative of the BioIndustry Association and could provide an independent view on manufacturing. Jeff Almond, eminent microbiologist and former Vice President of Global Research and External R&D for Sanofi Pasteur, brought specific expertise from leading thirty vaccine projects in industry.

All in all, it was a formidable army. What wasn't clear was how to deploy it.

To give a proper sense of what happened, I will describe the different elements relating to setting up the VTF and our work, but not always chronologically. So bear with me as I dig into each section.

2

AN EMAIL, A TEXT
AND A CALL

1 April 2020 – I was sitting at home in the Marches trying to hammer out emails and worrying about whether my pea seeds were being munched by mice. About midday another email popped up.

Alex Jones was asking me to be a member of Patrick Vallance's new Vaccine Taskforce – or the Vaccine Taskforce Expert Advisory Group to give it its full name. I was bemused. I knew Patrick well and respected him – but me? A 'vaccine expert'? What was he thinking? I have built companies developing medicines that cure people, but not drugs that stopped them from getting infected. Compared to the specialists, I knew nothing about prophylactic vaccines, as Patrick must have known perfectly well.

I called to check if this was an April Fool's prank.

I can't sit still when I'm on the phone, so I went out into the garden. I couldn't reach Patrick so spoke to Alex instead, stomping up and down. She told me they wanted knowledge and connections in the biotech sector since much innovation happened outside the mainstream pharmaceutical industry.

That half-hour changed my life.

Despite his galaxy of stars, it didn't take Patrick long to become concerned that he still did not have the institutional architecture required for his very ambitious agenda.

One problem was the large knowledge gap between the experts and the recently recruited civil servants. Conversations were frustrating. He was wasting a lot of time educating Whitehall on the basics.

Ian McCubbin, our manufacturing guru from GSK, noted in my first meeting 'we urgently needed to fit-out existing UK GMP clean rooms for drug substance and secure dedicated fill and finish capabilities to accelerate vaccine manufacturing.'

'GMP clean rooms; fill finish'? There was a lot of language that Whitehall didn't recognise. We spent more time explaining the acronyms and topics, like the breadth of safety standards demanded by the regulator, than we did figuring out how to actually secure and make the vaccines.

I was expecting to see elements of *Yes Minister* in these meetings, but there was no lack of intent, hard work or seriousness. Just lack of relevant skills.

Another weakness was that the Advisory Board was meeting only for an hour every other week. This seemed nuts to me – what can experts achieve in so little time? The bulk of these meetings were spent getting updates from Oxford University and Imperial College. I found it frustrating to have so little chance to develop broader plans to procure and develop vaccines. Yet more frequent deliberations would mean asking esteemed scientists, who were actively attempting to identify a vaccine, to stop working in their laboratories to educate officials on what they were doing.

There was also potential for tension and conflicts of interest. Oxford and Imperial College were developing different sorts of vaccines, both competing for government funding and attention. So the two teams felt obliged to make the best possible case for their own vaccine candidates. The scientists concerned could not always be as candid with the whole Advisory Board as might have been ideal in the circumstances.

In late April, I was surprised to read in the press that Oxford University had struck a non-profit vaccine partnership with AstraZeneca. I'd had no forewarning. I went back to the notes I had taken and wondered if I'd nodded off at the first meeting. But I'm sure we had not discussed this at the External Advisory Board. While this might reflect the pace of that alliance coming into place, it made me worry: if the advisers were being held at such arm's length from the real action, we could have no impact.

Public launch of the Whitehall-led VTF

Downing Street held a press conference fronted by Alok Sharma, the Business Secretary, on 17 April 2020. The announcement was full of official-ese: 'A new Vaccine Taskforce will drive forward, expedite and co-ordinate efforts to research and then produce a coronavirus vaccine and make sure one is made available to the public as quickly as possible.'

He announced the funding of twenty-one new research projects for treatments and vaccines and pledged to place the UK at the forefront of the international effort to fight the virus. It was, entirely intentionally, a strong news story.

As a holding device, Alok said the new institution would be led by Government Chief Scientific Adviser Sir Patrick Vallance and Deputy Chief Medical Officer for England, Jonathan Van-Tam (known universally as JVT).

Yet even at that time both Patrick and Jonathan had concluded that a new full-time individual was needed.

Fortunately for Alok, no one in the press conference decided to push him on what the executive leadership for his newly-announced organisation would really look like and how quickly it would be set up. Which were two very big unanswered questions.

To me, the balance between academic and industrial expertise for the Vaccine Taskforce did not feel optimal. I thought a lot about how to improve it. I would often use my exercise outside to think, whether on a mountain bike, a horse, or even just running on the hill.

I was concerned that, despite all these good intentions and stellar people, we did not have the right VTF model with authority and accountability to secure the vaccines we so badly needed. In the pandemic, with people dying every day, we didn't have time to get it wrong and pick vaccines that wouldn't work or wouldn't get delivered quickly. We had to do this properly from the get-go.

After my second hour-long Advisory meeting and a few thinking jaunts on the hill, I emailed Patrick on 25 April:

I want to flag an issue for you and the vaccine task force to consider. We have spent time discussing the scale-up, CMC, fill/finish etc of vaccine supply which is critical for our national vaccine strategy. The group of experts that the BIA has assembled with the leadership of Ian McCubbin – the coalition of the willing – is impressive and engaged. However, I do not know the process for formalising this group into a robust and durable capability for the UK irrespective of whichever vaccine may prove successful.

Would it make sense to create a central entity, e.g. 'Vaccines UK', owned and funded by the government which is responsible for all contracting and delivery whether adeno, mRNA [i.e. the different type of vaccines] or antibodies? That way we would have a single point of accountability, transparent use of public funds, experienced leadership etc. Vaccines UK would also be responsible for international licensing and deal making which arise from the UK science base so we have a single voice on the global stage.

What we needed was an expert group with the authority to go out to the vaccine and manufacturing companies and sign deals. I didn't need to explain the technical language to Patrick.

Luckily he had come to the same conclusion. He had also recognised that there could and should be a better way to operate.

He knew that the outside experts had to be brought much closer to the civil servants assembled within BEIS. A professional full-time team with a substantial external component rooted in industrial expertise would be more effective – perhaps much more. This team had to have the strongest possible mandate, ideally with a budget of its own, and the ability to make decisions at speed, fully aware that significant sums of public money might end up *not* producing any vaccines.

A VTF Version II had to be dedicated, protected and empowered.

With his current role as GCSA, I did not see how Patrick could be anything other than a part-time, temporary leader. It would be impossible for Patrick to devote the hours necessary to make progress. Dominic Cummings, then a figure of considerable influence in 10 Downing Street, supported the idea of an industry-led VTF. For Cummings, this whole idea had immense appeal; he saw it as part of his wider instincts on the need to shake up UK Government.

Invitation out of the blue

My invitation to chair the VTF arrived in a somewhat surreal manner, during that absurd simultaneous meeting on two computers as described in the prologue.

After I finished my call with Matt and started to calm down, I explained to Jesse and Nell about Matt's call and why this role wasn't for me. Nell rebuffed my excuses immediately. She reminded me that I had berated her for lack of a 'can-do' spirit when she had been struggling to find an internship abroad during her university studies. It was hypocritical of me not to bring the same 'can-do' approach to vaccines.

Compelling stuff, but emotion alone would not carry the day.

It was only after walking with Jesse in the hills, drawing on his experience of government and public service, that my mind began to shift, and some of my considerable concerns appeared more manageable. Matt had asked Jesse for my number beforehand, so he had an early hint about my potential appointment. Jesse told me that this was a national emergency, I would be brilliant for the job and of course I should take the role.

I was slowly becoming convinced I could do it, but I still needed some professional reassurance.

I called experts I knew in the field, including Patrick. I spoke to him while walking on the hill with Jesse. It was clear that he hadn't known until that call that I had been approached to take the reins from him. He was very supportive but sounded surprised by the pace of events; I too was surprised he hadn't been consulted. On other calls on the same walk, Jeremy Farrar and John Bell kindly insisted to me that my reservations were unfounded.

But even if this was persuasive, my colleagues at SV Health Investors, including my brilliant partner Houman Ashrafian, would have to agree if I was to lead this vaccine team for six months. Houman said he could manage everything at SV in my absence – which he duly did. He didn't miss a beat. For those who know him, that wasn't a surprise.

Withdrawing from commitments to SV was especially awkward as we had just raised a new investment fund. I had been named as a 'key person' in the fund, which meant that in theory our investors could suspend the fund if I was absent. It was to their enormous credit that our investors released me from a wide range of duties and didn't use their veto to trigger a fund suspension, but rather supported my taking on this role.

Despite this influx of support, there were still numerous reasons not to accept. Developing new vaccines would be likely to fail. Delivering them within a year felt like a hope against hope. And I didn't feel well qualified.

Ultimately, fully aware of how difficult the task was and knowing that we could easily end up with billions of pounds thrown down the drain, I decided I absolutely had to do it. A vaccine was increasingly likely to be the only reliable long-term route by which Britain and the wider world could be saved from the horrors of deaths and lockdowns. It would be an honour to be involved in the attempt, even if we were not successful. And besides, I had no desire to tell Jesse and Nell that I had turned the job down.

I told Matt Hancock the following day that I was inclined to do it, subject to some firm conditions in an engagement letter, which I had discussed at length with Jesse. These were that I had a clear mandate, a direct reporting line to the PM, would be located within BEIS with rapid decision-making, that I would be able to establish a dedicated budget with timelines, that it was a six-month term of office and that I would sign-off all communications in advance.

Looking back on it, I am not sure that I ever received a reply from Matt. It might have prevented a host of later problems if I had.

How was I selected?

The process that led to my being chosen as the first VTF Chair remains a bit of a mystery to me, even now. It seems as if it was very largely a decision made by the Prime Minister who asked for a list of those involved in the existing VTF External Advisory Board. Apparently when Boris saw my name, he immediately decided I should be asked to do it.

I understand that, separately, there had been a swift Whitehall process where a broader list of names was considered, where industrial experience and diversity of background were reviewed. There was no formal open selection process, which caused some adverse comment, but an open selection process was neither usual nor required for a temporary unpaid (at my request) advisory role such as this.

There was a personal connection, but it wasn't, as speculated, my husband Jesse Norman MP, who, as luck would have it, was then a minister in the Treasury where he was managing the pandemic furlough scheme. My mother's first cousin was married to Rachel

Johnson, Boris's sister, which meant that our paths had crossed on extended family occasions.

On one such occasion about fifteen years ago, Boris and I had a different view of how to spend a chilly summer's day near Largs in Scotland. Boris wanted to watch a rocket being fired, while I wanted to bike to a nearby beach, gather driftwood and cook a fish barbecue on the sand. Even though Boris tried to corral the group to join the amateur rocketeers, I was dead set on my beach barbecue with mackerel we had caught. As it turned out, everyone bar Boris enjoyed a slap-up fish lunch and Boris eventually joined us, bemoaning the fact that it was hard to see rockets in low, thick Scottish cloud. So Boris knew I could be stubborn.

It's rather hard to stretch this into 'friendship'. If this was any evidence of a 'chumocracy', as some suggested at the time and afterwards, then it was an elastic notion of chums.

Speaking to the PM

I headed to London by train on 6 May for a short meeting with Alok Sharma. As I looked across the Severn estuary, I wondered what had I let myself in for. The speed at which the pandemic had arrived and its impact were unreal. And now I had signed up to find vaccines for the UK? What was I thinking?

London lay empty. I changed out of my leggings and put on a skirt and clean shirt to look vaguely presentable. Wearing tights and heels again felt strange. It took no time to bike down to the BEIS offices on Victoria Street, but a lot longer to get into the building itself to meet Alok. The security guards did not recognise his name – after all, he was only the Secretary of State running the department – but after a few phone calls I was collected from the lobby. I was taken aback that Alok was joined by a retinue of advisers, who attended all his meetings. I now know this is normal. No official business is done unwatched in Whitehall.

Alok didn't tell me anything more than Matt had. We needed vaccines and Alok wanted me to speak to him every other day to update him on progress. I wasn't sure that such a frequent reporting schedule would be manageable, but I didn't argue. Predictably enough it turned out that Alok's diary was too busy to accommodate so many calls, so we mostly spoke at weekends.

I did speak regularly to Nadhim Zahawi, who was Parliamentary Under Secretary at BEIS. He was in charge of the life sciences sector, and genuinely committed to providing support wherever possible.

I biked home excited and a bit awed. Waves of text messages flooded in from officials from multiple departments wanting to speak about the VTF strategy and what I was planning to do.

Early that evening, I got the text 'can you speak?' from the PM himself. When we connected he said: 'Kate — I need you to get vaccines to save lives as soon as possible. We can't just shut down the economy. We need vaccines to tackle the invisible mugger and reopen the country and you are the person to do it.'

In a typical Boris way, he told me he wanted to wrestle the coronavirus to the ground. He also said he hoped that the vaccine would 'have a British flag on it'.

He set out three objectives: to secure vaccines for the UK, to ensure vaccines were distributed equitably around the world and to make the UK more resilient for next time. He wanted the UK to be at the forefront of vaccine R&D, manufacturing and supply globally.

I told Boris that developing and manufacturing vaccines rapidly was a massive uphill struggle and that there was a high chance that no vaccine at all would work. I was anxious to manage expectations from the start. Even PPE procurement, which on the face of it was much more straightforward, had faced substantial logistical and procurement challenges. I was willing to give it a good go but made no promises at my end. He would need to provide upfront cash at risk. And I was certainly not making any guarantees about flags.

My appointment would not be publicly announced for another week. This was to allow for what was an impressively intensive process of 'on-boarding', including a forensic examination of anything that might conceivably constitute a conflict of interest, with the consequence that I stepped off a couple of boards and committees where such a misalignment might possibly occur. It took a further four weeks before my formal letter of engagement was sent. This was, apparently, fast for Whitehall.

It was an exhilarating but exhausting day. I didn't sleep much that night. I kept going over and over all the things I needed to do, the people I needed to recruit and how the UK could be a major player on the world stage of vaccines.

I had Steve Job's mantra echoing in my head. 'Great things in business,' he once said, 'are never done by one person; they are done by a team of people.'

Building that team was vital if the VTF were to stand a chance of success.

3

A TEAM AT SPEED

'The good news is that you have got Nick Elliott – he's great,' Sir Stephen Lovegrove told me. I was in my kitchen with my eighth cup of tea that day. Stephen, the Permanent Secretary at the Ministry of Defence, was one of the many people who called me that evening of 6 May. He told me lots of things about Nick Elliott, but the one that stuck in my head was that Elliott was a bomb disposal engineer. That sounded pretty good to me. Calm, decisive and brave. Key qualities we would need in the Vaccine Taskforce team.

My first task would be to recruit others with the same vision and passion as I already felt. By both accident and design, we managed it.

The largest 'accident' was that critical appointment of Nick as Director General. We needed someone who had an extensive understanding of how Whitehall operated, coupled with strong commercial skills. And someone who could work well with me. If our relationship foundered the Vaccine Taskforce would have a short and unhappy life.

The British Government is not necessarily a case study in co-ordination. Coinciding with Sir Patrick Vallence's decision to reshape the Vaccine Taskforce and recruit an independent Chair with extensive industrial experience, Cabinet Secretary Sir Mark Sedwill had been considering the options for Director General of the Taskforce. These two recruitment processes occurred entirely separately. The PM decided personally who to ask to become VTF Chair, and the Cabinet Secretary, also in Downing Street, albeit in a different office, chose the VTF Director General. Stephen Lovegrove at the MoD had made a firm recommendation of Nick Elliott, then the Director General Commercial and Deputy Chief Executive of Defence Equipment and Support (the professional acquisition and support division of the Ministry of Defence, responsible for several massive capital programmes), for this latter role.

Nick and I discovered the identity of the other only *after* we had been appointed. It was lucky we happened to see eye to eye.

Nick

While Nick and I share a love of spandex, our backgrounds couldn't be more different. We worked even better together because of this.

My paternal grandfather had become a pupil teacher aged fourteen — teaching the younger children in return for his continued secondary education. He had risen to be a public health doctor of some distinction. Nick's paternal grandfather, one of twelve children, was a self-educated miner who had become a Pit Deputy before being killed in a mine explosion shortly after the end of World War II.

I had been educated at the prestigious — and private — St Paul's Girls' School in London, leaving at seventeen to read Biochemistry at Christ Church, Oxford. Nick had been to a state school in Leeds which was so rough that one of his form tutors had only one eye, the other having been removed by a disgruntled pupil with the aid of a screwdriver. This didn't stop Nick from being the first in his family to go to university and then on to Sandhurst.

From there, Nick had enjoyed an extraordinary career in the military. He had opted to be a bomb disposal officer. He had served in the old West Germany, Northern Ireland, the 1991 Gulf War and then the Balkans. In the run-up to the war in Iraq in 2003, he had put together a plan to invade from Turkey, rather than Kuwait. Although not ultimately adopted, it had so impressed the Americans that he was embedded as the only British citizen in their strategic planning unit for the conflict. From there he was awarded command of a battalion of 1,200 soldiers, including a substantial contingent of Gurkhas. This was in many ways the highlight of his time in uniform.

He then left the army for a key role at Network Rail, only to return to the MoD on secondment as Commercial Director (and later overall Deputy Director) of Defence Equipment and Support, a crucial unit with massive responsibilities.

Nick was in his final stretch at the MoD when Covid-19 struck, and he found himself drafted into Skipton House, head office of NHS England. Nick, like others with logistical expertise, was asked to resolve issues such as PPE and ventilator supplies. He was the right person to be the 'bodyguard' to the new VTF Chair.

Most of my career had been in venture capital, creating, building and funding small start-up biotech companies developing life-changing medicines. Nick's path combined danger with colossal projects. It was far from clear that, having been cast together as a *fait accompli*, we would click as a pair.

As soon as I had been told about Nick, I did what I always do when introduced to new colleagues with whom I will work closely – tried to find out about him from people I knew and trusted. It was an unusual situation for me as normally I recruit people directly. But I called a friend in the army who knew Nick and any doubts were allayed.

Later in my busy 6 May evening of texts and calls, Nick texted to introduce himself and we arranged to meet in Queen's Park the next morning. I bike everywhere in London so arrived on wheels in my black Lycra leggings. Nick turned up in similar-looking running gear. At least we had sport and exercise in common.

What followed was a slightly bizarre socially distanced talk around the park for the better part of ninety minutes. 'I am working for you' was his gambit; 'We are a team' was my riposte. By the end of that chat both of us were convinced that we shared a 'can-do attitude' and had very similar instincts about how to approach the immense challenge facing us, including rapidly building the core VTF Steering Group.

I chatted to Nick about the millions we invested to build new companies to develop new drugs. While Nick was used to much greater sums in the military, we established a common ground managing serious risks and budgets.

This 'spandex summit' would prove a seminal moment.

We clicked and it was clear that in Nick I'd found the perfect partner. He freely admitted to knowing little about healthcare. I was blissfully ignorant of the inner workings of Whitehall. Although people thought otherwise, because I am married to an MP, I am uninterested in politics. Fusing our skill sets was a blessing.

On the train back home, I started to map out the sort of team we would need to lead the VTF. Whizzing through Didcot Parkway, I knew the team must combine industrial expertise and skills in science, manufacturing and clinical development. A team with trusted relationships with industry. A team with the energy and determination to move mountains.

But without the parallel experts from government for contracting, project management and delivery, and diplomacy, we wouldn't be able to get things done. And that was where Nick could lead.

He had to sort out some basic matters immediately. It turned out that BEIS did not have a licence to purchase vaccines. BEIS did not have the authority from the Treasury to spend much money independently, so Nick had to work with the acting Permanent Secretary to acquire a reasonable operating budget for the VTF. Nick needed money to recruit and to pay people. I, quite rightly, had no authority to spend any public money at all.

Introducing Clive Dix

One of my other calls on the evening of 6 May was from Clive Dix, who had heard I had joined the Vaccine Expert Advisory Committee in April. He phoned to ask whether he could help in any way. I was still reeling from being dropped in the deep end of government, Whitehall and vaccines, and from the barrage of calls and texts.

But Clive's call struck a different note. We had known each other for over fifteen years, warts and all. I had backed Clive to lead two biotech companies, which he did brilliantly, in a quiet and understated way.

To get a sense of why Clive was so valuable to the VTF, it's worth understanding a little about his past history and the events that influenced him. And why I trusted him implicitly.

Born and bred in Birmingham, he had pursued first a BSc and then a PhD in Pharmacology at Leeds University. Leaving academic research at the Royal Free Hospital in London, he applied to work at Glaxo Wellcome, given his strong interest in industrial drug discovery. He rose to be the Head of Research but was far from convinced that big R&D units were best able to innovate and discover new drugs.

When Clive moved to a small new biotech called PowderJect Pharmaceuticals as Head of Research and Development, eyebrows raised. I had not met him at that point but knew of his stellar reputation. This was a notable move for someone so senior, and a great catch for PowderJect, a company created by Oxford University scientists in the 1990s. The CEO was Paul (later Lord) Drayson, whose father-in-law Professor Brian Bellhouse had developed a needle-free injection system for delivering drugs and vaccines.

Paul was a very effective and creative entrepreneur who I liked a lot, and I explored whether SV could invest in PowderJect when the company started. Paul called me at home one weekend to discuss terms. When Jesse told him I was well into labour with our first child and so couldn't come to the phone, Paul sent the largest bunch of sunflowers I'd ever seen. Sadly, we did not get a chance to back PowderJect as it turned into a very successful investment.

Running R&D at a small, nimble biotech was precisely the pioneering activity that Clive enjoyed and excelled at. PowderJect was then acquired by Chiron, a large US company. Chiron was most interested in PowderJect's revenue-generating products, less in the earlier-stage drug delivery technology. Recognising its potential, Clive aimed to buy this technology platform and create a new company to develop it further. He approached SV to seek funding for the acquisition.

It seemed like a great investment opportunity, so SV funded Clive as CEO to refocus the company to develop and manufacture therapeutic and prophylactic DNA vaccines for viral diseases and cancer. Instead of spending lots of money on rebranding, we decided to come up with a new creative name in the pub one evening: PowderMed.

Clive secured an attractive corporate partnership with GSK. The company then generated compelling data on the lead clinical programme for influenza, showing it could be used as an annual and pandemic flu vaccine. PowderMed's products were based on delivering DNA-coated gold particles to the immune cells in the epidermis, which stimulated a strong immune response. The company's goal was to manufacture and deploy its flu vaccine within the first three months of a pandemic.

Less than two years later, in November 2006, Pfizer made us an offer to buy PowderMed that we could not refuse. I remember seeing Clive's commercial acumen come into its own. He successfully negotiated the price up nearly fifty per cent from the opening bid. No transaction price was disclosed, but the *Financial Times* reported that Pfizer had paid up to $400 million. SV and Clive did well out of it. Pfizer said 'this acquisition is a strategic opportunity to enter the vaccine market and is part of our focus on broadening healthcare solutions for patients.'

I'd like to think that this early entry into genetic vaccines paved the way for Pfizer to play such a critical role in the Covid-19 pandemic.

In February 2010, GSK announced plans to exit research in depression and pain, resulting in major job cuts and the closures of six sites across Europe and Canada, in order to save £500 million by 2012. Clive had built the chronic pain drug discovery group at Glaxo Wellcome, recruited Simon Tate to lead it and thought there was a great opportunity to spin this out and create a biotech company with new, non-addictive pain treatments. Clive called me and asked whether I was up for backing this team with its project codename of Silver Arrow. I was.

SV helped shape the new company's business plan and team, and we raised over $35 million in Series A financing of what became Convergence Pharmaceuticals.

A key figure who worked with Clive and me to make the sale happen was GSK's Head of R&D, Patrick Vallance. While GSK's spin-out process was pretty slick, I needed Patrick's help to get the deal over the line and started to get to know him well. I was very impressed by Patrick's foresight even then. GSK asked for the right to send an observer to attend Convergence's board meetings, as part of giving their highflyers intimate exposure to a rapidly growing biotech company. I told Patrick that I was happy to have a GSK observer on the board, but that if they were any good we would be likely to try to poach them for our own companies. Patrick didn't mind. In his view, if GSK helped support people's careers into biotech, then this might ultimately help GSK in the future. Cool guy.

We funded Clive and his team to run a series of preclinical and clinical trials and were able to show our drug worked to treat trigeminal neuralgia (TGN). This is a really nasty chronic disease causing debilitating, episodic facial pain – sometimes called the suicide disease. It took a little longer to repeat Clive's previous success – five years not eighteen months – but once again it was sold on at a handsome multiple to Biogen in 2015.

On New Year's Day 2020, the morning after his daughter's wedding and a little worse for wear, Clive noticed media reports about a new and unexplained virus that had come out of China. Unlike many of us, he had a hunch that this would be the 'big one', the long-predicted pandemic that despite all previous doomsaying was yet to materialise. A decade before, he had volunteered to collaborate on the pandemic prevention plan developed in the final year of the last Labour Government (2009–10).

Clive joined several pandemic planning workshops, although he never knew if any recommendations were taken forward. Clive felt he could make a real contribution to dealing with the fast-developing coronavirus calamity. That sense of responsibility would harden when a close friend who had attended the wedding died of the virus. He called around to find out who he could speak to in government to volunteer his services. A friend then tipped him off that I was involved in the Vaccine Taskforce External Advisory Board.

When Clive called me to suggest that he serve as my Deputy, I bit his hand off. He was, in my view, the obvious person to bring together a small team of experts to identify the most credible vaccine contenders and to help advise me on the broad VTF strategy. Smart, networked, practical and committed.

In barely forty-eight hours, Clive had recruited a stunning team to assist him in due diligence and prioritisation of the most promising vaccines. He recruited people with proven technical and industrial expertise and entrepreneurial flair. This was a line-up that Whitehall officials simply could not have mustered in months of trying. It needed the personal connections and goodwill that only experience in the industry provided.

Steve

Steve Bates was the CEO of the BioIndustry Association (BIA), the trade association for innovative life sciences companies and people in the UK. I have known him ever since he was appointed as CEO. Steve's job in the VTF was to use his extensive network across the sector to bring an industrial perspective to our long-term pandemic planning work. We did not simply want to put this fire out only for future pandemics to create a more intense inferno. Having been a former special adviser – a 'spad' – in the Labour Party, he also instinctively understood how to work with government.

As CEO of the BIA, Steve had overseen an initiative in 2014 to find out what the UK could do if a worrying Ebola outbreak required a scaled-up vaccine response. The short answer was 'not much'. So, Steve set up the BIA Bioprocessing group to bring together experts to address the UK's medical manufacturing challenges. In early 2020, after an urgent request for aid from the Oxford University vaccine team, Steve received a much more encouraging response from the UK's bioindustry offering immediate practical help. But Steve needed a manufacturing expert to drive this – Ian McCubbin, head of the BIA Bioprocessing Group, stepped up.

Ian

Ian's role in the VTF was to oversee the scale-up and manufacturing of the vaccines, ensuring we had all the skills, equipment and supplies needed for population-wide vaccination.

Ian is a soft-spoken and completely charming Scot and a widely recognised authority in the realm of advanced medicine manufacturing. With a zeal for clinical pharmacy, he settled into a role at Organon after graduating. He threw himself into his work and mastered the many practical aspects of pharmacy manufacturing.

After about five years he moved on to Glaxo at Barnard Castle, a town now famous for Dominic Cummings' 'Barnard Castle eye test' and climbed up the ladder until he ended up at GSK's head office, staying there until 2001.

Like Clive Dix, Ian found the endless corporate mergers a disconcerting distraction. He left for Ivax in East London, a generics pharmaceutical business. Unlike Clive, though, he was drawn back to what was now GSK and spent the rest of his career there, manufacturing supply lines globally for new products. Ian worked closely with Patrick Vallance, who he also came to know better still as he sat on the Corporate Donations Committee which Patrick chaired. In 2017, Ian retired from GSK but continued to be active in the cell and gene space, not least as the Chairman of Roslin CT, an advanced cell therapy organisation based in Edinburgh.

Ian maintained a range of interests outside his companies. He played a leading role in the UK's BioIndustry Association in liaising with the Government about life sciences. He had worked with George Freeman as Minister for Life Sciences, helping to shape the Advanced Therapies Manufacturing Taskforce designed to create a distinctive UK approach. It was not surprising then that Steve and the BioIndustry Association would ask Ian in February 2020 to pull together a vaccine manufacturing blueprint.

In March 2020, Patrick tapped Ian to join his Vaccine Taskforce External Advisory Board as the BIA representative, to help on manufacturing advice and planning. I first met Ian in April. I remember scribbling notes frantically to capture everything he told us in those meetings. He brought an incredibly impressive degree of expertise, combined with calm reassurance on what could be delivered.

In one of the last VTF Advisory Board meetings, Ian presented his blueprint for scale-up and bulk manufacturing in the UK but his video went down midway. He couldn't see us and didn't know if we could hear him properly and see his slides. Rather distraught, he called me afterwards to ask how he had come across. I told him that he had not only been heard but extremely well received. Ian was quiet and convincing, and reassured us all that these monumental manufacturing challenges could indeed be tackled.

Immediately after my appointment, I made him my 'Mr Manufacturing' for the VTF.

Like Clive, Ian had to pull together a team swiftly to assess and support the due diligence and manufacturing of the new vaccines.

He built as strong a manufacturing assessment team as could conceivably be acquired, particularly with respect to advanced biological manufacturing, quality and regulatory compliance. They were widely known and hugely liked, which really helped when we needed to call in favours.

Giovanni

From our very first conversations in our respective roles, however, Clive and I knew that something important was missing. We badly needed an industrially experienced vaccine clinician with a track record of running pivotal clinical trials to secure approval of novel vaccines from global regulators. We needed someone with these skills fast.

I took on the task of finding that person myself. Life for the VTF would be much harder if this hole could not be plugged quickly.

I leant in. I used up a lot of my EE minutes making calls as I walked around the garden. I don't like sitting still. And I get a better signal outside.

I called and emailed a wide range of my contacts to try and find this industrial vaccine physician. There are plenty of UK academics with experience running vaccine clinical trials, but academic-run trials are typically very different from industry-led clinical trials, which are designed to generate data that the regulators want, not what the editors of *Nature* would like to publish. It turned out that there were few, if any, of the stature required in this country, largely because there were no truly substantial vaccine companies based in the UK.

It was time to go international.

I called Rino Rappuoli. Rino was Chief Scientist and Head External R&D at GSK Vaccines in Italy, having previously held a similar role at Novartis Vaccines. Patrick had introduced me to Rino in 2016, telling me he was an exceptional vaccine developer with one of the best records in the industry.

I had visited Rino a few years ago in Siena when my SV partner Houman and I were building a cancer company, Enara. This new company was based on science at the Francis Crick Institute in London, and we visited Rino to explore whether we could partner with GSK Vaccines. Houman and I discussed whether vaccines could be used to boost the immune system to help the body fight cancer. We debated the potential role of mRNA as a vaccine format over a lovely Tuscan dinner of *ribollita* with Rino and we formed a bond.

I described my new role and asked Rino for help. As well as giving me some crucial vaccine advice, Rino steered me towards Giovanni Della Cioppa, who had led clinical development at Novartis Vaccines and more recently at GSK. Giovanni was now back in Italy acting as an independent consultant. Giovanni had exactly the range of skills we needed, as well as industrial credibility. I rang Giovanni who nearly choked on his cappuccino when I told him I was calling from the British Government. I explained what we needed. Giovanni was friendly and accommodating and said he would do what he could to help. I introduced him to Clive and he agreed to be part of the VTF due diligence team.

This was a merciful turn of events, though not seen as such universally within government. Sections of the civil service had something of a collective coronary at the thought of an Italian national being such an important player and, unavoidably, being placed where he could see the entire UK approach towards vaccines. If the normal rules around security clearance had been in force, then I don't think we would have secured his services within the lifetime of the pandemic.

As it was, even in the emergency of spring 2020, it took six months before a formal contract was issued and Whitehall was forced to find some distinctly unorthodox devices to pay him. I tore my hair out at the roadblocks erected to prevent us working with Giovanni – it was a textbook example of Whitehall process getting in the way of outcome.

If he had not been so patient and trusting, civil service rules would have prevented us from working with him. When I finally met Giovanni face-to-face in 2021, I asked him when he got paid; it turned out that it was not until Christmas 2020. I remain enormously grateful that he was willing to work for free without a contract for so long. His arrival provided the last expert required for our exceptional industrial and due diligence team.

★

There have been a lot of positive comments about the benefits of bringing industrial experts into the Vaccine Taskforce. But this expertise wasn't enough. We also needed a team who knew which levers to pull in government to make things work. And to be pushy in getting what they needed quickly. Nick Elliott built the Whitehall VTF leadership team, to cope with government, as well as to ensure that everything we did was kosher. Specifically, we needed project management and contracting experts and diplomats. That presented me as Chair with particular challenges, juggling relationships within the emerging team as well as broader relationships within government.

Neither Clive nor I had formal legal qualifications, although we had negotiated scores of legal deals to set up, finance, partner and sell biotech companies. But doing deals in government proved rather more complicated. We needed a legal and commercial expert to drive the detailed negotiations for our vaccines and ensure the contracts were compliant with government guidance. Another moment where we were racing to acquire the best possible talent in the shortest possible time – judged by two metrics often in tension with each other. A wrong turn early would mean painful unpicking later, obstructing our primary goal: getting the vaccines.

Maddy

Madelaine (Maddy) McTernan was our star commercial and legal negotiator and deal-doer. As another north-west Londoner, we got to know each other on the occasional walk around Regent's Park together, or dinner outdoors at the amazing Brazilian barbecue in Belsize Park during the 'eat out to help out' era.

Maddy had read law at Trinity College, Cambridge, and initially entered private sector commercial law in the banking sector. Having shone in banking, she switched career and became a board member and the legal mastermind at UK Government Investments. Maddy was drawn into the original Vaccine Taskforce when the philanthropic agreement was being established between Oxford University and AstraZeneca in April. While the Government was not, strictly speaking, a party to that deal, Oxford had indicated that they would not enter an arrangement with which Whitehall was discontent.

In one sense, the Government was delighted with the Oxford/AstraZeneca alliance. Oxford had thought about striking a bargain with the US giant Merck. The potential benefits were obvious, but the risks were real too. Allying with Merck would require the vaccine to be manufactured in the US, exposing the venture to the erratic nature of the Trump administration. In a worst-case scenario, the US Defense Act would enable the White House to seize vaccine production for itself.

AstraZeneca, as an Anglo-Swedish institution, was preferable. Sir John Bell, an Oxford professor and the Government's life sciences champion, had brought the two of them together. Yet the alliance had been struck extraordinarily quickly, with discussions that had only started in mid-April 2020 resulting in non-binding but wide-ranging heads of terms (main terms of a commercial agreement) signed within a week. A more definitive document was signed a little more than two weeks later. There was, therefore, a sudden scramble to ensure that Whitehall's short- and long-term interests were guarded. This was doubly important in that at this stage the Oxford vaccine appeared to be the clear frontrunner.

Maddy had dealt with AstraZeneca and Oxford highly effectively and both Nick and I were confident she could do the job we needed. As the new VTF bedded in and started discussions with vaccine companies, it was crucial to have tip-top legal representation.

In our previous roles, we would agree the deal terms directly and would then bring in lawyers to turn these headline terms into binding contracts. That was not possible when taxpayers' money was part of the process. Clive and I found ourselves in the unusual situation of shaping and negotiating the heads of terms with the various vaccine companies and then handing over to Maddy, assisted by Steven Reece of Clifford Chance, to hammer out the final agreements.

Although I played no role in his appointment, it was extremely helpful that I had worked closely with Steven in his previous role at Olswang, when he had advised me on several biotech companies, including Convergence Pharmaceuticals.

Maddy's visible success in the commercial contracting for the VTF was rewarded by being appointed Director General of the VTF, succeeding Nick Elliot shortly after I too had stood down in January 2021. In April 2022 she stepped up to become the Government's hormone replacement therapy (HRT) tsar.

Divya

The ability to run clinical trials quickly was one of the UK's selling points, and we needed an expert to help turn this into reality. I called Jonathan Sheffield for advice; he had recently stood down as the Chief Executive of the National Institute for Health Research (NIHR), the oversight body for NHS clinical trials. I Zoomed with Jonathan – he is the spitting image of Sean Bean in *Game of Thrones*, especially with that flowing Covid hairstyle. He had just been to the fish stall in Leeds to select the freshest catch to make his wife dinner that evening; I loved the fact he was a foodie, like me.

Jonathan patiently walked me through how various parts of NHS research actually worked and introduced me to the right people when I needed them – incredibly helpful.

He was the one who recommended Divya Chadha Manek to me. A bold, even contentious, suggestion. Divya's existing role was to build strategic partnerships with global life sciences companies and persuade these pharmaceutical and biotech companies to run their trials in the NHS's national clinical trials network. Combined with this, she was responsible for smooth clinical operations for the studies, working across the NHS sites. She knew the pharmaceutical industry as well as the people leading the different NIHR trial sites, and knew from the inside how well they recruited and ran trials. I had met Divya a few years earlier when she had come to tell me about the UK's national clinical trial capability. She reeled off the stats supporting their experience and was clearly keen for my little biotech companies to run trials in the UK, so I was delighted when Jonathan reminded me of her.

When Divya enters a room – even a Zoom room – energy levels rise. Having represented India in rowing, she was used to relentless hard work. Although relatively young, Divya was appointed to the NIHR as a clinical studies officer, which involved recruiting and managing volunteers for trials.

Her big break, and one of immense subsequent consequence for the VTF leadership later, came when Divya took on a six-month secondment within the NIHR Co-ordinating Centre. They wanted to see whether they could increase the number of high-profile and high-impact clinical trials by having an external-facing Head of Business Development who would focus solely on encouraging global pharmaceutical companies to run their trials in the UK.

In short order, Divya made herself and the position indispensable. In 2013, NIHR conducted around three hundred commercial studies with pharma and biotech. It soon surged to seven hundred studies annually, and these studies were also a lot larger in scale as well. Divya grew her team of one (herself) to twenty-five and expanded her remit beyond mental health, to include all clinical indications, whether pharma, biotech or medtech.

Divya had an astonishing ability to assemble the trials at speed. She pledged that she personally would supervise an end-to-end approach from recruitment to delivery. Anyone seeing her in action would know that her single-minded commitment contributed to this stunning increase in UK clinical trials. Her absolutely magnetic charm and personality must have helped as well.

Divya was widely regarded as a rising star, but in the NIHR hierarchy she was not especially senior. Hierarchy has never bothered me. What matters is whether they can do the job. I soon found that certain noses had been put out of joint by the secondment. I rang her on a Saturday morning to announce that I needed a lead on clinical trials for the taskforce. Divya was staggered but sympathetic, replying that she would need to speak to her Chief Executive. 'I will do that,' I said. 'Well, when would I start?' Divya responded. 'Monday' was the answer.

This didn't faze her one bit.

She had a small child and a new baby. A usual conversation between Divya and me would include lines like 'Can you join a call on Sunday at 7 p.m.?', 'I will be breastfeeding then, how about 7.30 p.m.?' Divya's capacity to multitask staggered the men on the steering committee. We would watch her spoon-feed her toddler during calls, coming off mute to make key points. And even when she took a few days' holiday, she never switched off. I got calls from her at all times of day and night, updating me on the latest developments and endless troubleshooting to get volunteers enrolled and trials completed rapidly.

Divya also had a strong working relationship with Kirsty Wydenbach, an expert medical assessor in the clinical trials unit at the UK regulator, MHRA. Divya had worked closely with Kirsty for years so was familiar with how the MHRA worked and the crucial people involved.

June Raine, the CEO of the MHRA, told me Kirsty was top rate and one of their highflyers. Kirsty was able to describe the likely approach that the MHRA would take to assessing the vaccine candidates and ensured that all the connections our vaccine companies needed with the MHRA were in place. While all discussions between the vaccine companies and the MHRA were confidential, I took enormous comfort in Kirsty's presence at our early VTF steering committee meetings. Far from being an outsider looking in, she really felt like a fellow member of the team.

Sorry, folks – I know this is a heavy-duty list of names but building the VTF team was critical. Steve Job's quote echoed in the back of my mind: 'What I'm best at doing is finding a group of talented people and making things with them.' We needed those talented people to find and make vaccines.

Ruth

Ruth Todd would lead the VTF delivery and project management, and she boasted a unique line on her CV: submarine manufacturing.

Once vaccines had been identified and manufactured, then they needed to be delivered efficiently. This would require extraordinarily complex programme management, co-ordinating a substantial number of different organisations in Whitehall, many of whom were often strangers to each other.

At the start of what would become the pandemic crisis, Stephen Lovegrove found his services and that of the MoD being called upon more widely. 'Bring in the Army!' is a favourite tabloid headline in many a national crisis, but beyond the rhetoric the MoD and armed services were a vast resource of logistical and commercial expertise. Stephen was also serving, via the Whitehall version of a 'buddy system', as a mentor to the acting Permanent Secretary at

BEIS. Having already recommended Nick Elliott from within the MoD to become the VTF Director General, it struck him that Nick would need someone like Ruth to back him up.

Stephen asked Ruth whether she could help out on vaccines. Not exactly appreciating the vast commitment in prospect, she replied that she would be happy to assist. One rapid meeting with Nick later and she'd switched from submarines to the VTF leadership.

I spoke to Ruth during this speedy recruitment process, stomping about in front of the house since it was a hot day, though keeping well away from the chirping guineafowl in the field. The more we spoke, the more excited I became. Here was someone with astonishing experience in leading complicated manufacturing projects, running factories and working at companies like MG Rover, BMW, Babcock, and Jaguar Land Rover, before her role at the Submarine Delivery Agency. And she was willing to join our team.

Building submarines might seem a long way from vaccines, but Nick understood from his own career that the VTF needed very sophisticated project management skills. Someone to help devise, manage and present to the NHS a detailed vaccine distribution plan that wouldn't go wrong.

To limit possible security beaches or inadvertent disclosure, Ruth renamed the vaccines and antibodies with codenames drawn from the British submarine fleet, including Ambush, Triumph, Astute, Audacious, Victorious, etc. I had to keep a cheat sheet at the back of my notebook to remind me what each name referred to until we narrowed them down to a shortlist I could remember unaided.

Ruth, as a Manufacturing Engineering graduate, worked with a wide variety of clients from Marks & Spencer to Tarmac as an external 'fixer'. With the exception of a three-month project for AstraZeneca on a warehouse that needed an overhaul, Ruth had little experience of anything to do with the pharmaceutical sector before the VTF. In 2016, Ruth was ready to commit herself to a full-time employer and joined defence company Babcock International Group. This was her stepping stone to the Ministry of Defence.

In 2018, Ruth was recruited as the Commercial Director of the Submarines Delivery Agency. Submarine delivery turned out to be the perfect education for getting vaccines into human arms. The process of manufacturing vaccines would involve forging an intense relationship with a select number of very large prospective partners and getting the best out of them – a good analogue for large military projects as well. Ruth's style was to form unusually close working relationships with her suppliers. She found that regular and transparent communications helped to identify, pre-empt and address any issues that might disrupt the smooth running of her projects.

Her seniority at the Submarine Delivery Agency meant that she had often come across Stephen Lovegrove. In a chance corridor conversation, she once told him that she had been responsible for building and fundamentally remodelling no fewer than four factories and twenty-five warehouses, starting in 1995 when she transformed an old paint plant into an assembly line. This was clearly not the sort of background information that he received every day, as he made a mental note.

Once Nick had been hired on Stephen's recommendation, Stephen's next great call was to put forward Ruth to lead the delivery and project management for the VTF.

Given her experience, Ruth was also responsible for the security of the entire VTF operation. She worked closely with the security services and military intelligence to ensure the UK's vaccine work wasn't hacked and to identify potential threats to the UK's vaccine supply. There were solid reasons to suspect that at least one major state would, and in fact did, attempt to interfere with what the UK was doing – Chapter 7 will shed more light on this. There were also, and alas impossible to detail here, separate efforts by serious organised crime organisations to steal vaccine information.

Tim

Tim Colley was our VTF lead working with countries around the world, dealing with our international intergovernmental and NGO relationships.

This was the last full-time appointment to the inner team to fall into place, as the role was openly advertised in a competitive Whitehall recruitment process.

Tim had been with the Foreign Office for more than thirty years. He had worked on EU enlargement, served in the Caribbean and Pakistan, and had even been seconded to the Bulgarian Government as a Special Adviser to the Minister for Public Administration Reform. Most recently, Tim had been the UK Ambassador to Latvia, but was now in BEIS.

Almost the same age as me, Tim was brought up in Birmingham, Stafford and Cumbria. I discovered only later that he had studied Natural Sciences at Durham University – he kept his scientific credentials quiet.

Tim took on the international aspects of the taskforce agenda. Ensuring vaccines were distributed globally was a core goal of the VTF and the UK wanted to be seen as a major player on the global vaccine stage. Tim's broad international experience and connections would prove critical.

When I first joined the meetings with other countries that Tim had arranged, I was struck by how well he understood the machinery of governments around the world, along with his enormous patience and tact. I joined Tim for one meeting with a verbose European health minister and was amazed by how well he handled the meeting, getting his points across and finding areas of mutual interest.

Whitehall loves nothing better than to find out what other people are doing. That's why vaccine emails could end up with more than sixty people cc'd. Endless departments wanted progress updates the whole time. Tim provided partial relief to Nick in his obligations to provide these continuous reports to Whitehall.

JVT and Dan

For the sake of completeness, it should be noted that the VTF steering committee was the size of a football team.

The additional player was Professor Jonathan Van-Tam, Deputy Chief Medical Officer for England within the Department of Health and Social Care and an emerging media darling. He did not have the time to make the sort of commitment to the VTF as the other members. He was, however, an outstanding advocate for the VTF within the bureaucratic Whitehall jungle.

Jonathan's contribution went beyond his press conference routine of memorable metaphors (Covid 'is a goalkeeper that can be beaten'; vaccine development is 'a train which has stopped in the station; don't 'tear the pants out of' the guidance). He played a crucial role on the joint steering committee with Oxford and AstraZeneca, leaning on his experience in both industry and the public sector. JVT was very well networked in Europe too, having chaired the Expert Advisory Group on H5N1 human vaccines. These connections would prove valuable to help co-ordinate the approval of the Oxford/AstraZeneca vaccine. And he was great fun to work with: pragmatic, sensible, thoughtful.

Nick also co-opted a senior BEIS civil servant called Dan Osgood to the VTF steering committee to help manage the BEIS team to prepare the endless demand for dense Business Cases (of which more anon). Dan did a great job leading the team and improved the process of Business Case preparation and approvals. He brought real stamina, which made sense when I discovered his love of road biking, where riding 100km before breakfast was not atypical.

This top-tier team would be supplemented by a rapidly rising number of civil servants within BEIS, so that by the time I finished at the end of 2020 more than 150 people were operating in the broad VTF team.

We built the team in a few weeks. When I look back at it, I now realise that we did not have a traditional set of backgrounds. Instead, we were relying on the likes of a bomb disposal expert, an Indian rowing star, an Italian consultant, a submarine delivery agent, a former ambassador, a football pundit and a venture capitalist to get the UK out of the pandemic.

We were striking in our diversity. Nick and I had not consciously engineered this but it proved a considerable asset. This was one of the most effective teams I have had the pleasure of working with. As Maddy said later, 'We're all problem-solvers, we tend to be "heads down and get on with it". With the right people, right mission and right attitude, you can achieve an awful lot.' She was right.

4

WORKING FROM HOME

In ordinary circumstances, I would have been expected to lead the VTF from the somewhat austere offices of the Department for Business, Energy and Industrial Strategy (BEIS) on Victoria Street, London. With a little luck I would have been able to escape periodically to our rather modest offices at SV Health Investors: a crowded single floor near Holborn station, with some hot-desk space upstairs called the incubator. We don't have the trendy bean bags, ping-pong tables and exposed brick walls, but it's an open, buzzy office with glass walls and a large graffiti wall painting highlighting all the successful drugs we have invested in. And a great place to work.

The conditions of May 2020 were, though, anything but ordinary.

Like so many other companies, we had closed our offices and were all working remotely. Our IT systems for remote working had already been tested in an emergency in 2015. An underground electrical fire in Kingsway forced all the offices in the area to close for weeks and we were banished until carbon monoxide levels subsided.

Even before we were married in 1992, my husband Jesse and I had bought and started to rebuild a ruin of a cottage near Hay-on-Wye. Beginning in early March 2020, that became our base.

Apart from seeing Alok in London for that first meeting at BEIS and Nick Elliott for the walk around Queen's Park in May, I didn't come back to London a lot. Nor did my VTF colleagues. This was a genuinely national effort. We all worked from home across the country, making calls and joining video meetings. It was far more efficient than if we'd had to meet physically. We didn't waste any time travelling and the polite chit-chat at the end of meetings was gone. We redefined productive working.

Résumé recap

You may be wondering how I was chosen to become VTF Chair. To give a sense of the background and credentials leading up to my appointment, here are some of the highlights of what by 2020 had been a near thirty-year career.

My own route into the world of biotech had conventional and unconventional aspects. I wasn't particularly serious about academic study at school and spent a lot of time finding ways to minimise the number of O levels to take. After my seven O levels, I was so indecisive about my A levels that I was more or less told to study Biology, Chemistry and Physics by Heather Brigstocke, the very forceful head of my school, who wanted more girls to study sciences.

Mrs Brigstocke had recruited some outstanding male teachers in Physics and Chemistry, with the result that there were more girls in my year studying Chemistry at A level than English. And of course, none of us wanted to look stupid in front of these teachers so we all worked hard and did well. Even so, my Biology A level was weak: possibly because I was more focused on lacrosse matches, playing the oboe and chasing boys than on homework.

I took the 'fourth term' Oxford entrance exam in 1982, applying to read Biochemistry at Christ Church. I got on very well with the entrepreneurial tutor there, Tony Rees, an expert in protein engineering and biophysics.

At that time Biochemistry was a small, unfashionable and male-dominated degree course. There were three Biochemistry students in my year at the college and about seventy-five students taking the course across the whole university. Christ Church, mostly known for producing prime ministers, had only recently admitted women so the student gender ratio there was about five to one male to female. This did not bother me. Frankly, it was an inducement.

Terence Kealey, a biochemist and physician who subsequently became Vice-Chancellor of the University of Buckingham, taught me clinical biochemistry and was a big influence nurturing my interest in the molecular basis of disease.

By then I knew that I enjoyed the conceptual science and was really excited by clinical biochemistry, particularly by the real-world applications of emerging biological breakthroughs.

Through Terence's work in the Nuffield Department of Clinical Biochemistry, he gave me a fabulous grounding in applying basic science to everyday clinical challenges. Terence taught me how mutations in genes encoding chloride ion channels, which regulate a host of biological processes, cause cystic fibrosis. Such small genetic changes causing such profound consequences! I learnt how dysfunctional immune processes attack the insulin-producing pancreatic islet β cells to cause Type I diabetes. I was fascinated and really dug in. Predictably, I was very happy when these topics came up in my finals.

Biotechnology was coming of age, and it was ever more exciting. Biotechnology is a rather vague catch-all phrase that refers to the use of living processes, or organisms, to manufacture products to improve the quality of human life. It includes genetic engineering and making biological products that can be used as drugs or diagnostics.

The US Food and Drug Administration (FDA) approved the first genetically engineered protein drug at this time, the first 'transgenic' animals were made by transferring genes from other animals into mice, and Genentech, the first 'unicorn' biotech company, went public and was a wild success.

It was then that scientists invented the polymerase chain reaction (PCR) for sequencing DNA and RNA. How many people had even heard of PCR before this pandemic? It amuses me to think how far we have come that we now routinely talk about PCR or antigen Covid-19 tests – whereas in the 1980s it was the latest of the quasi-sci-fi technologies being developed.

This was a wild time, with inventions and advances coming daily. I got really pumped up by the progress and potential opportunities for biotechnology. Despite never under any circumstances admitting to being a geek, I would get to the biochemistry library early on Thursdays to read about the latest advances in the top journal, *Nature*.

I was less interested in spending hours at the laboratory bench, however, and much more interested in figuring out how new insights into biological processes could be tapped to develop new drugs. I followed the progress of the new biotech drug Activase, a bioengineered form of tissue plasminogen activator being developed to dissolve blood clots in stroke and heart attack victims. This appeared to be a game-changing new treatment approach – biotechnology in action.

Having decided not to be a pure scientist, I took an utterly conventional route and applied to become a management consultant. I ended up having to choose between McKinsey, then as now a big name in the industry, and Monitor, a tiny new outfit founded by a Harvard Business School professor. McKinsey tried to woo me with a trip to Switzerland while Monitor took me to an Afghan restaurant with Formica tables. To the stuttering incomprehension of the senior McKinsey partner involved, I opted for the latter. McKinsey sent me a letter delivered by taxi to Oxford.

In my own mind, Monitor is not a serious choice for anybody beginning their career in management consultancy... There is a serious question about the quality of your potential colleagues. No other undergraduate with an offer from McKinsey will join Monitor – indeed your colleagues will have been turned down by these firms.

Wow.

A little stunned, I used a payphone to call Joe Haim at Monitor. It was Joe who had correctly thought that Afghan dining would appeal to me. We chatted about McKinsey's letter and he reassured me that Monitor was not the career cul-de-sac claimed. I had met lots of people at Monitor, and he confirmed they were whip-smart, driven and entrepreneurial – just as I thought they were. These were people I could learn a lot from. Relieved, I stuck to my guns and I worked for Monitor very happily for two years in London, Holland and Germany.

Working at a smaller company, I was exposed to far greater and more diverse commercial challenges. Why was a market leader suddenly losing market share in Germany? How could a former coal mining company diversify into science-based high growth markets? Which pharmaceuticals should an Italian family-owned company buy to bolster their pipeline and how much should they spend?

At Monitor, I even managed to wangle a trip to the Balearics when working with Thompson Holidays. We were sent out to do 'research' to help develop tailored holidays for different types of people, beyond the well-trodden routes for families and couples.

Monitor didn't boast a large pool of consultants so I was very lucky to end up at the coalface of these varied international assignments, which taught me a ton. My apparently incomprehensible decision paid off.

A Masters in Business Administration (MBA) was more or less required in those days to get promoted in management consultancy companies. So I applied to Harvard Business School to do one in 1988. I was by then sure that I didn't want to return to consulting, but felt an MBA would give me a broad training across all aspects of business. It would be my launch pad to get into biotech.

As part of the admissions process, I had to prepare my own 'story', setting out why I should be accepted. My pitch was that I wanted to combine my interest in clinical biochemistry and genetic engineering with the business skills I had learnt at Monitor. I wanted to live in the heartland of the global biotechnology industry, namely Massachusetts, and rather presumptuously I said I would take these new-found biotech building skills back to the UK. In 2021, when invited to give an address to a group of Kennedy scholars from Harvard and MIT (Massachusetts Institute of Technology), the chairman of the meeting, Sir Mark Walport, embarrassingly introduced me by reading out sections of my application form to the audience. I cringed as Mark recited my rose-tinted ambitions, uninhibited by the benefits of experience.

I was in. As part of my MBA, I wanted to get experience in a biotech business in the lengthy summer break between the two years of the degree course. I was expected to secure this for myself. There was no internet then. I found by a process of trial and error that, using directories to find telephone numbers, I could phone senior people first thing in the morning, and that appeared to be more effective than writing letters that would lie unread in who knows whose in-tray.

I rang Vicky Sato, Vice President for Research at Biogen, an established biotech company in Cambridge, MA. Helpfully she picked up the phone, but when I told her about my quest for an intern role, she told me she didn't have any such opening. Generously she suggested that 'Rich at Vertex' might want a cheap pair of hands to help him in an ambitious start-up.

Vertex proved to be a very hot young biotech company, and Rich turned out to be Rich Aldrich, who has since become one of the biggest names in the sector. Both Rich and the CEO Josh Boger wanted to raise a lot of cash to enable Vertex to grow rapidly. So, Rich struck a series of very large partnerships with different pharmaceutical companies and was extremely successful in raising capital. He's now a venture investor and we work together to this day.

Vertex was a fantastic place to land, conveniently only a few blocks from my flat in Central Square in Cambridge. Even so I still biked as it shaved three minutes off an eight-minute journey. Vertex was shooting for the stars and welcomed publicity. It had opened its arms to a writer called Barry Werth. I posted the first article he wrote about Vertex's story in *Atlantic Monthly* back to my parents. Dad then told me that he had been roommates with one Jeremy Knowles at Balliol, who was then the Chairman of Vertex's Scientific Advisory Board. Then, as now, biotech is a very small world. The advantage is that it's possible to build a network quite quickly. One drawback: there is always the danger of groupthink.

★

I adored Vertex and thought I would settle there on a full-time basis once I had finished at Harvard. Personal factors intervened. Jesse, by then my permanent boyfriend, had spent several years in the US and was very keen to return to Britain. Huge commercial opportunities were opening up in Central and Eastern Europe with the fall of the Berlin Wall. He had been running a project giving away new medical textbooks and other educational materials to doctors in Poland, Hungary and Czechoslovakia (as it then was) during the Communist period. That was a way to build networks and free institutions. Now these countries were welcoming international investment and advice, Jesse wanted to return and help build market-based economies there.

What to do? My mind was made up after a conversation in Harvard's famous Baker Library with their legendary Agriculture Professor, Ray Goldberg. I told him my dilemma – 'boyfriend or Vertex?' Goldberg just gave me a friendly hug and said that if I had found the right man then I should go home as I would always find a great job. He was right.

Even so, it was with some reluctance that I prepared to leave Vertex, with no solid plans for another job. I threw myself into planning a post-graduation US tour with Jesse and decided to worry about what happened next, later. Then one day I came back to my room to find a Post-It Note on the door saying 'something adventure company called – please ring back' with a London telephone number.

With no other information – such as the person or institution making the request – I didn't call back. After a few days, they called again and proved to be the venture capital and private equity group Schroder Ventures, who had used a rather direct approach to hiring. They had simply got hold of the Harvard Business School Yearbook to identify possible new recruits for London.

I was hired.

The name of the firm has changed a few times over the years, but the essence of what I do for a living has remained much the same for almost three decades.

I was recruited as a generalist, but when I arrived we had a lively debate about sector specialisation. We decided to merge two small healthcare teams in London and New York to create a unified life sciences investing team. I did a lot of the legwork to help launch our first $100 million dedicated life sciences fund in 1994. I built detailed models analysing our historical biotech investment performance, a resource that investors would need to judge our competence. I researched possible investors, preparing presentations to show why they should be interested in making this high-risk investment. I designed elaborate charts showing the potential of biotechnology in developing life-saving medicines. I worked hard, often staying up late into the night on the phone with my colleagues in New York. I was the newbie on the team and was keen not to make any mistakes.

This was a heroic fundraise. This sector specialisation was an entirely new approach and so required a lot of justification to persuade investors to commit to a fund that was seen as narrow and high risk. Our sole focus as a team was on investing in and building biotechnology companies alongside my US and UK partners investing in the other life science sectors, including healthcare services and medical devices. The early investors took some big risks based on our arm-wavey promises about the potential growth in biotech and healthcare. But we have raised nine more funds since then so we must have been doing something right.

We backed the precociously young Professor Steve Jackson in Cambridge to develop targeted cancer drugs. He was the poster child for Cancer Research UK, publishing seminal academic papers in the field of DNA repair and DNA-damage signalling. He helped define how their dysfunction yields cancer.

When I did due diligence on this start-up opportunity, one senior pharmaceutical exec told me 'This is for the birds… but if it works it could be important.' His career in pharma had largely been based on making incremental improvements to existing drugs, often addressing the disease *symptoms* only and selling these drugs to as many patients as possible, even if not every patient benefited.

Steve's new approach was riskier: he wanted to develop 'disease-modifying' drugs, targeting unproven biological mechanisms and treating the underlying *causes* of the different cancers. These drugs would help only those patients whose cancer was triggered by that aberrant biology. Targeting the *cause* of the disease meant the cancer could be slowed or even cured. The benefit to those patients could be significant. Their lives could be transformed.

Fortunately, it wasn't for the birds. We backed Steve and funded his company KuDOS Pharmaceuticals. Their first drug, olaparib, is now approved for ovarian, breast and prostate cancer patients with an inherited genetic predisposition to suffer from these cancers. It is a game-changing new treatment – prolonging survival for many patients who had no options before.

One New York start-up presented such exciting early data in experimental models of blindness that we joined as the first institutional investor. They developed the first drug to treat age-related blindness caused by macular degeneration. Competitors followed and this new type of drug now helps protect the sight of hundreds of thousands of patients globally.

We have done this repeatedly in cancer, inflammation and infection. Our investments resulted in the launch of twenty novel medicines.

In 2015, I was at my desk in Kingsway, London, watching double-decker buses narrowly miss the overhanging branches of the plane trees. This was a quiet day. Recently protesters had marched outside, complaining about climate change with fancy dress and loudspeakers, disrupting our meetings.

My phone rang. It was a senior exec I knew from Biogen. He asked whether SV would be interested in creating and managing a venture capital fund focused on dementia investments that they were supporting. 'Hmm…' I thought. Dementia had so far proved a graveyard for investing, so this wasn't something immediately ringing my bell.

Then I was called by Pfizer asking the same question. Then Janssen. Then GSK. All these pharmaceutical companies coming together in a venture capital fund to develop new dementia drugs? It was pretty unusual. Based on this unexpected deluge of calls, I thought I should take a harder look at whether this was something where we could really make a difference.

It turned out that this new dementia fund was being anchored by six pharmaceutical companies, the UK Department of Health and the charity Alzheimer's Research UK, aiming to invest in and develop new drugs that would actually slow or stop the course of dementia.

Few diseases evoke more dread than dementia. Most people think their life is over if they receive a diagnosis of it. As Western countries age, the numbers affected grow too. Right now, over fifty-five million people around the world have dementia, with ten million new cases a year. And there is no cure.

All disease-modifying drugs to treat dementia had failed. A few drugs were available that relieved some of the symptoms for some patients for a short time. That was it. In my business, money is invested to try and turn heroic scientific breakthroughs into new drugs. But biotech investors recognise that most ideas fail. Losses are offset by the occasional successes, which can be enormous. But no one had ever made money developing dementia drugs that worked. Consequently, we had not prioritised investments into dementia companies and nor had other venture capitalists.

I dug in, my noncommittal attitude evaporated and I concluded that here was a massive global opportunity to make a difference. The clinical need for effective dementia drugs was huge. I discovered that experts predicted there would be 135 million people worldwide with dementia by 2050. Deaths from Alzheimer's were rising dramatically, even as deaths from breast cancer, heart disease and stroke diminished. Since we were living longer, this was only going to get worse.

I duly threw SV's hat into the ring to be considered as fund manager. The formal process fell bang in the 2015 general election, where I was expected to make at least a cameo appearance with Jesse in Hereford. But I made it work and we won the mandate. And Jesse won convincingly in Hereford too.

Jesse and I took a long weekend's holiday after the election to recharge. While he was catching up on sleep, I spent hours basking in the warm Spanish sun writing a detailed dementia fund presentation and drafting the first placement memorandum for prospective investors – away from interruptions, with the added benefit of Jabugo ham and cava.

For the next two years, I travelled the world seeking investors for this new fund and potential investment opportunities. I designed the fund strategy with my people at SV and started recruiting a new team. I completed the rather arduous £250 million fundraising for the Dementia Discovery Fund in 2018. This was as much of an innovation as the 1994 exercise had been.

By the final close, we had Bill Gates behind us, seven pharmaceutical companies and prestige supporters such as the American Association of Retired Persons (AARP) and NFL Players Association as investors. This was the world's first fund focused solely on discovering and developing dementia therapeutics. It has invested in forty-five novel dementia drugs, of which six are already in clinical trials.

The original idea of a dementia fund had come from David Cameron when he was the Chair of the G7. He felt that the UK, supported by the G7, could spearhead new treatments for dementia. The Department of Health became a small investor in the fund, represented by Sir David Cooksey, a renowned venture capitalist and businessman. This was my first real exposure to Whitehall. A very benign start.

Developing precision medicines

In the year before Covid-19 emerged in the UK, I had spent much of my time corralling investors into our seventh SV fund, called SV7 Impact Medicine Fund. It was focused solely on creating and investing in biotechnology companies to discover and develop high-impact precision medicine drugs to either cure or have a significant impact on patients, their families and society, while still making attractive returns.

This biotech VC fund was intended to make the most of what has been described as a 'Golden Age' of scientific discovery. The latest gene therapy technologies can now replace missing or mutated genes to treat blindness or muscle wasting, cancer patients' cells can be engineered to kill their cancer and increasingly precise medical data and tools can be developed to treat the underlying causes of disease. CRISPR technology is now so advanced that some new drugs are being designed to cut and edit DNA, just as we do a Word document, to remove or replace disease-causing genes.

The potential of all this is truly transformative. Biotechnology has the capacity to allow people to live longer and healthier lives. Disease could be stopped in its tracks before it has even started. We will move not just from cure to prevention but from prevention to pre-emption.

This is a complicated area to understand, let alone to invest in. I still marvel at the genius of revolutionary medical science and am proud of the part we play in developing medicines with a real-world impact. The essentials of what I do have not changed much over the years, but the market has changed a lot. When I first started investing, we were focused on identifying drugs that could treat symptoms but would not necessarily affect the underlying disease. With the massive advances in biology and genetics, I and my team at SV have increasingly focused on finding drugs that specifically target the aberrant biological processes that cause the disease. We can now aim to cure or at least slow disease – not just treat the symptoms.

Over the years the biotech world has also altered, so the best venture capitalist funds do not merely put money behind a new idea, but now actively assist in building a business around it. In the 1990s up to a third of our investments required the creation of companies from scratch. These days almost two-thirds of SV's investments are into start-up biotech companies that we have built ourselves. That's why we put the incubator space above our office: entrepreneurs, scientists and experts can meet there and work together to develop their business plans, build teams and start to develop life-changing new drugs.

In a typical year we might review a thousand opportunities, of which a quarter would be deemed worthy of digging into more thoroughly. A large number of in-house ideas based on cutting-edge science get an airing too. After an intense triaging process, we will arrive at a shortlist of around twenty to thirty needing a more substantial review. In the end we may make investments in five to ten new companies.

Our style at SV is to be a very active participant on the boards of our companies. That means I'm involved in drug discovery and development decisions, financing and corporate strategy discussions as well as agreements on how to build the organisations. Even then, despite all this due diligence and portfolio company support, we have to build a twenty-five per cent loss ratio into the funds, recognising that many of these early companies will fail; we hope these will be more than offset by the major winners.

The nature of the healthcare sector is that, even with experienced venture capitalists, or pharmaceutical companies for that matter, there will be very many failures. These losses hurt, not least because I have my own money at stake alongside that of my investors.

Risk runs through everything we do in biotech. Almost every new drug that enters clinical trials will not work in the end. More than ninety per cent of all ideas for new drugs fail even to reach clinical trials. At the VTF, my experience of investing in biotech proved important: I didn't feel unduly daunted by the issues in delivering a Covid-19 vaccine. It was bound to be the biggest challenge of my professional life – the stakes were stratospherically high – and we had to be willing to take some long shots to secure success and I was extremely comfortable with that.

We try to minimise failure, but if we don't fail a bit, it means we probably aren't taking risks on the investments with a big potential upside. We need the big returns to offset our losses. Our strategy has been to build portfolios and manage our investments very carefully against the risks we can foresee. We don't throw good money after bad. We build the strongest possible teams. And we agree explicitly with management what we are collectively trying to achieve. If we win, they win. We work day and night to try to make our companies winners.

★

Back to the VTF. The weather was getting better. On one of my longer runs up on the hill, I reflected on my new role and my instinctive initial fear that I was an 'imposter' when it came to vaccines. I was now a few weeks into the job and felt more in control. The team around me was beginning to hum and we were making real progress. I realised that I was better qualified for the role than I had first thought.

I was entirely comfortable with risk, and risk would be the VTF's oxygen. I was used to being involved with extremely experimental ideas, uncertainty and innovations. I had a long history of building expert teams from nothing very quickly.

The notion of taking what might be a lengthy list of candidate vaccines and swiftly whittling it down to a shortlist of the most promising isn't intimidating. It's an activity I have been doing for decades. At the VTF, as at SV, I had experts who knew this stuff inside out.

Finally, my relationships across the biotech and pharmaceutical industry seemed to be a massive advantage for us. I had been around for nearly thirty years, as had Clive Dix, so we knew a lot of the key players – and we could easily get to any we did not already know.

I had sold many of our small biotech businesses to huge pharmaceutical companies such as Pfizer and AZ. I had helped forge partnerships between our biotech companies and pharmaceutical businesses to develop new drugs.

Perhaps most importantly, I had recruited extensively within the industry over many years to build our management teams. That meant I had built up a vast personal network across the pharmaceutical and biotechnology sector in the UK, the United States, Europe and around the world. It was clear to me that this network could be a critical advantage for the VTF, if we acted quickly.

The Marches

Stunningly beautiful. Very warm people. But not the obvious place to be launching a counter-attack against a new, rapidly spreading and deadly coronavirus.

I started going there in utero. My recently married parents had bought a small cottage as a second home just inside Wales in 1965 for just under £1,000 before I was born. They chose a remote spot on top of Cornhill in Powys. They wanted open spaces for their family. And an antidote to fast-paced London life.

My father had been at Sedbergh School in Cumbria and acquired a love of hill and mountain walking. He became Lord Chief Justice of England in 1996, and insisted that the title be expanded to 'and Wales' as the principality fell under his jurisdiction but was unrecognised. When in the same year he became a life peer he assumed it as Lord Bingham of Cornhill. Sadly, he died in 2010 and chose to be buried near to the cottage in St Cynog's Churchyard.

The phrase 'second home' might leave the wrong impression. This wasn't a classic quaint cottage in the country. Pencommon – the house on the hill – was a small, unmodernised, stone, farmer's dwelling. We didn't have indoor water or sanitation but used an outdoor tap to fill large water drums. The tap used to be at the bottom of the drive two fields away, so it was a relief and much less of a chore when my parents moved it closer to the house. We warmed the water on the Aga and had a hip bath in front of the fire. We used a chemical loo called an Elsan in the privy at the top of the back garden, with unmatched views. In the summer it was framed by lilacs and roses.

Mum once found a nest of squirrels in our bunk bed, so Dad decided to put a smoke-bomb in the roof to force the squirrels to leave. The smoke-bomb unfortunately set light to the roof and as kids we watched in awe as the flames went up. Not having water anywhere near the house complicated the response. Luckily the Talgarth fire brigade were able to get it under control. The most exciting thing for me and my brothers was camping in the field for weeks until the house was habitable again. We cooked sausages and toasted bread on an open fire.

After Jesse and I were married in the field below the cottage in 1992, there was a housing census and inspection. They concluded that the house was unfit for human habitation on every count.

Jesse wrote a lovely article shortly after Dad died entitled 'Mr Justice: A Portrait of Lord Bingham', which describes some of our home life.

[Pencommon] originally had just a single bedroom, but two more had been added and Kate and I were billeted in one of these. Since our room lay on the opposite side to the staircase, with the Binghams' own bedroom in between, this raised the interesting question of how to deal with the need for a nocturnal Harry Slashers. Getting to the garden seemed to require a Colditz-style escape out of the window, but even this was preferable to the prospect of tiptoeing through the main bedroom and past the sleeping parents. Luckily the solution was to hand: a stout china chamber pot, with a lid.

The eccentricity of our arrangements did not end there. As Jesse noted:

All meals were eaten in the kitchen or, in any but arctic weather, on the slabs outside. There being no water and so no dishwasher in the house, at the end of the meal the plates were taken outside and washed up in a tin basin with water from the water butt heated on the Aga. This operation was generally led by Tom. 'The plates can apricate in the sun,' he would remark on a balmy day, delighting in this rare word, with its air of apricots. More often, however – this being Wales – he would wash up in the freezing cold, dressed in his ancient green army greatcoat.

I have wonderful memories of these strangely tough conditions and it never occurred to me that washing up outside, or going to the loo in the back garden, was unusual. We never had a TV or radio in Wales so read books and entertained ourselves with cards, singing and ping-pong.

In 1996, the house in Wales was comprehensively renovated. My parents built a lovely sitting room as well as new bedrooms and four bathrooms. Running water had come to Pencommon at last. While Dad had to spend time in London for professional reasons, there is no doubt Pencommon was his home. Wales would be all but in my own bloodstream too.

Like father, like daughter. Up to a point. Having come back to the UK in 1991, Jesse and I got engaged and started planning our wedding. We were looking to buy a home but were shocked by London property prices. We decided that we would be better off renting in London and spending what money we had on something outside the capital. Where better to start than where I had grown up, and where my parents lived?

In 1991 we found a ruined watermill for sale, upstream from my parents. This included a tiny miller's cottage which would have had one room upstairs and one room downstairs, but the walls had largely fallen in after the roof collapsed. Attached to it was the watermill itself with two pairs of grinders. It had the overshoot water wheel still intact which would have been fed from the mill pond behind.

We put in an offer and exchanged before our wedding. And then spent the next few years rebuilding it to meet the latest regulations on heating and insulation.

★

When the Covid-19 crisis exploded, I thanked my lucky stars we had installed new EE mobile broadband shortly beforehand. There was no mobile signal other than at the top of the hill, or a few miles away. No broadband was possible through the phone lines as we were too far away from the switch, which meant that there was too high a loss of data through the line.

Decent access to the internet was an absolute prerequisite. While I was overseeing the VTF from the bedroom, my husband Jesse, as the Financial Secretary to the Treasury or FST, was managing the detail of the furlough programme alongside other emergency measures designed to soften the impact of the virus on the UK economy. As FST, he was ultimately accountable to Parliament, alongside the Chancellor of the Exchequer, for providing about £100 billion through the tax system at HMRC to protect jobs during the pandemic: £70 billion on the furlough scheme to protect nearly twelve million jobs and a further £28 billion to support about three million self-employed people.

This was an enormous undertaking. On top of that, he was managing a ton of tax policy, setting a digital strategy for HMRC, working on infrastructure strategy and taking a lot of emergency financial legislation through Parliament. It was unbelievably hectic.

But he also made a huge difference to my VTF work. Without Jesse, I could not have taken on this role. I completely relied on his wise and calm advice. He knew Westminster and Whitehall inside out. Every time I hit a bump or roadblock, he would suggest a path forward or offer a useful number or email address for me to find a solution. And he kept me positive when I was gloomy and brought me back down to earth when I was overexcited.

As Jesse wrote in the *Hereford Times* when he left office in September 2021, 'We worked round the clock, me on furlough, her on vaccines. Someone described us as Mr Tax and Mrs Vax.'

Mercifully, it was not just Tax and Vax, or insanity might have beckoned. Our daughter Nell was sitting her final exams and our younger son Noah was completing the remainder of his second year at Yale by Zoom – on American hours. Sam, our eldest, had to stay in the United States given the US laws restricting foreign nationals from re-entry. Sam was living in a quasi-commune where he spent most of his time collaborating in composing musicals; at least that was more social that my own lockdown life.

One evening in June I was feeling particularly stressed, and Noah and Nell introduced me to *Saturday Night Live*'s Funniest Cats sketch to cheer me up. Adam Driver, as host Finn Raynal-Beads, brought on guests who took a comically French approach to narrating cat videos. That made me laugh a lot and still does. Look it up.

Nell and Noah then did their own spoof – even better. Watching them is still my best antidote to stress.

★

My dominant memory of those months is the sheer amount of work involved. My days would usually start with emails at 7 a.m., meetings from 8 a.m. to 8.30 p.m., a brief break for food and calls and meetings continuously all day, often with a closing 10 p.m. call to Nick or Clive before bedtime. The timetable rarely changed at weekends, though we didn't have the early morning group calls. My SV assistant, Alanya Calleja, kindly agreed to step in to make sense of my schedule and liaise with the VTF private office at BEIS.

We held 8 a.m. meetings on Mondays, Wednesdays and Fridays on MS Teams – apparently the most secure of the different video options. I now understand that others in the VTF would have preferred to start later but I turned a deaf ear to that. There was no time to lose. I felt vindicated when, during early calls with US company Novavax, they mentioned how surprised they were by our speed and flexibility. No one in the private sector had experienced any government working like this before.

As other departments in Whitehall became interested in the VTF, they joined the Monday meetings. On Wednesdays it would usually be just the Steering Group and one or two outsiders, depending on the issue under consideration. On Fridays, we would review the progress that had been made to date and identify future priorities. Anyone who committed the crime of speaking while still on mute would be fined for the communal beer kitty.

I doubt if any of those involved will ever forget it – I certainly won't. Nick largely worked in Whitehall, with daily meetings with Cabinet members and frequent encounters with the Prime Minister. Clive recalls working fifteen-hour days without a single day off for about nine months. Ian spoke of the mental strain he felt at the start as too few people were trying to do too many things. Divya talked to me almost daily at this time, while managing her toddler and baby.

Anyone who says that working from home is some sort of holiday and inevitably associated with lower productivity should take one look at the VTF's work. We endured more stress in our own homes than we had faced in decades of office work.

We were all completely focused and our motivation remained incredibly strong. We were not put off by the fear that no vaccine would be secured and so many hours potentially wasted. But Clive and I felt an extra degree of pressure. There was no one to whom we could pass the buck.

5

SETTING THE STRATEGY

One of the challenges of the entire VTF experience, reflected in the structure of this book, is that so many significant issues had to be dealt with simultaneously rather than consecutively, but to make sense of the overall story they need to be teased out. At the same time as I was assembling a team, I was also setting the strategy and trying to navigate my way around government. This chapter outlines the key decisions taken to develop the VTF strategy from the start.

6 May: 'Ping…ping…ping'. I was getting ready for bed and glanced at my phone. I saw a host of texts from unknown numbers. I was being bombarded by strangers wanting to discuss my plans for the VTF. What a twenty-four hours! It had all happened so fast. I hadn't even had space to think.

On the train home the following day after my walk with Nick Elliott, I decided to set out some initial thoughts in a PowerPoint presentation. Of course, I didn't have any firm plans at that stage but I did have some high-level punchlines.

I reiterated my simple mandate: to secure and deliver vaccines quickly to the UK and abroad. Speed was of the essence because people were dying every day.

I knew I was not dealing with drug discovery experts in government who were familiar with the risks and challenges of clinical development and manufacturing. So, I set out the facts in very clear black and white. And easy metaphors.

I described what the VTF was attempting to achieve as 'harder than Everest'. No vaccine had ever been successfully developed to combat any human coronavirus.

Ever.

We knew precious little about SARS-CoV-2, except that it causes Covid-19. The Chinese had released the draft genetic sequence of the virus suspected of causing the Wuhan pneumonia outbreak on 11 January 2020 – surprisingly quickly. But we had no good data about the level or method of transmission, fatality or infectivity – or even who was most at risk. Vaccines usually take years to develop and manufacture. Viruses mutate. While there were some intriguing new vaccine formats and approaches that might deliver results, they were untested and unproven – two qualities you just can't have in medical science.

I made it my routine to revise this VTF Update document every ten to fourteen days, keeping a running 'what we are doing and where we are at' briefing document to share with the PM, ministers and wider Government figures. As I started to build the team up and bring external industrial, scientific, technical and deal-doing experts into its work, I documented their credentials in order to reassure the Government and Whitehall that we knew what we were doing.

In setting the strategy, I knew that success was far from certain. If anything, outright failure was more likely. If we failed to secure the best vaccines or if people were not willing to take the vaccine, the result would not just be the loss of my own reputation, but a massive impact on public health. However, I still felt an acute responsibility to my co-workers at SV whose own fates would be affected by my failure.

But I'd made the decision to take this on, so decided not to worry but just get my head down and try to do a good job.

Likelihood of success

In my first VTF Expert Advisory Committee meeting, on 3 April 2020, I asked the vaccine experts for their assessment of the likelihood of success of any Covid-19 vaccine. They told me that it was only fifteen per cent likely in each case that any vaccine would prove effective, and then only if the vaccine was already in clinical trials. In all other circumstances, the odds shrank to ten per cent or lower. I wasn't shocked by this: it was not wildly different from the development of new drugs. While fifteen per cent is plainly not zero, it is clearly a long way short of a majority chance.

I did not know what level of protection we would get from a successful vaccine. Even if a vaccine 'worked', there was the likelihood that, like many flu vaccines, it would protect only about half its recipients from infection, leaving the other half vulnerable to infection. The likely duration of any effectiveness was also unclear. While I wanted these vaccines to provide protection from serious disease, hospital admission and deaths for a period, this remained only a hope.

All of this made for some cold realism. Spreading our choices across a portfolio of different vaccines would increase the chances that at least one of them might be of value, but it did not make it anything close to a probability. If you put a £10 bet on ten numbers on a roulette wheel, this does not ensure that you get your stake and more back. It would be entirely possible that none of the ten numbers would come up, and all cash would be lost.

The messages in the press appeared to be rather optimistic, both in terms of how long it would take to generate decisive clinical data, and the likelihood of the vaccines' future efficacy. I don't think the message of how unlikely any vaccine was to succeed was well understood in the spring of 2020.

Scientists and doctors were paraded before the media during March and April 2020, and frankly I was worried by how positive they were. I was concerned that no one appreciated the serious challenges of using vaccines to control Covid-19. We did not want to raise false hopes which might even increase risky behaviour.

As for me, I was definitely not in the glass-half-full camp. I agreed with the more sombre view shared by SVB Leerink, a specialist American investment bank. They published a report on 21 April 2020 entitled *Sober Up! 25 reasons not to count on COVID vaccine for Herd Immunity in 1–2 years*. It said:

> We view the current expectations for a vaccine in this timetable (12–18 months) as the equivalent of standing 24 feet (the usual distance is 8 feet) from a dartboard, with one dart in hand and counting on a bullseye with one throw. It is theoretically possible but highly unlikely that such expectations are correct.

The publication's twenty-five reasons why it had come to this view seemed so strong as to almost end any argument that might be had on the subject. Optimism could barely be punctured more forcefully.

This bleak outlook was rooted in the historical record. There were numerous examples where the infectious agent behind a disease had been identified but it had taken decades to create a successful vaccine, such as tuberculosis where the cause had been known since 1882. In some cases like HIV, we still don't have a vaccine.

While new vaccines have of course been developed, the average time from identification of the disease-causing pathogen to a vaccine being licensed is sixty years. The lab-to-jab recordholder was the mumps vaccine developed by Maurice Hilleman in the 1960s, which took four years. And this was in an era where the requirements made of clinical trials were less onerous.

Even that breakneck pace of vaccine development obviously wasn't going to work here. We needed a step-change if the VTF was to have any impact on the pandemic. We didn't have four years. There would be too many deaths, both in the UK and in the rest of the world.

A report for the Ministry of Defence in June 2020 (*Covid-19 vaccines; from lab to patient*) bluntly stated that 'Overall vaccine science and manufacturing has not modernised in the same way as the wider pharmaceutical and biotechnology industry.'

This was undoubtedly true for the so-called 'first generation' virus vaccines where vaccines were made in eggs.

Yes – literally chicken eggs.

I couldn't believe we were even talking about this in the twenty-first century.

Most flu shots are made in eggs. This involves infecting millions of fertilised chicken eggs with live virus, which replicate in the yolk sac before being harvested. Live virus is then inactivated to form the vaccine. This process had not changed much in decades.

This seemed crazy. This method was far too slow and laborious to be useful for Covid-19. The vaccines produced weren't even that good, as viruses produced in eggs are often quite different from the original viruses. Clive and I both felt strongly that eggs weren't the solution.

The one chink of light was that recent innovations offered quicker and more modern ways to make vaccines.

In this world, a 'platform' is the word used for the base technology – the underlying system – that can be used to develop a number of different vaccines. I knew a little about Oxford's 'adenoviral' vaccine platform already. I had visited Adrian Hill at the Jenner Institute in 2016 to see whether his platform might be suitable for cancer vaccines. He showed me how Oxford's adeno platform could be engineered to include the genetic code for a harmless protein to stimulate the immune system against cancer or infectious pathogens. Adrian is encyclopaedic when it comes to developing vaccines so I had been given a good briefing. That meant I already had a reasonable idea that these adeno vaccines could be manufactured and I hoped they would be successful.

Hope is not, however, by itself a strategy. The BIA bioprocessing taskforce had been working hard since February 2020 to develop options for the scale-up and manufacturing of the early vaccines. The Coalition for Epidemic Preparedness Innovations (CEPI), a global body led by Dr Richard Hatchett, a prominent American physician at the Wellcome Trust and the Gates Foundation, had also performed early work scoping out manufacturing capabilities in the UK and globally.

When I arrived in May, I discovered that the VTF officials in BEIS had handed over responsibility for surveying the vaccine landscape and making recommendations to a high-profile management consultancy firm. This company no doubt employed very bright people but had no evident expertise in evaluating and prioritising the most promising vaccines.

I wasn't up for this. I didn't want to hand over the critical judgements to an arm's-length consulting company with no specialist expertise in a highly specialist field. I wanted the experts – real experts – I knew and trusted. The select band of VTF industry experts that Clive Dix was putting together was the team I wanted to hear from.

So, my first significant decision was to ask Nick to move the management consultants off the project.

There were other key questions to address early on. Each had major strategic ramifications, both in terms of the goals we had to deliver and the team we would need to do this. I also didn't want to create waves before I even started, by putting the wrong people's noses out of joint.

Do we focus only on vaccines, or expand to therapeutics and antivirals?

A vital issue was the overall remit of the VTF. Should it be responsible for treatments for those who had *got* Covid-19 as well as for vaccinations *against* it?

The agenda for the first formal meeting of the new VTF steering committee held on 11 May 2020 had actually referred to the organisation as the 'Vaccines *and Therapeutics* Taskforce' (my italics). If we were indeed to include therapeutics I would need to build a very different team, with different skills.

The path of least resistance would be to include therapeutics – that's the area I knew best. I had worked in drug discovery and development for decades. I knew the people and I knew what to do. It was the fine detail of prophylactic vaccines where I lacked experience.

Alok Sharma as Business Secretary was keen for us to incorporate therapeutics. We had phone calls to discuss this. I remained dubious.

There were strong reasons not to expand beyond vaccines. Taking on vaccines *and* therapeutics was a considerable mission. They were quite different. They could easily end up competing with one another for time and attention. Would we be stretching ourselves too thin?

On a journey to London in early May to meet Alok I learnt that there were already substantial tensions in the official world of therapeutics. There had been, not unlike the VTF, an initial attempt at something akin to a Therapeutics Taskforce, which started as a drive to foster closer co-operation between industry and academia, much as the UK BioIndustry Association had done for vaccines. In this case, however, the partnership proved less harmonious.

My signal on this journey was not good so I kept dropping off the call. But I heard enough to know that there had been a heated debate over how to manage the smaller Phase 2 studies that were being proposed to explore whether there were existing drugs that could be repurposed to treat the new coronavirus. Any drugs showing promise in the early clinical studies could then be moved into large Phase 3 pivotal studies.

The industry had been very keen on moving swiftly ahead to lead the exploratory Phase 2 studies. The academics were far more wary. There were some very senior officials in government who had instinctive suspicions about the motives of the industry experts.

One official even asked an industry volunteer: 'What are you personally going to get out of this?' as though every commercial expert in the area was in it for the money.

This reaction from Whitehall soured the atmosphere. The industry and academic volunteers felt that they were becoming marginalised and distrusted. I didn't want to step into what was already turning into an ugly turf war.

I knew the later-stage pivotal therapeutic trials were under control. Professor Martin Landray and Sir Jeremy Farrar, Director of the Wellcome Trust, had designed the world's largest Covid-19 therapeutic trial in February – on a Number 18 bus. Jeremy agreed to provide funding and Professor Peter Horby in Oxford joined Martin to lead this trial called RECOVERY.

The RECOVERY trial had several treatment arms of about 2,000 patients each, evaluating different approved drugs versus the usual standard of hospital care in parallel. The drugs tested included antivirals, antibiotics, corticosteroids and anti-inflammatories. The scale of this trial was large enough to generate unequivocal data on which drugs saved lives and which didn't. The trial was launched in nine days. By 19 March they had recruited their first patient. Within three months they had proven the first drug worked.

So, I didn't think there was any need to interfere with what was being done in these very slick, large repurposing trials. It was all running smoothly.

Repurposing existing drugs is quicker than developing drugs *de novo*. For example, when Pfizer was running clinical trials on a new phosphodiesterase type 5 (PDE-5) inhibitor drug to test its effectiveness in treating hypertension and angina, they noticed one side effect of the drug was to induce penile erections. Pfizer changed the clinical indication of the drug: sildenafil was launched as Viagra to treat erectile dysfunction.

Even without this backdrop, therapeutics was manifestly a very politically sensitive space. Not only was there a big gap between the industry experts, the academics and the officials, but I recognised there was also a huge risk of open warfare between BEIS and the Department of Health over who was in charge.

There was a decent case to say that the VTF was rightfully at home within BEIS because our focus on manufacturing and development lay closer to industrial strategy than conventional procurement. That case would be weakened if therapeutics were incorporated as well, and the Department of Health would feel even more bruised. Vaccines were the big hole in our efforts to control Covid-19. I spoke to experts including Patrick and Jeremy Farrar and agreed with them that vaccines should be the primary focus. Therapeutics were out and went back to the Department of Health.

However, I felt strongly that the VTF should take the lead in reviewing antibody products against Covid-19, known as antibody cocktails. These cocktails consisted of two antibodies that bind to the spike protein, basically to provide a 'synthetic immune-response-in-a-syringe'. Antibody cocktails could substitute for vaccination for those people without a functioning immune system, such as cancer and HIV patients or those on immunosuppressive drugs. Antibody cocktails are used as a treatment to improve the survival of Ebola patients. The immunocompromised population might not respond to a Covid-19 vaccine and we needed to protect them too.

Antibodies were likely to be safe and effective. But they were also expensive to make, and so more suitable for specific vulnerable groups than for the population as a whole. And like vaccines, they were vulnerable to changes in the virus that might render them ineffective. Finally, as well as being used prophylactically, antibodies could be used as a therapeutic for those who were already infected, as a boost to their immune response.

I argued that rather than two teams separately evaluating the antibody candidates, the VTF should take the lead on all due diligence. We would make recommendations for which antibodies, if any, should be included in the VTF portfolio for prophylaxis, and which should be included in Oxford's RECOVERY trial to be assessed as therapeutics.

Primer on the different types of vaccines

I found it amazing that there were so many different ways to create a vaccine. How many ways are there of skinning a cat after all? But the answer is: a lot. And each approach generates a somewhat different immune response – we had to look at all of them.

This description is drawn heavily from the excellent primer on the topic produced by the Wellcome Trust on its website, which I recommend reading. Wellcome notes:

> All vaccines work by teaching our bodies to recognise and fight the pathogen in a safe way. They encourage our immune system to produce antibodies, T-cells or both, so that if we encounter the infection later our immune system knows how to defend against it.

There are four main types of vaccine (*listed in order of discovery and years of use*):

Whole virus vaccines are old-fashioned but well understood. (The Chinese Covid-19 vaccines were predominantly whole viral-based vaccines.) There are different types of whole viral-based vaccines, either inactivated/dead viruses or weakened live viruses, combined with an adjuvant. (An adjuvant is a vaccine ingredient used to create a stronger immune response.) A virus can be inactivated by being exposed to heat, chemicals or radiation, or formed into so-called Virus-Like Particles (VLPs), a form of the virus that closely resembles the real thing, but which has been created artificially. An inactivated virus vaccine typically does not trigger as strong an immune response as a weakened, live, *attenuated* virus-based vaccine. Examples of inactivated whole virus-based vaccines include polio and flu. Given the potential risks, weakened live virus vaccines have not been prioritised as vaccines for a lethal pandemic, though this format has been used successfully for the chickenpox vaccine and the measles, mumps, and rubella (MMR) vaccine. Not all viruses can be grown at scale, and strict containment facilities are required.

Protein subunit vaccines employ pieces of the Covid-19 virus, namely fragments or peptides of the spike protein itself. This is also a very well-established vaccine approach. When injected, it triggers an immune response. The proteins are grown in living cells in advanced bioprocessing factories and then the protein is extracted, purified and deployed as the active ingredient in the vaccine together with an adjuvant which acts as a general immune stimulant. Examples of protein subunit vaccines include Hepatitis B and meningococcal vaccines.

Then there are two new types of vaccine which rely on the *host* cells to manufacture the protein, namely viral vector vaccines and mRNA vaccines. No viral vector based on the adeno platform or mRNA vaccine had ever been approved for use when I started as Chair in May 2020.

Viral vector vaccines use a harmless virus which is altered to contain certain parts of Covid-19's spike protein genetic code. Once injected into the body, the virus infects the cells and harnesses their protein production machinery to produce the spike protein. This then triggers a response to alert our immune system to recognise the real virus. Almost all vaccines in this group use different types of adenoviruses, the sort that cause the common cold, as their carriers.

mRNA (nucleic acid) vaccines contain part of Covid-19's spike protein genetic code (messenger RNA) encased in a fatty envelope. Messenger RNA is a sequence of genetic code which our bodies use to tell cells what proteins to construct. Like the viral vector vaccines, once the mRNA vaccine is injected into the body, it instructs the cell's protein production machinery to generate the spike protein. This triggers an immune response. As with viral vector vaccines, the host cells are stimulated to create the Covid-19 spike protein and then attack it. DNA-based vaccines follow the same approach. mRNA vaccines are simpler to make since they use an enzymatic process before being wrapped in a greasy shell and there is no need to remove cells or host cell proteins. mRNA vaccines are unstable and have to be kept at ultra-low temperatures.

I called the latter two vaccines the hairy, scary, sexy vaccines as they had not been approved before, unlike the tried and tested whole virus-based and protein-based ones. Of course, in May 2020, we did not know whether *any* vaccine formats would work against Covid-19, or whether we could even manufacture them at scale.

Clive and I agreed that we should build a portfolio with the most promising vaccines representing each of the different formats, so that we could increase our chances of securing at least one success-ful vaccine. Each vaccine format was likely to stimulate a slightly different immune response of antibodies and T-cells.

In the happy event that more than one vaccine worked, it would make sense to have a choice of vaccines so as to maximise the breadth of immune response in different parts of the population. Older people's immune systems are getting a bit weary, a bit less active and alert, so tend not to respond so well to vaccines. A choice of different vaccines would improve our chances of finding a more effective one for the elderly. Also, I thought that the more estab-lished vaccine formats (protein and whole virus) might be more suitable for vaccine-hesitant people, who might be resistant to receiving a new-generation vaccine.

How many vaccine doses to buy?

While all the VTF work was ramping up fast, I was also trying to be a good mum. My daughter Nell was starting her finals in late May so I made lots of extra-tasty pearl barley, home-grown beetroot and feta salads to keep her going for these four-hour online marathons. I stocked up on Maltesers too. I wanted to make life as easy as possi-ble at a rather stressful time. The weather was stunning, so on a couple of evenings we rode out onto the hills in the golden late-evening sun. That kept all our spirits high.

The morning of Nell's first exam on 25 May, we discussed the Joint Committee on Vaccination and Immunisation (JCVI) at our VTF Steering Group meeting.

Clive and his team were busy deciding which vaccines to buy, but we needed to know how many doses to buy. We asked the JCVI who in the population should be vaccinated.

The JCVI had been formed in 1963 from an existing advisory board on polio immunisation and had acquired statutory status in 1981. It was structurally very different from the MHRA in that it was essentially a set of experts to advise the Government on vaccination. These experts had usually met only about three times a year and were unknown outside the medical community.

Figuring out who to vaccinate proved anything but straightforward. Unbeknownst to me, this obscure body had a fraught political status.

First, the devolution settlement in the UK meant that the JCVI wielded different authority in different places. Since 2009, the Secretary of State for Health was largely required to implement its recommendations in England. In Wales, the findings offered to ministers were advisory. In Scotland and Northern Ireland, the JCVI had no formal statutory clout but ministers mostly accepted its counsel. This would not be the only time when devolution would confound me.

Second, the JCVI's Chair since 2018 had been Professor Andrew Pollard from the Oxford Vaccine Group. As he was the Principal Investigator leading the Oxford/AstraZeneca vaccine development, he had a conflict of interest. A Covid-19 subcommittee was created and its Chair would be Wei Shen Lim, a consultant respiratory physician and honorary Professor of Medicine at the Nottingham University NHS Trust.

Finally, although they were advising us on who to vaccinate, we knew a lot more about the emerging vaccine contenders than they did since we were reviewing the detailed data on them all. Clive Dix regularly briefed the JCVI on our assessment of the different vaccines and Wei Shen would attend our VTF meetings on this issue.

By the time we got to July, the JCVI told us that their highest priorities were the frail elderly and frontline health workers. After that came adults over fifty and younger adults who had underlying medical conditions that made them especially vulnerable to the virus. These represented the Groups 1–9, widely discussed in the media by early 2021.

Only if very safe vaccines came on stream in the future, they said, would the JCVI consider vaccinating younger people to stop infection and asymptomatic transmission, but at that point, healthy adults and children were not a priority. Since no vaccines were being trialled in children in the summer of 2020, considering whether to vaccinate them at that point remained entirely hypothetical.

Of course, the official advice changed as the pandemic progressed, with variants emerging, such as Alpha, Beta, Gamma, Delta and Omicron. New clinical trials on teenagers were launched in late 2020 and by mid-2021 trials on children as young as six months were underway. But in the summer of 2020, we were talking about an adults-only vaccine.

We asked the Department of Health to confirm how many individuals were represented in Groups 1–9 and were told to use a planning assumption of thirty million people for all of these 'at risk' cohorts. Most vaccines required two doses for protection. JCVI shared estimates for take-up and wastage based on experience with flu, which proved to be pessimistic.

Having thirty million people at risk meant that the UK would be a small customer relative to the US, the EU and Japan. This weak bargaining position might seriously harm our ability to secure the most promising vaccines. What to do? We took a very commercial line, which proved absolutely fundamental. We decided that the only way we could compete with these massive buyers was by turning the UK into the best possible client, doing everything we could to make this country the most attractive place in the world to develop and manufacture a vaccine rapidly.

Defining the six-month goals

After testing my home-cured bacon with Jesse and Noah for breakfast on 28 June, without a great deal of take-up, I decided I needed to define exactly what success would look like for the VTF. The headline goals the PM had given me were fine but, as with my biotech venture investments, I wanted more detail that could be used to measure our work.

I would be leaving my temporary role as Chair by the end of the year, so setting goals for my tenure made sense to me. The whole VTF effort was now moving at a breakneck pace and the team was growing rapidly. Now was the time to get everyone aligned on the detail.

I wrote and circulated seven headline goals for the VTF to reach in six months, both to focus the team and to signal to the Government what to expect.

1. *Procure rights to a diverse range of vaccines which have the potential to vaccinate safely to protect the high-priority populations in the UK by the first half of 2021.*
2. *Establish robust supply chains where necessary to ensure there is sufficient supply for the high-priority populations by the first half of 2021; build plans for longer term supply.*
3. *Provide funding for all prioritised vaccine clinical trials to be run through NIHR with industrial scale diagnostics and MHRA regulatory support to enable rapid demonstration of clinical safety and efficacy in the high-priority populations. Ensure the pharmacovigilance systems are in place for long-term clinical follow-up of everyone vaccinated.*
4. *Develop and evaluate detailed operational plans with Department of Health for deployment as soon as a vaccine becomes available.*

5. *Collaborate with other countries (where appropriate) to improve access to develop, supply and distribute the most promising vaccines internationally to low- and high-income countries.*

6. *Establish long-term vaccine strategy plans to prepare for future pandemics within the long-term industrial strategy for life sciences.*

7. *Educate and inform government, parliament and commentators about Covid-19 vaccine development, challenges and the science involved.*

For each goal, I defined a range of key measures on a separate page to measure how far we had gone towards meeting that goal. For example, for Goal 1, I set December 2020 as a target to have signed supply agreements for six vaccines, both domestic and international, from at least three of the four different vaccine formats.

I also added further tests. The VTF portfolio would need to include at least two of the first four vaccine candidates (if any) to receive approval from the MHRA by the end of the first half (H1 in the jargon) of 2021 *and* must have the manufacturing capacity to deliver at least sixty million finished doses to the UK by September 2021. I knew this was very ambitious.

I included an additional 'stretch goal', namely to secure emergency approval for the Oxford/AstraZeneca vaccine for dosing by the close of 2020.

In or out of Europe?

Before I was writing down my initial thoughts on a VTF strategy, senior advisers to the President of France had reached out to their equivalents in London. Emmanuel Macron had suggested that France, the UK and Germany merge their efforts to acquire vaccines. I was sent a short note entitled a 'Covid-19 EMA Pandemic Task Force' later to be called the 'Inclusive Vaccine Alliance' or 'E3'. Not only was President Macron champing at the bit over this notion, his officials stressed that he wanted to make a public declaration of intent as soon as possible.

When I joined the VTF in May I was asked what I thought about Macron's suggestion. Not a crazy proposal by any means – in fact it could be quite helpful alongside our own VTF work.

The UK, France and Germany each had substantial capabilities for an end-to-end vaccine approach, but all of us would have to spend time and money completing what was missing to be wholly self-sufficient. A co-ordinated division of tasks could be a smart shortcut. All three countries also had national companies developing promising vaccine candidates.

A combined population of more than 200 million people would wield more collective bargaining power with vaccine companies than the UK alone, which was a third of that size. With limited supplies, a pact could change the odds for success substantially since we could broaden the size of the VTF portfolio. The depressing fifteen per cent judgement of success might have a chance of heading towards a fifty per cent shot. It had its political difficulties with respect to the EU, but Paris was hinting to London that it too would prefer to keep the concept entirely separate from the European Commission.

There were some very significant players in Whitehall and beyond who sympathised with the idea. As he has publicly acknowledged in his own book on the coronavirus crisis (*Spike: The Virus vs The People*), Sir Jeremy Farrar, Director of the Wellcome Trust, strongly favoured a pan-European vaccine policy. I was certainly not opposed to co-operating with the EU.

Jeremy made his case forcefully to the Cabinet Office and elsewhere. If the VTF went forward on its original, unilateral mandate he could foresee some very awkward challenges. The UK might have to enter contracts by itself with multiple companies at high risk and uncertainty. This would involve the commitment of large amounts of money to unproven vaccines at a worryingly early stage in their evolution. He rightly feared that the companies concerned, many of which were very large institutions with a strong sense of their own interests, would hold all the aces in negotiations. They could dictate terms – the threat hanging that, if the UK did not accept, plenty of other countries would.

The only means by which the UK might avoid that trap was by entering into more contracts with more companies than it could possibly need. Not an outcome anyone wanted. That would bring real financial and ethical costs. A pooling approach such as the E3 would reduce the risks.

I discussed with Jesse the disadvantages to this expansion of strategy. I was pretty concerned that the VTF might be about to be folded into something else in a matter of weeks after being created, and well before we had the chance to really get going. I knew we had a special team whom I trusted and it might just be better to get to the top of Everest independently. What did an E3 deal mean for Oxford/AstraZeneca? The French proposal was disturbingly vague in terms of the extent to which it would prevent any of the three governments selectively pursuing their own agendas, as well as co-operating with others.

Would the rest of the EU really be relaxed about France and Germany aligning with the UK outside of it? What would it mean for their own vaccine supplies if one were to be licensed? How would other players with whom the UK Government was conducting an ongoing vaccine dialogue – the United States and China – regard this initiative?

On the day before our mutual appointment was to be announced (15 May) Nick Elliot and I discussed the situation. Nick had been asked whether he had any comments on a memorandum on the E3 idea being prepared for the Business Secretary. He had emailed me saying 'The international dimension is something we are going to need to agree a strategy on and there are lots of fingers in this particular pie around government.'

In some ways senior UK officials and special advisers were spooked by the French initiative. It had 'very hot potato' written all over it. They certainly did not want to do anything which would lead to the UK being bounced by France into an alliance that subsequently could not be kept under control. I wasn't even sure whether the Prime Minister would allow it. Nick's sound advice was to take the *Yes Minister* approach, namely to keep talking to the French privately and put the matter off until we had a better sense of whether the alliance could work.

For the better part of a month the procrastination continued. BEIS officials attempted to find a set of words that their Secretary of State could send on to 10 Downing Street for consideration. The French were still pushing hard, but had they really signed up Berlin? Officials operating for the Prime Minister were firm in what they would and would not be willing to put in his weekend red box. They wanted more detail and BEIS was finding it hard to provide this.

I did not object in principle to working with other European countries, and in fact had plenty of discussions with my counterparts on the continent during my time as VTF Chair. Neither Nick nor I, though, wanted in any way to limit our capacity to act independently. We had no wish to lose our agility by becoming subject to a clunky decision-making process.

I was particularly disconcerted that the Cabinet Secretary seemed to be veering towards accepting the French-led approach and abandoning the VTF entirely. I remember going for a walk with Jesse in the hills discussing this, and he firmly encouraged me to draw a line in the sand on this question. I said to Patrick directly that any such collaboration with other countries had to happen alongside the autonomous activities of the VTF and must not serve to shunt us into an administrative siding.

Playing for time turned out to be an asset as it let the VTF show it could make swift advances and thus ease some of the concerns that the UK might be too small an actor to procure, develop and manufacture its own vaccines. The bureaucrats sent proposed language back-and-forth, so that it was almost up to the VTF itself whether it wanted to be independent or aligned with France and Germany.

The possibility of this three-way pact now entered the public domain. The potential membership had been extended to involve Italy, the Netherlands and Norway. This may have made it more inclusive, but it undermined the logic of the opening Gang of Three proposition. The structure grew even more amorphous. Full-blown UK involvement now seemed unlikely..

The very idea was also a source of aggravation to others within the European Union. On 12 June the European Commission announced its own plans for a €2.7 billion programme to fund Covid-19 vaccination development and procurement in the EU. This slammed the door shut on a UK Gang-of-*now-more-than-*Three agreement. It would place Brussels in charge of procurement for the EU bloc and let Brussels set conditions for the UK's participation if we wanted to be part of this, since in 2020 we were still part of the EU.

I had supported Remain in the 2016 referendum on the UK's membership of the European Union. To that extent the notion of an understanding with France and Germany as a supplemental part of the VTF's strategy was welcome. Being subsumed into it completely was a different matter altogether. The European Commission seizing the reins and making it clear that it would operate on the basis of its standard procedures crystallised the situation as totally unacceptable. As I would say to a meeting of the House of Commons Public Accounts Committee on 11 January 2021:

> The conditions that the EU set to allow us to participate were conditions we felt were not attractive. We were not able to join any decision-making on which vaccines to choose; we had to abandon the negotiations we either already had underway or had concluded with AZ [AstraZeneca]; and we also were not able to talk to future potential vaccine companies that they [the EU] may be talking to now or in the future. We felt that the conditions were too tight and that we would be able to act more quickly if we did it independently.

As matters turned out, the whole episode would be something of a fortuitous escape for the VTF. Even had the initial UK–France–Germany tripod remained intact, discussions as to who did what within the three countries would be bound to absorb more time and probably involve more friction than the UK opting for its own distinctive stance. Jeremy Farrar was gracious to state in his book:

> While I was initially disappointed that the UK had opted out of the European Union procurement scheme, the UK's Vaccine Taskforce, led by Kate Bingham, has been one of the standout successes of the country's pandemic response. While I don't like saying it, it was the best possible example of British exceptionalism approaching a challenge with a mixture of urgency, risk-taking and pragmatism. I am sure many in Europe wish the same approach had been brought to bear on behalf of the bloc.

I was also certain by this stage that we had to drive the 'best possible client' approach, making the UK an irresistible customer to the vaccine companies – offsetting our relatively small size. I wanted to show the UK could help develop and manufacture these vaccines fast and professionally. Being a good customer did not seem a priority for the EU.

There was now no going back. The UK had committed to its own vaccine strategy and proving the wisdom of that decision would rest squarely on the VTF steering committee. Next challenge: to reconcile our strategy with the Byzantine procedures of Whitehall.

6

THE WAYS OF WHITEHALL

Surprisingly, I don't have a lot of pillow talk with my husband on the workings of the government machine. He knows that I am not that interested in engaging in conversations about politics. I brought little prior experience of Whitehall to the Vaccine Taskforce.

It may sound counter-intuitive, and running contrary to my cherished focus on outcomes not process, but please bear with me when I describe some of the official bodies, alongside Whitehall processes and tongue-twisting acronyms. It does offer some insight as to how government actually operates.

Other than a role on the UK Life Sciences Strategy Advisory Board, I hadn't spent much time schooling myself on how our administration worked. Three decades in the private sector hadn't armed me for what I would face during my seven-month tenure.

But I was blessed with two important assets. The first was Jesse. He brought experience in both industry and academia, but he had been involved in politics in one way or another for the previous fifteen years. He had, by 2020, been a Member of Parliament for a decade. He was serving as Financial Secretary, the number three minister at the Treasury, right at the heart of one of the most powerful institutions in Whitehall. He had been Paymaster General and before that worked as a junior minister in BEIS (my host department) and at the

Department for Transport. Having been a philosopher of politics, he understood thoroughly how it was supposed to work, as well as how it actually worked. His ability to explain how fiefdoms in government interacted was invaluable. Jesse had nothing to do with my VTF work; he could give constructive advice without any risk of conflict.

The second was Nick Elliott, who from the outset sought to shield me from the worst aspects of bureaucratic complexity and intrigue. Frankly I couldn't have done the role without both of them.

My position as VTF Chair was novel, probably inconceivable, outside the context of a pandemic.

As mentioned, I had discussed the role at length with Jesse and we wrote a list of conditions to help ensure success. Two conditions, agreed with the Cabinet Secretary in my engagement letter, proved especially valuable.

The first was that I would report to the Prime Minister. This was an important card to hold as it meant that, if I felt that I was enduring delay, disruption or obstruction, I could attempt to break the deadlock by reaching out directly to the PM, and this would not breach the bounds of permissible procedure. It was a card that I knew that I would have to play sparingly or it would diminish in effectiveness.

On a periodic basis I would exchange text or WhatsApp messages with Boris to let him know about our progress, but I only deployed the 'nuclear option' of asking to talk to him when all other routes seemed blocked – I pressed the button only two or three times during my tenure. He had his own concerns of course, mostly around whether China or Russia might acquire a vaccine before us, or whether the vaccines would be 'British'. But for the record, when Boris was Prime Minister, he offered me consistent and strong support during my time as VTF Chair.

The second new feature was the process by which the VTF could spend money, given that speed was of the essence.

In ordinary times it is hard to make risky spending decisions in Whitehall. Any such proposition would start off within its home department, then sequentially move around other affected departments and finally be sent to the Cabinet Office and the Treasury, who would have no compunction in totally ripping a proposal apart. Of course, there is merit in several sets of eyes running over public spending, particularly if it involves high risk. Yet if this process had been imposed on the VTF then we could not have done what we did.

Quick government decision-making. Really?

I was keen to avoid a very long and painful bureaucratic approval process and wanted assurances that the UK would be willing to take appropriate risks and provide upfront funding to rapidly build a portfolio of vaccines *before* we knew which if any of them might work.

To do this, the VTF needed something much closer to the risk-tolerant investment committee model seen in venture capital. I wanted an investment committee to scrutinise our proposals robustly but also ensure nimble decision-making. Speed was another of my conditions for taking the role in the first place. And remarkably, this is what we got.

We established an unusual but highly effective structure to allow the VTF to prioritise and to recommend the purchase of vaccines and related activities in manufacturing and clinical development, without bypassing the normal controls of government.

First Clive and his SWAT team of experts would evaluate and shortlist the most promising vaccines. Then we would explore what sort of deal the vaccine company was seeking and bring Maddy in to help shape the legal terms of the deal. Typically, the smaller companies wanted more help with upfront scale-up, manufacturing and clinical development than the larger multinational pharmaceutical companies. Those smaller companies needed more cash up front, but that was not necessarily a bad thing since we would hold more influence over their manufacturing activities, helping us build capabilities in the UK and long-term skills to provide resilience against future pandemics.

The VTF team would then dig in to define exactly how to deliver the help that the vaccine company needed for scale-up and manufacturing as well as the level of support needed for clinical development and regulatory approval. Ian and Divya, working with Clive, were in the hot seat together with Maddy who would turn all of this into a legal contract, which would explicitly define doses, timing of delivery (including priority access) and costs, plus all the contractual terms.

Finally, Nick would take the proposed Business Case plus the 'execution ready' legal contracts first to the Permanent Secretary at BEIS for approval as the relevant Accounting Officer, and from there to a Ministerial Panel. This Panel effectively operated as the VTF 'investment committee' – just as we have in venture capital.

The Ministerial Panel consisted of the Business Secretary, the Health and Social Care Secretary, the Chief Secretary to the Treasury and a Minister of State at the Cabinet Office. Meetings popped up at comparatively short notice. Scheduling within forty-eight hours wasn't unusual, and in an emergency shorter still. Meetings were often held on a Friday evening or over a weekend. Nick would send the recommendation – invariably over a hundred pages of the Business Case together with the detailed legal contracts – with a request for a decision. I would attend these meetings together with Nick, Maddy and others to answer any questions Ministers might fire back. This nimbleness was one of the best aspects of working with Whitehall.

But for all the ministerial responsiveness, we were required to use a rigid Whitehall Business Case template. It might well be right for other aspect of government business, but I really did not think it fit for purpose when dealing with vaccines. The VTF was compelled to cram the document with a strategic case, an economic case, a commercial case, a financial case and a management case. In other words, we had to argue almost every case out there except for the one that mattered: the scientific case.

Making the scientific case for vaccines was critical. It gave the rationale for the proposed vaccine. It summarised our evaluation of all available data, future development and manufacturing plans, and it anticipated risks – all, one might have thought, of some value.

Using the Procrustean bed of the Whitehall Business Case template, with all its unnecessary repetitions, wasted time. Misplaced too was the slightly surreal requirement for detailed proofs of 'value for money'… when we were in the midst of a pandemic. Of course value for money was important. But any vaguely competent modeller could sketch out the elements required to remove all doubt in a few hours.

That grumble aside, the accelerated decision-making, both with respect to spending and industrial strategy, was game-changing for the UK. Although the way the VTF had been set up – with a direct mandate from the PM, external experts working with a civil service team, and a dedicated Ministerial Investment Committee – was a radical departure from Whitehall's usual processes, we always respected the key principles of civil service practice. The VTF outside team gave expert advice. The core VTF staffing, project management and negotiation functions were carried out by civil servants led by Nick. And ministers, and only ministers, took decisions and committed public money.

Before we could reach the point where public money was spent on vaccines, there was an immediate hurdle, and one that absorbed a considerable amount of time. We had to make the overarching VTF Business Case to the Treasury, describing the whole programme, to ring-fence funds to deliver the VTF's goals. With the overall VTF Business Case approved, we could then move to individual recommendations.

I had no experience of how a Business Case might be assessed in the public sector. I was well acquainted with private sector business plans – I have spent my life assessing them – but it soon became clear that a Government Business Case was very different.

Building a Business Case for the Treasury

In principle, it was entirely reasonable to ask the VTF to develop a Business Case and a budget and submit them for official consideration. Simply being handed a blank cheque from the Government was, rightly, not on the cards.

The difficulty came from the fact that the VTF's mandate was entirely different from public expenditure norms. Yet apparently no one in Whitehall was willing to accept that standard calculations and methodology were not appropriate. The VTF Business Case had to tick a lot of bureaucratic boxes that required a mixture of imagination and improvisation.

One might have thought that the value for money of an effective vaccine campaign was pretty obvious. Apparently not.

In early June 2020 – only a few weeks after the dedicated VTF had been created – we estimated that we would need to spend about £5.2 billion between June 2020 and the end of 2022.

However, this estimate relied on assumptions based on very little hard data, since we were so early in the process. We had to estimate how many vaccines we needed to buy, at what price per dose, how many doses and when they would be delivered, the numbers of people to be vaccinated and all the additional costs we might need to incur in manufacturing and clinical development – all of which were impossible to predict in June 2020.

We had to assess the chances of success of everything we did in the Business Case for the Treasury – and apply a highly improbable degree of statistical precision.

Not only was it clearly too soon for the VTF to have prioritised the most promising vaccines, completed due diligence on them and agreed terms of pricing and delivery, but the vaccine companies themselves did not know what those numbers might be. At that point, no vaccine company was anywhere near the manufacturing scale that would be required to deliver millions of doses, and so their costs/path to get to that scale were very uncertain. Prices were tentative too.

What we knew then was that the Oxford/AstraZeneca vaccine would be cheap and the Moderna vaccine expensive. So, we picked an average number in between. But that's not exactly a scientific way of building a cost model.

The standard Whitehall case required us to quantify the benefits to the UK economy based on the extent to which vaccines put a stop to the pandemic – also impossible to determine in June 2020. Somehow our VTF civil service team calculated a 'minimum' benefit of £10 billion and a maximum of £200 billion.

£10 billion to £200 billion – that's quite a range! It seemed nonsense to me. But whether you went for the small or the large number, it was obviously value for money.

Looking back at this now, I am amused by how Nick and the team managed to retain a straight face while writing those numbers. Let alone the Treasury officials reviewing the Business Case.

As far as I remember, these calculations implied that the VTF would provide 'significant value for money' with a Whitehall-defined cost benefit ratio of between three and fifty. With such a large range, the whole exercise seemed pretty meaningless, but apparently no project would get funded without a benefit–cost ratio of at least three.

This massive level of uncertainty was the result of trying to fit numbers into a standard Whitehall template, despite not having any costs or benefits we could be certain about. It was like being asked to write operating instructions without knowing the product.

We needed to produce estimates of where the economy would be without a vaccine and how much larger it might be following vaccination, but without yet knowing how effective the vaccine was at saving the lives of different age groups, or who would be vaccinated and when. A graph was inserted for the sake of form. I am not in any way an economist, but the notion that this was robust data on which to make decisions was laughable – and not something I would have accepted in any investment recommendation at SV.

There also had to be a counter-factual, namely what would be the outcome if the UK decided *not* to take up vaccines, but instead let the virus rip until herd immunity was achieved. The Treasury informed us of, and seemed to have respect for, an LSE study (based on the work of the esteemed Professor Benjamin Moll, who was at pains to point out how tentative his conclusions were) that suggested August 2022 as the date for reaching herd immunity, but the reality is that there was no reason to prefer this date to one reached by throwing a dart at a calendar while blindfolded.

In a morbid twist, it turned out that there was and still is not a single accepted measurement across Whitehall for the benefit of *not dying*. The Department for Transport apparently estimates the cost of one life at £2 million, which would mean that only a few thousand lives saved by the vaccine would allow the VTF to 'break even'. The Department of Health and Social Care via NICE (the National Institute for Health and Care Excellence) has an alternative scheme in which for every 1,000 deaths they would lose 9,045 'Quality of Life Years' (QALYs) with a value of just over £500 million, meaning that the VTF would have to show that vaccines saved rather more lives to come through the cost–benefit analysis unscathed. The difference between these estimates comes from the fact that car crashes affect a varied age range, while those who expire as the result of other causes tend, unsurprisingly, to be elderly, with fewer 'natural' years left. All in all, these disparities were yet another reason to be cautious about bogus attempts at accurate assessment.

These highly speculative numbers had to be reinforced by a BEIS analysis of the risks involved in the VTF mission. The relevant Programme Management Office duly applied a Risk Appetite Statement (RAS) to assess how the VTF fit with BEIS's departmental accepted range of risk appetites. It deemed the risk level to be 'very high'. A Risk Potential Assessment (RPA) had also been conducted, although I don't understand what the difference is between a RAS and RPA, which also showed that the VTF was 'very high risk'. My view was that the cost in money and time of doing this nonsensical and irrelevant work for the Treasury was too high.

The final VTF Business Case was the better part of a hundred pages long when it was finished – it certainly passed the weight test. I would have cut through the lot and sent a single paragraph to No. 11 Downing Street. It would have read:

> The cost of the vaccine taskforce is relatively small (0.22% of pre-Covid UK GDP) compared to the economic and social impact of this pandemic, hence the taskforce only needs to marginally increase the probability of finding and manufacturing a vaccine to be positive to the UK economy. The size of the benefit–cost ratio is less relevant.

'Irrelevant' would have been even more succinct. In this Alice in Wonderland situation, and with more than a hint of Monty Python to it, the VTF made its Business Case and its outline budget and presented this to the Treasury. We wanted to ring-fence the funds so that we did not have to waste more time down the line arguing over where the budget money came from.

★

I remember attending my first meeting in the summer in the big green Cabinet Room in Downing Street with some ministers on

MS Teams, and I complained that our budget had still not been approved. Boris turned to Rishi Sunak, who was on video, and challenged him as to what was going on. Rishi had no idea. This was my first inkling of the power of officials, who get to decide exactly what they show to their ministers for approval and decisions. Vaccines had clearly not been high on the list of priorities for the Chancellor's office.

I visited Downing Street only two or three times during my role as Chair, but that first occasion was pretty eye-opening. I arrived on my bike, showed my passport to the policeman and parked inside the gates. The policeman directed me to the Portakabin to get scanned, as in an airport. None of the policemen doing the scanning inside were wearing masks. I asked them whether they were in a bubble, since they weren't wearing masks. They said 'No', and that they constantly rotated between teams.

My second surprise came in Number 10 itself. Waiting in a side room, I was met by the Prime Minister's assistant; she told me that the PM was ready to see me, and I could take off my face mask.

'Really?'

'Yes,' she replied, 'masks are not required for business meetings.'

SARS-Cov-2, it seems, now respected professional commitments. I had not been aware that the virus was capable of so cleverly discriminating between those it infected. But apparently being in a business meeting conferred immunity.

I've never heard anything so ridiculous. I'm probably not alone.

Three months later, the Treasury officially endorsed the VTF Business Case and budget, and I think final sign-off came at some point in September. In fact, this did not matter much as it turned out that we could continue with our work unimpeded; the Government needed to approve only the binding legal commitments to spend large sums of money, and those came later.

Nick had taken most of the bullets in this warped tale, but he could not shield me and the team from everything. The VTF had been in existence for barely a matter of weeks. Micromanagement and distracting demands for data and forecasts grew all too common. Not only were we building the plane as we were flying it, we were flying in the dark and simultaneously writing the instruction manual, and fielding endless petty questions from air traffic control asking about the strength of the orange juice we were serving to passengers.

I had entered a world where process apparently mattered more than outcomes.

Endless government distractions

Fending all this off was a serious waste of time when we should have been concentrating on the day job.

The Cabinet Office quickly became the bane of our existence. They kicked off by requiring that VTF officials in BEIS send Excel spreadsheets with status updates twice a week, populated with data that seemed irrelevant at best.

Officials in the Cabinet Office kept attempting to rope senior VTF members into meetings from May 2020 onwards about how a vaccine roll-out might be organised – before the team had even made the decisions about which vaccines to prioritise.

I received repeated emails about Commissions, government jargon for reports on assigned subjects.

As I wrote to one enthusiastic Cabinet Office junior official in early June, responding to her third email requesting a Commission on vaccine deployment with her deadlines highlighted in bold:

Dear —: I admire your persistence! As I am sure you know we have a Secretary of States' meeting this Friday at which we will share a presentation and seek an aligned position between BEIS and the Department of Health for vaccine deployment. As I've said before, we have a robust process and team in place and I'm afraid I am not willing to allow this to be distracted by external requests for information. Alok Sharma has already discussed this with Michael Gove after you first made this request so I trust this is all in order.

This was by no means the worst example of sheer short-sightedness. No; the biggest waste of time and money came in the form of the National Audit Office.

I completely understand and recognise the importance of scrutiny, accountability and transparency. That's how we work in venture capital. We hold our investee companies to account through our board seats and equity ownership, as our investors hold us to account to ensure their money is invested wisely. Like any citizen I don't want the Government spraying my taxes around willy-nilly. But this was different.

In July 2020 Gareth Davies, the civil servant who headed up the National Audit Office, decided to take this moment to launch an investigation into how the VTF was performing, apparently to demonstrate that public money was being spent wisely. Specifically, he wanted to review whether the VTF used 'their resources efficiently, effectively and with economy'. His letter went on to say that he:

hoped that by undertaking this investigation now, whilst your officials are making these important decisions, his team will be able to help sharpen your thinking and bring to your attention any risks that could significantly impact on the programme. He hopes that this approach to our work will enable you and your officials to gain insights and benefits throughout the whole process.

Amazing. This was July. We had launched the VTF in May.

As I have said, no one was against obtaining value for money. And I welcome scrutiny and expert advice. But the idea of doing an audit before there was anything *to* audit, let alone the suggestion that the NAO's youthful generalists would be able to 'sharpen our thinking' when we were working absolutely flat out 24/7 to find and develop vaccines in the face of a national emergency was – and remains – a foolish and expensive joke.

This absurd proposition forced me as Chair to throw my toys out of the pram, otherwise the audit would have ground the VTF team to a halt. My intervention postponed the start of the NAO audit process, but only to August – a point at which we had not yet signed *any* vaccine procurement contracts since they were still at term sheet stage. Yet even so, the NAO's insistence on an audit took up our scarce resources and diverted our team from the real work they were charged with.

In the event, the NAO sent a team who knew nothing about vaccines, manufacturing, clinical trials or pandemic preparedness. So, again, I was bemused about what insights they thought they might share that would 'sharpen our thinking'.

The NAO's report was published in December 2020 and in January 2021 the Public Accounts Committee (PAC) – the Select Committee charged with reviewing government spending – assessed the NAO's report in public.

The PAC meeting was fine. My supposedly sixty-minute appearance ended up being closer to 2.5 hours but, broadly speaking, apart from some partisan questioning about cronyism, the hearing was reasonable.

But the NAO had sent numerous requests over five months from August to December 2020, which took a lot of time to respond to. Several of these demands were so ridiculous and inane that, after the PAC meeting, I sent a six-page letter to Gareth Davies, as the Comptroller and Auditor General of the NAO, describing in detail what an unnecessary and wasteful exercise it had been. Again, Jesse's advice on it was invaluable.

My letter was virtually radioactive.

I am writing to highlight some serious concerns relating to the quality of the recent NAO audit of the Vaccine Taskforce (VTF) and the Government's preparations for the Coronavirus vaccine programme.

Let me say up front that I hugely welcome effective scrutiny and accountability, and both are ever present features of my work as a life sciences investor and business builder. I also strongly believe in the importance of Parliamentary scrutiny of public expenditure: it is essential to democracy, and in the UK the NAO has a crucial role in providing expert input to that scrutiny.

The NAO report into the work of the VTF provides some useful public information, which the VTF would in any case have been pleased to publish on request and in a timely way. But as an instrument of scrutiny the investigation was poorly conceived in its outline and inadequate in its execution, and the report reflects both failings. To that extent, this audit has not served Parliament and the public good.

In the normal course it is not possible for civil servants to draw attention to these concerns. But it is important for someone to do so. The NAO's weak performance in this area demands proper review, and without that review such wider concerns would likely go unaddressed. I am sure that as Comptroller and Auditor General you will appreciate the importance of the NAO and you yourself being properly held to account.

I went on to list the multiple shortcomings of this audit, including a profound lack of understanding of what the VTF was doing, the timing and scope of the audit and a failure to understand, or adequately to reflect, the extraordinary environment in which the VTF has been operating.

If the Government or the NAO had asked us to disclose the overall costs of the contracts we were committing to, I don't see why we couldn't have just published those numbers, without the five months of time-wasting.

I concluded by asserting:

I have no previous experience of the NAO nor of working in government, so I do not know how its other audits have worked. I do have experience, however, of audits of public and private companies and also of charities through being a member of numerous audit committees. But, as you can see, I did not see the benefit of this particular audit.

I hope these comments can help you to focus the work of the NAO so that it can better serve Parliament and the public good in future. The NAO's performance in this case in turn raises a range of more fundamental questions, and I am copying this letter to the Chair of the Public Accounts Committee, the Chair of the Health and Social Care Committee, the Secretary of State for BEIS and the Speaker for information.

I did not get an adequate response. I'm told my letter did the rounds of senior civil servants. However much they may have relished the contents, I hope they all realised the seriousness of the points made.

I have no political ambitions and my style is to be candid and straightforward. It was easy for me to call out this failing since I wasn't jeopardising a political or civil service career. But frankly I don't know who audits the auditors. Civil servants are the ones who work with the NAO and they certainly won't rock the boat. So, who will?

If I had ever been asked the question 'What is the biggest threat to the success of the VTF?' the honest answer would have been 'Large parts of the rest of Whitehall'. People were queueing up to conduct investigations into us.

A ray of government sunshine

I should stress that I had absolutely no issue with being held accountable in an intelligent fashion. Nor was this impossible. By far the best inspection that I participated in was done by a team from the IPA, or Infrastructure Projects Authority, the expert body which manages and audits infrastructure projects across Whitehall, reporting to the Cabinet Office and the Treasury. This inquiry was held at the end of November 2020, logical since most of the main decisions on vaccines had been made. It was a relatively short exercise.

Importantly, the individuals conducting the review clearly had expertise relevant to what the VTF was seeking to do, in spectacular contrast to the NAO which made a host of elementary mistakes in its report. It would be easy — but perhaps not inaccurate — for me to suggest that this was because the IPA Review Team were all women. In my day job I am fanatical about having senior women leading my companies and on boards since I find diversity helps make better decisions. But in the IPA case, it was their actual experience in healthcare, manufacturing and project management which meant that their questions and suggestions were genuinely helpful.

Furthermore, the objective of the Review Team was to look for positive aspects that could be divined from what the VTF had done, as well as constructively looking for places where we could improve, rather than to approach us in the spirit of a professional hitman. I was genuinely pleased when it awarded us a clean bill of health.

Jumping forward in time to illustrate further the point about endless interference, the Government reviews continued. Even months after I had left the VTF, I was asked by the Cabinet Office to speak to Nigel Boardman, a non-executive director of BEIS and former city lawyer who was conducting yet another review on government procurement, which looked into both PPE and vaccines.

I was surprised to discover BEIS had not seen fit to share with Nigel our VTF 2020 year-end report, nor had they shared the IPA audit. Both of these reports were very informative about how we worked and reached key conclusions regarding effectiveness and the challenges we faced.

It was clear, sadly, that speaking to me was an afterthought: the report came out the following day. The Cabinet Office Permanent Secretary confirmed to me, 'You're right in that a lot of the main points in the report had already been prepared.'

In other words, my response was a waste of time. Where do all these reviews end up and what changes are made as a result?

Called up in front of Select Committees

Besides these various watchdogs within Whitehall, there was Westminster to contend with. As part of my seven-month tenure, I was called as a witness to five House of Commons Select Committees, including the Select Committee for Health and Social Care, the Select Committee for Science and Technology, those two bodies together and the Public Accounts Committee. Somewhat oddly I was not asked to appear before the Select Committee on Business, Energy and Industrial Strategy even though it was my institutional base.

I thought the Select Committees were pretty good. The members from different political parties seemed well prepared, polite and asked probing questions. They seemed genuinely interested in understanding the detail of what we were doing, the challenges we were facing and what we should expect to achieve.

For the first one, on 1 July, I stuck yellow Post-Its on the window all round my laptop screen giving me all the stats I might need. More of a psychological prop, since I knew my stuff. I balanced my laptop on two Amazon boxes to get the camera at eye level. I was pleased to be joined by Sarah Gilbert and John Bell.

I rather enjoyed the opportunity to talk about what the VTF was doing, finally able to answer the questions without fear of the BEIS communications team feeding me lines. Greg Clark, Chair of the Science and Technology Committee, was particularly probing in November 2020. He pushed hard to find out exactly how many vaccine doses we expected by when.

Helpful, as I was able to give a clear and direct view on when I thought vaccines would be ready for deployment, information not yet public. It reminded me of meetings with investors in my venture capital funds who want to know exactly how we have invested their money and why. I enjoy that sort of interrogation – and shame on me if I don't know my facts or can't convince with my responses.

Many career civil servants I met as Chair regarded an appearance in front of a Select Committee as an utterly terrifying ordeal. They clearly feared that it could be a one-way ticket to personal career destruction. It cannot be beneficial to the public good for such testimony to be viewed as entering a lion's den. It's much simpler in life to know what you are doing, tell the truth rather than attempt to spin, and be held to account for what you do.

By far my worst encounter did not involve process or Parliament. It was an extraordinary ambush in a Cabinet Office meeting room, early in my time at the VTF, at the hands of Matt Hancock.

Surprise attack

The occasion was a video meeting of the Covid-O (Operations) Committee chaired by Michael Gove, the Chancellor of the Duchy of Lancaster, in June 2020. My first time before this body. In advance, like all good stakeholder management in the private sector, I asked Matt Hancock for advice about likely questions and on how I should conduct myself. The tone of our conversation then was friendly and I thought helpful.

When it came to the Committee discussion itself, the Secretary of State for Health and Social Care had traded in Dr Jekyll for Mr Hyde. He started by suddenly asserting that he could not under-stand why I thought people his age, namely mid-forties, would not want, indeed demand, a vaccine.

I reminded him that the VTF was not responsible for determin-ing *who* would be offered a vaccine. That was a job for the Joint

Committee on Vaccination and Immunisation (JCVI), as he well knew, since they had a statutory duty to advise him. My role was to secure the vaccines for those the JCVI recommended should be vaccinated, not to develop policy.

I also reminded him that, at the time, there were no vaccine clinical trials being run on children. It was literally impossible to contemplate vaccinating children until those trials had been run, the safety assessed and the vaccines approved for use by the regulator for this age group.

Matt's second tirade was that he 'could not believe' that I had ordered only thirty million doses of the Oxford/AstraZeneca vaccine for delivery in September 2020.

In fact, that deal had been largely agreed between Oxford and AstraZeneca in April just before I landed at the VTF, so I had inherited this contract. When I observed that it would be a miracle if we received thirty million AstraZeneca doses by Christmas, he snapped. Matt told me that he kept being told by experts that things were impossible, only to find out later that they were perfectly possible if enough effort was made. He was openly accusing me of a lack of ambition, questioning my competence, and doing so in front of his Cabinet colleagues and key officials.

The meeting didn't end well. Michael Gove could not have looked more embarrassed. Alok called me immediately afterwards to apologise. Others sent messages of support.

I was more angry than you can shake a stick at. I was almost stuck to the ceiling with fury and exchanged angry WhatsApp messages with Matt who had said: 'You can't just tell me I'm wrong'. Well, it turned out that I could, and he was.

It took all of Jesse's considerable charm and husbandly love to calm me down and make me appreciate the context of my treatment.

I immediately called Ian McCubbin, my manufacturing guru. I told him I had stuck my neck out on the likely delivery of the AstraZeneca vaccine and wanted to check I hadn't got it completely wrong. First Ian reassured me that receiving even thirty million AstraZeneca doses by Christmas was indeed extremely optimistic.

I asked him whether there was literally *anything* else we could do to accelerate the delivery of the vaccines. Ian paused. Then in his wonderfully charming Scottish way, he said: 'You could try singing to the cells and ask them to grow faster.'

It was pure politics. It seemed to me that Matt was still aggrieved that responsibility for vaccines had been taken from him and his department and moved over to BEIS instead. I thought that perhaps he was determined to refight that battle and, if that involved throwing rocks at me, then so be it. He also knew that he would always win in a verbal punch-up with the mild-mannered Alok, who was nowhere near as aggressive. Alok was not as political an animal and was certainly insufficiently devious to take on the Health Secretary.

Would I have to endure constant sniping at my leadership of the VTF, even though the vast majority of those with whom I worked had confidence in my abilities? My first instinct was to brush this all off as political theatre. But then I reasoned that, were I to let myself become a punching bag, we ran a real risk that political obduracy, an army of procedural investigations and, potentially, parliamentary critique, would undermine all that the VTF was doing.

To protect against ongoing criticism, I made a further decision that set the strategy for how the VTF would function. Again, Jesse's advice and experience were crucial: hire an expert of unimpeachable authority and expertise to review the VTF strategy, team and actions. This audit of the VTF could then be shared with ministers, or indeed anyone else who needed to see it.

I called Sir Richard Sykes and asked him to mark our homework. He had a record in academic life and in industry second to none. He had at various times been Chairman of GlaxoSmithKline and Rector of Imperial College, London. He co-founded the Jenner Institute for vaccine research and was intimately familiar with all the challenges we were facing.

'Distinguished' hardly began to describe him. Sir Richard was also known to be fiercely independent. If he did not think much about any aspect of the VTF operation then he would say so, loudly. For that reason, Clive, who knew him well, thought that I was taking something of a gamble in recruiting him.

My view, however, was that given the stakes, if there was any room for improvement in our strategy or team, I wanted to hear that from Richard. And we might as well get that specialist and expert feedback early so we could amend our course. A seal of approval for the VTF from Richard, if that was indeed his conclusion, would be as close to body armour as I could acquire.

When they found out that I had commissioned him, BEIS were plainly appalled, Matt was incensed and the Cabinet Office had a seizure. Things were not done in this way. The Cabinet Office called Nick and told him that they had not approved this audit. Thankfully Nick stood firm. He pointed out that I had complete authority to hire anyone I chose to help with the VTF, so conducting this audit was entirely within my rights.

Sir Richard's review was released on 4 July 2020. It was unambiguous in its conclusion. This was:

> The team leading the VTF is of extremely high quality and once again highlights the depth of talent and expertise we have in the UK. Time will tell as to the results, but they have made an excellent start. They are in my opinion perfectly suited for the complex task ahead, being a group of smart pragmatic highly experienced individuals. If anyone can do it, they can.

Sir Richard emphasised the work we were doing around Human Challenge trials (see Chapter 11) and encouraged us to do more here. Otherwise it was a very strong endorsement.

I would not be challenged by Matt Hancock or anyone else in government in this way again. Indeed, my relationship with the Health Secretary did recover and at times he offered me valuable backing. Alas, there would turn out to be other means of attack, including hostile leaks to the media, for those who remained sceptical of me.

I had come to appreciate that there was a near-total ignorance in Whitehall as to what vaccine manufacturing actually entailed. Vaccines, which are basically biological materials, have to be grown in living cells, and that takes time.

Subsequent Covid-O meetings were better, including the one on 23 June, Jesse's birthday. It was another stonking clear, blue-skied day and wonderfully warm. We had a lovely outdoor birthday brunch. I picked a huge bunch of sweet peas and we wore white and red pointy paper hats.

So I was very calm when I dialled into the Cabinet Room Covid-O meeting that afternoon. And this time everyone behaved properly.

Working with international agencies and governments

If the ways of Whitehall could involve minefields, I would soon find that dealing with multinational and international institutions was more like quicksand.

Although my first goal was to secure vaccines for the UK, my engagement letter had also referred to a second goal, namely: 'To ensure adequate global distribution of vaccines to bring the quickest possible end to the pandemic and to the economic damage it inflicts.' This was immensely important to me, not just because it had been made a VTF goal. Morally and practically, I could not see how we could truly bring the Covid-19 crisis to an end and be confident that it would not flare up again later without a genuinely global vaccine campaign.

We had a strong steering committee member, Tim Colley, a former UK Ambassador to Latvia, in place by July 2020. Tim was ably supported by Chris Minchell and there were a number of impressive figures, notably Saul Walker, at the Department for International Development, who were experienced and provided valuable support. Saul challenged some of my assumptions about vaccine take-up with data and I listened hard to his advice on all global health issues.

We needed a plan for if and when vaccines became available for international distribution. Making it reality hinged on many other countries and international organisations, which became an issue. Globalisation and international supply chains meant that no single country had all the elements to discover, develop and manufacture vaccines on its own. We needed countries to work together rather than against each other to counter nationalism.

The diary entry for my first meeting as VTF Chair in May read 'Call with Canada', alongside Patrick Vallance. We spoke to Patrick's opposite number there and explained what our nascent plans were for the VTF and explored how we might co-operate. This was the first of several exchanges with other nations' public health teams to share thoughts about how to tackle the pandemic with vaccines.

Just after my call with Canada, Downing Street came on the line. They asked whether I was free to attend a meeting with the PM that afternoon. 'Yes – that's fine.'

That meeting turned out to be with Bill and Melinda Gates. The agenda was to determine the UK's level of commitment to sharing vaccines, and specifically the UK's funding pledge to the Global Alliance for Vaccines and Immunization (GAVI).

GAVI was founded in 2000 with funding from various governments plus the Bill and Melinda Gates Foundation. The UK had been the largest single financial contributor to its 2016–20 round before the coronavirus emerged and had just indicated a further commitment of $2 billion for 2021–25. Before the pandemic, GAVI had helped to vaccinate almost half the world's children against deadly infectious diseases, reaching the most challenging places in the world.

The UK was also about to host a remote Global Vaccine Summit in June 2020. The goal was to create the Covid-19 Vaccines Global Alliance (COVAX – sorry, another acronym!) as the vehicle to acquire and send vaccines to low-income countries. We also hoped that COVAX might become a permanent facility ready for future pandemics. The UK put its money where its mouth was and pledged £548 million, the largest at that time. Ultimately, world leaders made commitments of more than $7 billion at this summit to provide equal access to vaccines for all people.

I put on a pink '*Zoom*-shirt' (though not actually Zoom since this was Bill Gates) and joined the MS Teams meeting. On the screen, Boris was on the top right in the Cabinet Room in Number 10. He started by explaining to the Gateses that obesity was the real driver of developing serious disease. He told us that this was why he ended up in intensive care.

I'm not sure that this was part of his briefing.

But then the call moved into a more comical mode. Boris became animated and waved his arms wildly. He said to the patient Gates couple: 'The trouble with the UK, Bill and Melinda, is that we don't have any enzymes.'

What?

No enzymes?

What does that even mean? What has that got to do with the UK's commitment to equitable access to vaccines? Were enzymes a topic in his briefing notes?

He must have had something else in mind. Luckily, we soon got back onto track. Bill and Melinda, as expected, were hugely knowledgeable and interesting. We discussed the critical need to get vaccines to those most vulnerable around the world. And the funding needed to pay for this.

We discussed the problem of vaccine nationalism. The rest of the world was always going to be a second priority behind securing vaccines for and in any individual country. This was the case in the

UK as well, although I think our actions at least showed an understanding that out there was the bigger picture.

The world of acronyms in global health

Global health is a very difficult landscape to navigate. It's highly political. A number of institutions believed that they had a special authority when it came to vaccines. One was the World Health Organization (WHO), with which the Trump White House was virtually at war, accusing its head Tedros Adhanom Ghebreyesus of being under the control of China. A toxic situation. The other key organisation alongside the WHO and GAVI was the Coalition for Epidemic Preparedness Innovation (CEPI).

CEPI was launched at the World Economic Forum in 2017. While GAVI was primarily focused on the global distribution of vaccines, CEPI was more interested in R&D. Its goal was to identify and help fund research projects to develop novel vaccines against emerging infectious diseases. Especially focusing on those new vaccine formats suitable for global health distribution.

CEPI's initial fund of $460 million was drawn from the Bill and Melinda Gates Foundation, the Wellcome Trust plus support from several governments.

Richard Hatchett, CEPI's CEO, had been on the UK's Expert Advisory Group with me. Together with Jeremy Farrar, he brought superb knowledge of global health and vaccines and gave me great advice throughout. Richard had worked in the US Government at a high rank and had been the Chief Medical Officer and the Acting Director of the US Biomedical Advanced Research and Development Authority (BARDA).

The UK had, apparently, held back from CEPI at first, possibly because of our ties to GAVI. But in March 2020 it signed up and pledged £210 million specifically for the development of a Covid-19 vaccine.

I was impressed with Richard and his Director of Vaccine R&D Melanie Saville. Given this depth of vaccine expertise, it seemed to me that CEPI's knowledge and leadership in funding and developing new vaccines fitted very well with GAVI's expertise in distributing vaccines all round the world. Working together, these two groups provided all the expertise needed to drive COVAX.

However, to do this they needed money and unified support from governments around the world.

Sir Andrew Witty, a former CEO of GSK, had been appointed the WHO Global Vaccine Envoy. He had taken a leave of absence from his role running US company Optum Health to take on this role to co-lead the WHO's efforts to accelerate the development of a Covid-19 vaccine.

Andrew is enormously pragmatic, commercial and straightforward. We hadn't worked directly with each other before but had appeared on industry panels together at conferences. I'm a big fan. Andrew is one of the most articulate public speakers I know – a talent I greatly admire.

Andrew's role was to try to shape COVAX into a single co-ordinating entity which all the various groups could work through. Andrew reviewed proposals for countries to pool risks in developing and sharing vaccines. There was a lot of jostling for voice and power as far as I could determine, though Tim Colley and his team were on the front line here rather than me.

There were many proposed mechanisms for COVAX's vaccine procurement for low-income countries. Some struck me as impractical. Someone needed to bring this all together and get it into shape so that high-income countries would provide funding.

It was suggested that Andrew should be the Chairman of the Shareholders Council of COVAX to bring this leadership, structuring it in a way that the wealthy countries would support. Through his role as CEO of GSK, Andrew used to run a global vaccine company, striking commercial and supply deals all around the world.

So that made him a great fit for chairing the COVAX facility to buy and distribute vaccines worldwide.

In the late summer, I asked the PM to call Andrew to ask him to take on the role as permanent Chairman of the COVAX Shareholders Council and 'lean in' – the phrase Sheryl Sandberg coined in her best selling book to take greater ownership and responsibility.

Earlier that week Boris had texted me to ask 'When do we get a vaccine!!?' I responded 'End of the year if Oxford and BioNTech work'. Encouraging as always, Boris replied 'Fantastic. You and your team have been amazing. What more can I do to support?'

So, I asked Boris to call Andrew. Despite telling Andrew what a good job he was doing as WHO Vaccine Envoy, Boris somehow forgot to ask Andrew to take on the Chairman role for the Shareholders Council. This didn't matter since Andrew had by then agreed to step in as an interim.

By September, it appeared that GAVI was going to be in charge of COVAX. GAVI's director Seth Berkley told me he was planning to appoint one of his deputies to run this facility. I spoke to Aurélia Nguyen, the designated leader and suggested they needed a team with experience of negotiating with Big Pharma companies. Since GAVI's focus was on distribution of vaccines, I presumed they would also want experts to select the best vaccines for low-income countries. But instead of working with CEPI, who were demonstrable experts on pandemic vaccines, they asked us – the VTF – for help to assess potential new vaccines.

I never understood why GAVI didn't work arm-in-arm with CEPI. I was surprised to have received this request in September, five months after we had started. Of course, we were happy to help but why hadn't CEPI been put front and centre here?

The global political manoeuvring was intense. Relevant expertise was not sufficient. The question of who should be placed in positions of seniority was to be deeply politicised. Everyone wanted their own person to chair – to represent their country's interests. The COVAX shareholders were not willing to make Andrew a permanent appointment. Andrew couldn't wait indefinitely to discover whether he would be appointed permanent Chairman of COVAX. In December 2020, he accepted a role as CEO of the $400 billion UnitedHealth Group.

While the principle of global unity was admirable, achieving that co-operation would be very hard.

As the WHO was involved, the United States under Donald Trump wanted nothing to do with it. This political position changed when Joe Biden succeeded Trump. The US came into COVAX and became the biggest sponsor. But by then, the path was set.

It would prove a long and painful slog for the VTF team, which sought to frame a united and effective international response to Covid-19. Tim was superb and patient. But decisions here were political and out of my hands. Candidly, I was disillusioned by the machinations I witnessed.

I have to say that my engagement with the team at the Gates Foundation was always superb. The President of Global Health, Trevor Mundel, was extraordinarily thoughtful and strategic. Given its deep relationships around the world, the Gates Foundation identified areas of critical need and provided speedy funding to accelerate the delivery of vaccines to low-income countries. It acted much more strategically and quickly than any global health organisation or government. This wasn't a surprise to me since the Gates Foundation played a catalytic role in vaccinating nearly three billion children against polio, resulting in a decrease in the incidence of the disease by ninety-nine per cent. The funding and technical resources contributed by the Gateses meant that this effort has so far saved more than eighteen million children from paralysis and death.

7

OXFORD'S TRIUMPH

It was late May 2020, my appointment was in the public domain and expectations for action had been accelerated. I had no time. I had to get up to speed on vaccines fast. I dug into the data on the leading vaccines and research reports.

My venture capital and industry colleagues were pinging me non-stop with reports and ideas. I spoke to Richard Mason, a biotech entrepreneur seconded into Strategic Command, Defence Intelligence in the MoD, who brought additional insights. It was a very daunting task. I felt like I was back at school studying for exams.

The first task for the Vaccine Taskforce was to prioritise the best vaccine candidates from around the world to build a portfolio of vaccines for the UK. We wanted to find those vaccines most likely to generate the data needed to convince the MHRA that they were both safe and effective. But also that they could be manufactured at scale and could possibly be delivered by late 2020.

The immense responsibility for deciding which vaccines to pick for the VTF portfolio fell to my deputy Clive Dix and to the small collection of individual experts assembled by and around him. The VTF Steering Group spent hours interrogating Clive and his team's recommendations and deciding on the final portfolio. They are among the many unsung heroes whose judgement led to the VTF overall making the right decisions.

Due diligence and vaccine prioritisation would have to be undertaken in weeks, not months. There were tasks that Clive and his team had to tackle simultaneously. The first was to conduct due diligence on the two home-grown candidates which the UK Government had already started supporting. That meant assessing both the Oxford University/AstraZeneca vaccine, which was already in clinical trials, and the very different self-amplifying RNA vaccine which Professor Robin Shattock at Imperial College was developing.

By the end of April, the UK Government had provided £45 million of financial backing for these two 'UK bids' and the VTF had to decide how to rank them in the overall drive to find a viable vaccine.

We also needed to review all the non-UK vaccines and the different formats to prioritise the most promising. The Oxford aspect of that process is the story of this chapter.

Oxford becomes a clinical powerhouse

From the outset, Oxford looked like a serious possibility. To understand why requires a sense of the history of how the university has become such a force in medical research over several decades.

This was due to a man who died in 1963, two years before I and my co-author Tim Hames were born.

William Richard Morris was born in Worcester in 1877, the eldest of seven. His father, a clerk, moved the family to Oxford three years later. Morris left school at the age of fourteen, and in 1904 he married Elizabeth Anstey. She predeceased him in 1959 after fifty-five years of marriage. Crucially, they had no children to whom to leave a legacy. Her husband had started his career repairing bicycles, and then branched out to include the recently invented automobiles. He designed his first car, the bull-nosed Morris, at a garage on Longwell Street, Oxford, in 1912. This was properly launched the next year, and Morris was christened 'the English Henry Ford'.

The Great War interrupted business badly but in the 1920s his production lines were humming. In 1925, for example, the annual output of his factory in the Cowley suburb of Oxford was 56,000 vehicles. He had become extremely wealthy. A generation earlier, the American industrial magnate Andrew Carnegie had thundered: 'He who dies rich dies disgraced.' Morris absorbed the lesson and resolved to be a philanthropist. His first donation to his adopted hometown's university came in 1926, when he endowed a new Chair in Spanish Studies.

A twist of fate in 1928 made Morris reconsider where his money should be directed. He suffered a very bad reaction to anaesthetic while undergoing what should have been a purely routine operation to remove his appendix. Medicine now jumped to the summit of his personal priority list. In 1930, he donated £100,000, then a staggering sum, to allow the Radcliffe Hospital in Oxford to purchase the Radcliffe Observatory site. He also started making sizeable gifts to Guy's Hospital in London. By 1934 he had been made a baron. In 1937 he offered £1 million to build and endow Nuffield College. At about the same time, he endowed four Professors of Medicine at Oxford. In total, some £2 million was to be handed over. This allowed the Oxford Medical School to be established. He specified that one of these new Chairs was to be in Anaesthesia. This was the first such academic position in the British Empire.

In 1943, William Morris embarked on his most spectacular charitable endeavour to date. He created the Nuffield Foundation with the gift of £10 million in shares from the Morris Motor company. It was to support medical and health services, social well-being including scientific research, the care and comfort of the aged poor and other charitable purposes backed by him and, after his death, by his trustees. When that moment came in 1963, he left over £3 million from his estate to Nuffield College. His role in Oxford's emergence as a medical research superpower was transformational.

Oxford's focus on vaccines is largely due to the Jenner Institute in the city. But the Jenner Institute didn't start its life in Oxford.

The moving force behind what would be called the Edward Jenner Institute was Sir Richard Sykes, then the Chief Executive Officer at Glaxo Wellcome (later GSK). His vision was to establish and fund a three-way collaboration between academia, the pharmaceutical industry and the Government, in order to carry out the research required to develop and produce new vaccines. Between 1996 and 1998 it operated from the Institute for Animal Health in Compton, Berkshire, before being formally opened by Peter Mandelson, then Secretary of State for Trade and Industry. Glaxo Wellcome made a commitment to finance it for a decade. In addition to Glaxo Wellcome, the funding consortium included the Medical Research Council, the Biotechnology and Biological Sciences Research Council and the Department of Health.

Sir Richard was determined to keep supporting the Edward Jenner Institute, but other funding streams dried up. In the light of this, with support from the Jenner Vaccine Foundation, in November 2005 the Edward Jenner Institute became the Jenner Institute and moved to Oxford University and the UK Institute for Animal Health.

The Oxford Vaccine Group

There are a lot of players, acronyms and labels in the vaccine field which require a cold towel round your head to navigate. The Oxford Vaccine Group involved individuals from multiple institutions. The key professors would include Sarah Gilbert and Adrian Hill from the Jenner Institute, but also Andrew (Andy) Pollard, who had led the Oxford Vaccine Group since 2001. Andy was located within the Department of Paediatrics. Catherine Green, another important figure, was Associate Professor in Chromosome Dynamics at the Wellcome Centre for Human Genetics at Oxford, together with her colleague Teresa Lambe. Dr Sandy Douglas was a vital player in the planning and scale-up of manufacturing. Oxford had acquired an impressive pool of talent in the vaccine space well before the pandemic of 2020. Together, this was a group of experts in developing experimental vaccines for infectious global diseases.

Securing funding for vaccine research, despite the undoubted brilliance of the scientists involved, could be a frustrating exercise. An Oxford team had applied for WHO funding to fight a future 'Disease X' pandemic in 2018 but was rejected. We will never know if the world would have been better prepared if Oxford been able to make a head start.

Much would happen with the putative Oxford vaccine before I and the new VTF started work. On New Year's Day 2020, as she recalled in her own book *Vaxxers*, written with Catherine Green, Sarah Gilbert read about four people suffering from a strange pneumonia of unknown cause in Wuhan, China.

On 8 January 2020, the WHO confirmed that this new virus was a new coronavirus, SARS-CoV-2. The next day, by coincidence, Oxford University announced that they would start a new Phase 1 trial of their MERS (Middle East Respiratory Syndrome) vaccine in Saudi Arabia, led by Sarah Gilbert.

That team instead started work to design a vaccine for this new coronavirus using the full genomic code of the coronavirus just released by the Chinese. The Oxford team designed their Covid-19 vaccine on their ChAdOx1 adenoviral platform, which is a common cold virus, harmless to humans, found in chimpanzees, which can be engineered to incorporate new genetic sequences.

The Oxford scientists genetically engineered this chimp virus to include the genetic sequence encoding the SARS-CoV-2 spiky glycoprotein, known as the spike protein. Graphics departments everywhere created brilliant images to characterise these spiky invaders to help illustrate news reports.

As described earlier, this adeno vaccine, when injected into the body, would trigger the host cells into making the Covid-19 spike protein, which in turn would stimulate the production of antibodies and blood-based T-cells to defend the body against Covid itself. In barely a fortnight, Oxford had designed a vaccine against the new pathogen, based on their prior work in SARS and MERS, and were confident that it would be safe and that it would induce a protective immune response.

Oxford's call for help

Events had moved quickly from there and the VTF had to catch up. The Oxford team had struck a deal with an Italian manufacturer, Advent Srl, to produce the first one thousand doses for the initial clinical trials. That this happened so swiftly reflects the commitment and courage of Sandy Douglas, as it was not then clear how to pay for this.

It was increasingly obvious that Oxford would need outside help in this huge undertaking. No university had ever discovered, developed and manufactured a worldwide population-scale vaccine, let alone in a format which had not yet been approved. They needed to know urgently what sort of bulk manufacturing capacity might be available, ideally in the United Kingdom. The place to look was the BioIndustry Association (BIA).

Netty England, a bioprocessing consultant and leading figure at the BIA, was surprised to receive an email from Oxford's Dr Catherine Green on 15 February 2020. Netty said in a subsequent VTF podcast:

It was a Saturday while the football was on. Norwich v Liverpool. We got an email from Oxford University asking for support to scale-up their vaccine. At this stage, they could only make their vaccine at 10-litre scale. That was going to be enough to make material for the clinical trials for 10–15,000 volunteers but not more than that. So, I sent out an email on that Saturday evening asking for support to be able to get a group together to help with bulk vaccine scale-up and by Monday evening we had that consortium.

It was an astonishing response by the sector. Although very few companies in the UK were actively involved in vaccine manufacturing, the UK had built a vibrant cell and gene therapy community with skills and biological manufacturing capabilities that could be adapted for vaccines. Better still, these companies were now offering to set aside their existing commercial schedules to rally to the cause.

The scale and pace at which everyone contributed was remarkable. Over thirty companies and institutions came together to help. Steve Bates, as CEO of the BIA, was the mastermind who drove and co-ordinated this industry response.

In March, the Government had agreed to finance the £2.2 million cost of the Oxford clinical trials. In April and May, further awards of cash were pledged from Whitehall and the Oxford team raised hopes of the possibility of a positive result by September if the viral transmission rates remained high enough in the UK. It may seem counter-intuitive, but high levels of infection are needed to generate quick clinical results, showing whether a vaccine can indeed offer robust protection against disease.

The swift early funding decision allowed the Oxford Phase 1 and 2 trials to be conducted in April and May 2020. Normally there would be long delays endured while scientists sought funding and awaited their turn for regulatory consideration. But not this time. Far from it. The MHRA dramatically changed how it worked on Covid-19 trials. As its Senior Medical Assessor Kirsty Wydenbach noted:

At the start of the pandemic it was obvious we needed a process to ensure Covid-19 trials were able to be up and running as soon as possible in the interests of public health. This involved prioritising the processing and reviewing of all applications for Covid-19 therapeutics and vaccines trials.

Dedicated clinical assessors were established to review draft trial documents before they were formally submitted for regulatory approval, and immediate informal regulatory advice meetings were offered. This became the feted *rolling review* process which the MHRA so ably pioneered.

By April 2020, Oxford had decided that it needed an industrial partner able to scale-up and manufacture its vaccine and had sealed a deal with AstraZeneca. Astonishingly, AstraZeneca had not been known as a player in the global vaccine market and had very little prior experience in vaccine production. Nevertheless, it committed to act as Oxford's partner and work urgently to ensure the vaccine was manufactured and distributed globally.

The VTF team digs in

I was concerned that ministers were in danger of backing a vaccine without having a full picture of the risks and opportunities. We urgently needed to assess this, so that we could place the Oxford breakthrough in the broader vaccine landscape. We would shortly be asked whether to make a much bigger funding commitment and I wanted to ensure we made cool-headed data-guided decisions, not ones driven by rose-tinted momentum and patriotic flag-waving.

The VTF assessment came in integrated stages. The first: preclinical and clinical assessment designed to answer the question 'Is this vaccine safe?' The second question: 'How likely is it that this vaccine will work, especially for those at most risk, and will it win regulatory approval?' The third was the manufacturing review, where the question was: 'Can it be made swiftly at high quality and at scale?'

Clive's due diligence SWAT team included Steve Chatfield, then a non-executive director of the Vaccine Manufacturing and Innovation Centre (VMIC), and a real authority on vaccines. Steve had worked for more than forty years in the biopharmaceutical industry and the public sector developing and commercialising vaccines.

Clive also introduced another leading light in this area, Helen Horton, who was between jobs. She had just left Janssen Vaccines to take up a new role at Touchlight Genetics and was very happy to be seconded.

John Tite, a widely respected independent immunology and vaccine consultant, was also up for it. I knew John well already as he had served as start-up CEO of Bicycle Therapeutics, founded by Nobel Laureate Sir Greg Winter and backed by SV, now listed on Nasdaq.

We invited other heavyweight advisers such as Garth Rapeport, a physician and Visiting Professor at the National Heart and Lung Institute in London. I have known Garth for years, a brilliant respiratory drug developer and physician.

The Oxford/VTF diligence group consisted of Sarah Gilbert and Andrew Pollard for the university and Clive's 'dream team' of Steve Chatfield, Helen Horton, John Tite and Giovanni Della Cioppa. Together they reviewed all the preclinical and clinical data to answer the first two questions.

The manufacturing analysis was undertaken by Ian McCubbin and his separate 'dream team' of Andy Jones, Dave Watson and Steve Chatfield (again).

Andy Jones was the Challenge Director for Medicines Manufacturing at UKRI. I had met Andy before in my role on the Life Sciences Industrial Strategy Advisory Group so knew of his decades of industrial experience at AstraZeneca.

Dave Watson, a former Senior Vice President for Global Industrial Operations at Sanofi, was new to me. Dave had built and run manufacturing sites all over the world for Ciba-Geigy, Fisons and Wyeth before Sanofi. He was not a tourist when it came to advanced medicines manufacturing.

The VTF manufacturing diligence team worked with senior figures at AstraZeneca. They also worked with over thirty specialist companies including Cobra Biologics and Oxford Biomedica to review the data and plans for scale-up.

The Oxford/VTF outcome was overwhelmingly positive. It could be summed up in a single sentence from the report, namely 'The ChAdOx1 SARS-CoV-2 vaccine is a strong contender to prevent Covid-19.'

We spent time discussing the theoretical merits of a single high dose or lower two-dose schedule. It appeared that the side effects were related to dose and we thought there was a risk that a high dose with temporary side effects might deter some from accepting the vaccine. The clinical data ultimately suggested two doses.

I remember Andy's reaction in May when I asked him whether the VTF team could run the full due diligence so that we could have a complete picture of the Oxford data and plans. Although this was the last thing he wanted, he was generous with his time and explanations which massively helped our work. After that I would often have Sunday morning update calls with Andy after his early morning run, wearing a bright orange T-shirt. He probably took calls on his runs too, as he never stopped working.

The bonds of trust that were forged early on would be invaluable as we faced the inevitable bumps in the road later.

★

Oxford's clinical trials were also to throw up what would be an ugly side to the quest to find a vaccine. It was widely reported on social media by anti-vaxxers that Dr Elisa Granato, photographed receiving an injection as part of the trials, had died afterwards. It was entirely false, but many more lies followed both in the UK and around the world, stoked by the anti-vax brigade.

Much of what the VTF reviewed would become public knowledge when the results of the Phase 1 and Phase 2 trials were reported in *The Lancet* in July 2020. This prompted a media frenzy – and raised unrealistic expectations.

The data showed that the Oxford vaccine could indeed induce an immune response but what we did not know at that point was whether or not this immune response would actually protect against infection, hospitalisation or serious disease. The good news was the vaccine seemed to be safe and tolerated.

The Oxford data came as the lockdown restrictions were being eased. Foreign travel resumed, the controversial 'eat out to help out' scheme in August 2020 seized the public imagination and schools prepared to return in September.

It was obvious to all of us at the time that all this brewed the perfect storm for a second wave with winter in sight, so even if a vaccine were to be approved at the earliest possible moment, we feared it would probably be too late to stop the UK being plunged into lockdown again.

Manufacturing challenges expected

The manufacturing coalition seemed to be working well but we foresaw difficulties. The issue wasn't whether the vaccine could ever be scaled-up, but how quickly.

Our work concluded that the ChAdOx1 manufacturing process was well understood and well planned for by AstraZeneca and their Oxford and industrial partners. Inevitably a lot of the early plans were based on academic work in small volume bench-scale reactors that had yet to be scaled-up to regulatory-quality, bulk manufacturing levels. Moving from test tubes into 1,000–2,000 litre reactors is not for the faint-hearted. There were assumptions about how much of the vaccine would be produced by when, which depended on the mammalian cell culture continuing to behave predictably as the bioreactors got larger – which they never do.

All this work would have to be completed against extremely tight timelines. I was personally concerned that politicians might be tempted to overpromise and then blame those involved with the VTF for underdelivering when, as I sought always to say publicly, huge uncertainties were involved. We were attempting to do something that had never been done before and at an unprecedented speed.

The rate of scale-up was the biggest obstacle to the AstraZeneca plan. New tests needed to be developed to assess yield, quality and consistency at each stage. There could easily be unintended consequences every time the conditions were changed. We had to test and retest every iteration to make sure the living cells were growing as planned.

I had experienced manufacturing challenges before in my biotech companies. Unexpected stability failures set back a life-changing respiratory drug by over a year until we designed a more robust and scaled manufacturing process. We never thought we would not be able to scale up the vaccine, the question was how long would it take? There were plenty on the outside, including some very senior figures advising ministers, who were much more sceptical.

A degree of caution was rational. Four major multinational pharmaceutical companies – GSK, Pfizer, Merck and Sanofi Pasteur – were responsible for about eighty per cent of the global vaccine market. While AstraZeneca was an impressive company and could mobilise astonishing resources, it was not a dedicated vaccine company. The notion that everything would work smoothly for AstraZeneca to deliver millions of doses to treat the population rapidly with an unknown viral vaccine vector was, to put it mildly, very optimistic.

Nick was in a position to take a Full Business Case for the Oxford University/AstraZeneca vaccine (codenamed Project Triumph) to the VTF Ministerial Panel for approval.

We had an initial understanding to buy a total of 100 million doses (with 30 million proposed to be delivered in September 2020), but the contract was not finalised until late August. Given the massive work AstraZeneca was undertaking in establishing supply chains around the world and the associated commercial contracting, we allowed a pause until we got our heads down with AstraZeneca to complete the UK legal agreement.

There were still substantial risks, set out starkly within our densely packed document. We would provide upfront funding to reimburse the costs incurred by AstraZeneca and the various contractors working for them. This funding could not be recovered if the vaccine were ultimately unsuccessful.

AstraZeneca had volunteered to act on a not-for-profit basis, and its early estimate was that its vaccine would cost $3–4 per dose. Remarkably cheap. It was, however, precisely that, an estimate. It was hard to judge accuracy as the vaccine had not yet been manufactured at scale.

AstraZeneca, like all the Covid-19 vaccine companies, requested broad and unlimited indemnity from the Government for all losses arising from the product, including death and personal injury.

The financial commitment was hardly insignificant. The total sum negotiated by Maddy for the 100 million priority doses, including a generous contingency, was just under £500 million. As part of this, we would provide upfront payments totalling £130 million to pay for the scale-up and production of the vaccine, with further millions of pounds set aside to cover reservations and consumable orders that AstraZeneca had committed to and paid at risk.

None of this took account of the fact that the Government had to deal with the logistics and the expense of distributing the vaccine to tens of millions of people. That could easily double the cost. In fact, the NAO has since estimated that the cost of deployment was more expensive than the vaccines themselves.

Yet there was no hint of a wobble inside Whitehall. It has been a test case for their faith in experts. At the time that Project Triumph was signed off, it was not merely hoped but expected in certain quarters that the Oxford/AstraZeneca vaccine would be the first in the world to obtain regulatory approval, granting the Prime Minister his wish that a vaccine would come wrapped in a Union Jack.

Problems mount

The second half of 2020 would involve a multitude of obstacles. Most had been foreseen by the VTF.

There were three main difficulties. The first was that it became clear by June that the best-case scenario for scale-up was far too optimistic and that the yields would be substantially lower than anticipated. Hence the prospect of thirty million doses being manufactured for the UK by September receded almost overnight and securing that number by the end of 2020 now looked unlikely. Ian McCubbin had consistently expressed his doubts to the rest of the VTF steering committee that the thirty million doses could be delivered, and he was proven right.

Unfortunately, expectations had been raised to fever pitch following Alok's announcement of further funding for the Oxford/AstraZeneca vaccine on 18 May 2020, with headlines trumpeting that AstraZeneca would make up to thirty million vaccine doses available by September if trials were successful.

With such high hopes, I found myself obliged to fend off assertions about the real number of doses that AstraZeneca might provide in 2020 during relentless quizzing by Parliamentary Select Committees, initially in July and then again in November 2020. The problem, bluntly, was that everyone seemed to believe that what had been suggested as the most optimistic, best-case number of doses that could be manufactured quickly would indeed turn into reality, despite the known challenges with scaling-up these manufacturing processes. They thought that any failure to reach these challenging targets must be the result of conspiracy, deceit or incompetence.

It would have been better had AstraZeneca talked down what it could achieve earlier in the year.

I was surprised by the paranoia circulating in some at the very top of government, who seemed to think that AstraZeneca was not being straight with even the most senior of ministers and something sinister might be afoot. I knew this was not true.

When AstraZeneca announced their manufacturing and distribution deal with Russian drugmaker R-Pharm in July 2020 without informing the Government beforehand, it was met with cries of traitor. In fact, as I pointed out to ministers, AstraZeneca was required in its government contract to make its vaccine available to all those who needed it worldwide and they were merely fulfilling these terms. This contract did not dictate that they should supply vaccines only to their friends.

It was unfortunate timing since this deal was signed days after Western intelligence officials identified Russian hackers trying to rip off Oxford's Covid-19 vaccine research, linking the would-be thieves with the country's intelligence services.

There were several James Bond moments when Nick or Ruth, who both had high-level security clearances, had to physically meet AstraZeneca leaders in Cambridge to brief them personally without fear of being overheard. I didn't know the details at the time but knew something secret was going on.

In these briefings, Ruth and Nick told AstraZeneca about an upcoming propaganda campaign apparently from Russia that had been discovered, describing possible hostile interventions. Enemy states apparently used online platforms to undermine confidence in Covid-19 vaccines, including the AstraZeneca one. Shortly afterwards, the UK media pre-empted these misinformation campaigns by outing the negative propaganda images, which featured a chimpanzee in a white coat labelled AstraZeneca holding a syringe, with a toothy, scary grin. *The Times* headline on 16 October read: 'Russians spread fake news over Oxford coronavirus vaccine'. The paper gleefully described the interception of this planned bogus news and wrote:

> The crude theme of the distorted images is that the vaccine, millions of doses of which will be manufactured by the pharmaceutical giant AstraZeneca, could turn people into monkeys because it uses a chimpanzee virus as a vector. The campaign is being targeted at countries where Russia wants to sell its own Sputnik V vaccine, as well as western nations.

I was able to persuade AstraZeneca to let us know before they signed with China, which they did.

It was a shame that there was so little trust and understanding of industry within government and Whitehall. The fact that Jonathan Van-Tam and I sat on the Oxford/AstraZeneca Joint Steering Committee and so had full sight of all key decisions, work and analyses did not allay suspicion. I was amazed that I spent much of my time while Chair – and, rather strangely, even more *after* I had left the VTF team – being contacted about the shortfall of AstraZeneca doses and attempting to calm people down on this matter.

The second delay came through the effect of lockdown and the resulting fewer infections.

The first lockdown in 2020 was great at reducing viral transmission and saving lives. But this came with a downside: high levels of viral transmission are actually needed to be able to demonstrate statistically that vaccines can protect against infection.

Clinical trials on vaccines are designed to compare levels of infection in those who have received the vaccine versus those who have had the placebo. You need to have a sufficient number of infections to prove statistically that the vaccines have an effect. In the summer of 2020, too few people were getting infected to prove that the vaccine could provide protection.

The Phase 3 trial in the UK coincided with the imposition of severe restrictions. The level of public compliance with them was much higher than many had anticipated. People really were staying at home, social distancing was being observed, pubs were closed. The number of cases collapsed spectacularly. While this was obviously a great outcome for immediate public health, it made the placebo-controlled Phase 3 trials in the UK extremely difficult. This lockdown slowed down the Oxford trial, which was a shame since it had started at the front of the pack.

It was always intended that this vaccine would be trialled outside of the UK, both to get the scale of trial needed for regulatory approval as well as to demonstrate that the vaccine worked in diverse populations. Andy launched trials in Brazil, South Africa and Kenya. And had to manage the false news in those countries too, claiming the vaccine was killing people. But with low infection levels in the UK, we ended up watching very carefully the infection levels (and recruitment rates) in these other countries with the macabre hope they could make up for the reduced infections in the UK.

In September 2020, following a Suspected Unexpected Serious Adverse Reaction (SUSAR) in the UK Phase 3 clinical trial, AstraZeneca and Oxford voluntarily paused the Phase 3 trials worldwide, while the UK regulator the MHRA, all relevant international regulators and the independent Data and Safety Monitoring Boards investigated the event. This is a routine regulatory procedure employed to ensure any new treatment or vaccine is safe. Normally these events are not reported on the front pages of newspapers.

Dr Doug Brown, Chief Executive of the British Society for Immunology, noted:

What we are seeing with the news that the AstraZeneca–Oxford University Covid-19 vaccine trial has been paused due to ill health in one participant is one of these safety procedures kicking in. As we all know, people fall ill for a multitude of reasons, and the project team will now be reviewing in depth what is the cause of this person's illness and whether it is linked to having been given the vaccine or not. To be ultra-cautious, the trial is paused while this process is carried out – this is another of the safety procedures built into all vaccine trials.

Within a few days the MHRA became convinced that this SUSAR was *not* the fault of the vaccine itself, but of an unrelated condition, and allowed trials in the UK to resume.

The US authorities, the FDA, were more dogmatic. Even though Oxford/AstraZeneca had voluntarily paused the trial, the FDA raised the temperature by issuing a formal notice halting the study. Several in the university and the company felt that an element of vaccine nationalism was now in play. They were entitled to their concerns.

When Johnson & Johnson (an American company) later encountered a SUSAR in their US trial it was suspended for a week. Oxford/AstraZeneca, by contrast, were put on hold for two months. This was not the only example of apparent bias.

I was disappointed to learn later on that the FDA would not allow AstraZeneca to apply for an emergency use application but insisted on a full licence application. This increased the level of paperwork by at least tenfold. I understood that the FDA disregarded data acquired in the UK trials and apparently insisted on repeating the analyses themselves, even though the UK labs doing the testing were approved and inspected by the MHRA. The irony was that AstraZeneca was not likely to sell its vaccine in the US anyway. The enforced regulatory delays would make it too late. Instead, it had sought FDA approval as further validity of the vaccine for distribution to low- and middle-income countries around the world. There would be sniping from American quarters throughout.

There were also public comments about the efficacy of the vaccine from President Macron and Chancellor Merkel, which were ill-informed and at worst a terrible own goal in that they legitimised vaccine opposition and hesitancy. Macron suggested that the vaccine did not work in the elderly and it was reported that Angela Merkel wouldn't take AstraZeneca's vaccine.

Not content with claiming that the vaccine didn't work, the EU leaders then alleged breach of contract in early 2021 and sued AstraZeneca for non-delivery of the vaccine. When the redacted UK and EU vaccine contracts became publicly available in early 2021, Maddy's low-profile but crucial role became apparent.

Comparing the UK and EU contracts with AstraZeneca for their Covid-19 vaccine, Sébastien De Rey, a contract law specialist at Leuven University said, 'The U.K. contract is, on some specific points, more detailed.' The journal *Politico* wrote in February 2021:

> This core difference, according to a lawyer familiar with the development of the U.K. text, can be chalked up to the fact that the contract sealed with London was written by people with significant experience of purchasing agreements, specifically drug-buying deals. The European Commission's contract, by contrast, shows a lack of commercial common sense, in the lawyer's view… The U.K. contract makes it clear that London had thought through the entire Oxford/AstraZeneca supply chain, rather than just focusing on the delivery of the vaccines. The EU, by comparison, was more unclear, even as to where its plants would be.

Maddy's commercial acumen shone through these redacted contracts. She clearly relished her role as a tough commercial negotiator who takes no prisoners. Maddy was supposed to be taking a long sabbatical in 2020 but the pandemic got in the way. We were very lucky to have her on our side.

Consistency didn't seem to trouble the EU. The consequence was that 1.4 million doses were left unused in Germany when thousands of people were dying in early 2021. That is an extraordinary legacy for former Chancellor Merkel and her advisers.

As I said to the *FT* in April 2021: 'The bickering just layers uncertainty in people's minds, so it needs to stop. We need to get those people who are vulnerable vaccinated.'

Sir John Bell was more forthright, telling the BBC, 'I think bad behaviour from scientists and politicians has probably killed hundreds of thousands of people – and that they cannot be proud of.'

There is no doubt that politically motivated and ignorant comments, amplified by hysterical headlines in the media, slowed the vaccine roll-out on the continent and cost lives. It bitterly frustrated Oxford and AstraZeneca.

The final falter was perhaps a more self-inflicted piece of imperfect public relations, due no doubt to exhaustion at the relentless pace at which everyone was working. When AstraZeneca issued their Phase 3 results, after Pfizer/BioNTech had already released their amazing data, they offered three different numbers for efficacy – 62%, 70% and 90% according to the dose administered. This was confusing and it led to rampant claims on social media that the company was engaged in the pharmaceutical equivalent of party political 'spin doctoring' in an attempt to drive its own number closer to that of the 94% efficacy linked to its rival.

This messy episode was compounded in early 2021 when the company managed to find itself in a public spat with the US Drug Safety Monitoring Board over the accuracy of the data it was citing. Such an open clash was all but unheard-of and it no doubt soured relations between AstraZeneca and the FDA even more.

I got to know the charismatic Mene Pangalos, Head of Biopharma R&D at AstraZeneca, who was heavily embroiled in this unprecedented public argument. We texted and spoke frequently. He was involved in every aspect of the vaccine development as well as the Covid-19 antibody cocktail programme. I've no idea when he ever sleeps.

★

Even though the Oxford/AstraZeneca vaccine held enormous promise, it definitely did not signal mission accomplished for the VTF. We could not be certain that this vaccine would actually be approved or that it would work for everyone. We simply had to have a wider range of vaccines. We could still be badly exposed if we did not.

8

CHOOSING A MESSENGER

Patrick's gut feeling was on the money. At the very outset of the crisis, before the first cases had even been recorded in the UK, he had foreseen that messenger RNA (mRNA) vaccines could be our salvation.

Even though the technology concerned was new and untested, Patrick had worked closely with Moncef Slaoui who ran vaccines at GSK and had been a strong advocate of this new approach. Moncef subsequently moved on to take a non-executive role at Moderna to focus exclusively on mRNA and was later appointed as Head of Operation Warp Speed, President Trump's equivalent to the UK's Vaccine Taskforce.

It was always likely that potential mRNA vaccines would be part of the portfolio built by the Vaccine Taskforce. But which of the mRNA vaccines could realistically be rapidly delivered to the UK?

There were two main overseas candidates, Moderna and Pfizer/BioNTech. As I found out when I joined in May, the choice had almost been predetermined in the weeks before I assumed the VTF Chair.

There was, though, the possibility of an intriguing new vaccine approach based in this country. It was being promoted by Robin Shattock, Professor of Mucosal Infection and Immunity at the

Faculty of Medicine at Imperial College, London. I had been excited by Robin's early briefings on this technology platform in April when I was a member of the Expert Advisory Panel.

It was more enticing still in that the thesis behind this vaccine contender was that it would be a step beyond mere messenger RNA: self-amplifying RNA.

Imperial's RNA innovation

A self-amplifying RNA vaccine (saRNA) not only encodes the instructions for the host cell to make a coronavirus protein, but it also makes lots of copies of the RNA containing those instructions. Robin suggested that the dose needed could be as little as one-hundredth of that of an mRNA vaccine. A very low dose meant it should be easier and quicker to scale-up and manufacture. So potentially vast numbers of people could be vaccinated quickly and cheaply. A potential game changer if it could be delivered.

Unlike Oxford, which had been running trials on its ChAdOx vaccine platform for some years, the Covid-19 pandemic was the first real test of Imperial's self-amplifying technology. Also, unlike Oxford, they had not managed to secure a partnership with a major pharmaceutical company which could provide the skills, resources and capabilities needed to turn an academic project into commercial reality.

Since the initial funding had already been provided by the UK Government, I was especially keen to prioritise the due diligence work with Clive and his team to see whether the saRNA vaccine should be a core part of the VTF portfolio, given the flexibility and potential speed of the approach.

To prepare I watched Robin's videoed talk at the World Economic Forum 2019 titled 'Distributed production of RNA vaccines for agile response to outbreaks'. His passion and commitment to global health was infectious (no pun intended).

One of my early pieces of preparatory work here was to look at the Business Cases for funding the Imperial vaccine prepared by the Department of Health. I wanted to know exactly what had been done so far and what the plans were for developing this vaccine. What was the data that had been generated so far and what were the near-term milestones?

When I read the Business Case prepared by the Department of Health before my arrival it described a 'Phase 3: Large scale study in over 2m people'. Wrong by orders of magnitude. Blimey. That set major alarm bells ringing. In fact, I was gobsmacked that something so outlandishly and obviously wrong could have made it into the document. Given the public interest in how tax payer money is spent, did the team in the Department of Health really have any idea what was needed? And what about the people who read the Business Case? The language was wrong, and the scale of what they planned was patently absurd.

After that I insisted on seeing every single recommendation that was being prepared by the VTF so that I could read every word before it was finalised and submitted. I started to realise that I wasn't complying with the normal Whitehall hierarchical processes. My team at the VTF were surprised and probably appalled by the fact that I would take a lot of personal time to read, comment on and even rewrite future Business Cases to ensure they were accurate and balanced. But getting the words right really matters: to communicate, to bring people together and to discipline one's own thinking.

Clive and team set to work to get up to speed. Unfortunately, we were not convinced by the early diligence that this saRNA vaccine would be ready in time to form a central part of the VTF's vaccine portfolio. We found too much emphasis on the strategy, not enough on delivery. Despite the incredible commitment and hard work of Robin and the Imperial team, we did not believe that it was remotely possible to launch an approved saRNA vaccine by the end of 2020, or even by mid-2021.

We were particularly concerned about the proposed supply chains – one for the UK and another for the EU. Complicated did not begin to describe them. All of the experts on the team, Clive, Ian, Dave, Steve Chatfield and Andy Jones, worried that what was being proposed looked too fragile and that even if a vaccine emerged that fully met the immense promise of self-amplifying RNA, it would prove too hard to make it at scale.

They reported back, saying 'the scale and complexity of potential issues create risks for successful project delivery. A number of cumulative issues make this a challenging project.' They recommended that Imperial's programme would benefit from collaboration with a multinational pharmaceutical partner with the experience and resources they currently lacked.

Other aspects of the proposal provoked considerable anxiety. It relied more on Robin personally than the Oxford vaccine, which had a number of interconnected academic and industrial partners. Imperial College had created its own social enterprise, VacEquity Global Health, which would be the non-profit vehicle for delivering the vaccine throughout the world. Attempting to establish a management structure such as this on an almost pop-up basis was going to be challenging, even if the consultants recruited were credible.

Leaning in to try and help

At this point I started pinging my contacts to see how we could help plug the gaps. Clive and the team did the same.

I emailed a senior vaccine leader at GSK to ask whether the company might be interested in partnering with Imperial, just as AstraZeneca had partnered with Oxford. GSK duly dug into it and scrubbed the saRNA data and plans, but declined, saying they would have to rebuild the supply chain from scratch. Their feedback reminded me of the tale about a tourist lost in the West of Ireland asking a local farmer for directions to Dublin and being told, 'Well, if I were you, I wouldn't start from here.' I tried other pharmaceutical companies to no avail.

At that point, the government had provided about £10 million to secure resources, raw materials, equipment and production slots. Ian McCubbin had helped to bring in the highly innovative and effective government-owned CPI, the Centre for Process Innovation in Darlington, to help Imperial with scale-up.

The VTF team was seriously concerned that the milestones and plans were not deliverable. Much to Robin's understandable irritation, in July we told him that the VTF would pause negotiations on the vaccine supply contracts for a month to collaboratively conduct a Readiness Review to establish the risks, mitigations and a detailed cost model. This Readiness Review was something that Ruth had conducted throughout her career but was not a formal process I had encountered before in biotech.

Robin felt we were procrastinating. He wrote to me saying 'another major contract needs to be placed without delay and we continue to live on a hand to mouth basis. If we wait till the readiness review is completed before critical contracts are put in place, we will likely slip several months behind on our ability to deliver.' I was of course sympathetic to Robin's position. I didn't want to be the government foot-dragger. I was torn between trying to support this exciting new technology and needing to build a vaccine portfolio that could deliver for the 2020/2021 winter.

By October, it was clear that Robin's frustration was increasing as we fielded calls from the press and members of the public asking why we weren't supporting Imperial. I had a glimpse of the somewhat abusive mailboxes that MPs must face daily when I read the letter from someone called Harry Bradbury, Executive Chairman of the Imaginatives Group:

The manner in which this affair has been mishandled over months is a national disgrace. No degree of obfuscation and dithering by

BEIS and DH can mask what is happening here. Imperial College is deliberately being prevented from completing a successful trials program by being starved of funds… There isn't the slightest evidence at this stage that these big brands will achieve anything of lasting value to Covid vaccine development. Please help me to help others to see sense.

I wasn't exactly happy for the VTF's work to be labelled a national disgrace by someone I had never heard of, let alone ever met or spoken to. But this seems to be the run-of-the-mill way that disgruntled citizens speak to people in government. I talked to an anxious MP who called me to discuss this, explained what our due diligence had found and what we were doing to try and help.

We reluctantly decided that the Imperial saRNA vaccine was not an option we could pursue. There were too many doubts about the vaccine and we were confident that it would not be ready for mass production by the end of 2020. It took somewhat longer for the team at Imperial College to accept this outcome.

As it turned out, the initial saRNA clinical data generated towards the end of 2020 was not very encouraging. The ultra-low dose promised by the self-amplifying approach was not yet ready and there was more work needed to turn this into a commercial product. It was at the cutting edge of the cutting edge, but not yet ready for action. We needed vaccines that could be shot into arms as soon as possible.

That's not to say it will never be a serious technology. Far from it. In September 2021, VaxEquity Ltd, the sister company to VacEquity Global Health, had reached an agreement with AstraZeneca to license its self-amplifying technology. I hope that this promising approach will soon have an opportunity to prove its worth.

With Imperial not making it into the core VTF portfolio, it was the two messenger RNA options that mattered.

The Karikó–Weissman story

What is now called mRNA was identified in 1961. The practical consequences of this were not then obvious. And it remained a matter of academic interest to a very small set of scientists only.

One of them was Katalin Karikó, a young Hungarian at the University of Szeged, and by her gender alone a very unusual figure in the 1970s. She started thinking about the practical applications of mRNA from as early as 1978. After her doctorate was completed, she moved on to the Institute of Biochemistry Biological Research Centre of Hungary. Not long after that, though, this body lost its funding. She now had little prospect of becoming a scientist of distinction in her home country. Despite all the uncertainties involved, she moved to the United States.

Karikó's first three years in the US were spent as a postdoctoral fellow at Temple University. She wanted to use engineered mRNA to trigger cells into making the protein encoded in the mRNA genetic sequence. She believed that mRNA could be used to influence immune response. By the time she had arrived at the University of Pennsylvania in 1989, proving this formed the core of her research activity.

Karikó appeared to be banging her head against a brick wall. Try as she might, she struggled to produce engineered peptides, which are the building blocks of proteins, using her synthetic RNA. Her attempt to induce human cells to act as she wanted them to act kept failing. The mRNA was invariably detected by cells and destroyed. It was also an incredibly delicate substance to handle.

Karikó was fortunate to acquire a collaborator in David Weissman who had arrived at the faculty from Boston University. It was by no means his sole area of specialism but he brought new ideas. The experimentation continued until they made a scientific breakthrough. This changed everything.

Every strand of mRNA consists of four molecular building blocks called nucleosides. Cellular enzymes called ribonucleases recognise these mRNA nucleosides as foreign invaders and break them down. Karikó and Weissman found that they could evade the 'innate immune system' if they altered the nucleosides to stop this unintentional burglar alarm. This meant there would be a far better chance that the mRNA would be able to enter human cells without detection and play the part of a biological postman, delivering instructions to those cells to produce certain proteins.

The Karikó–Weissman combination had cracked it. There was now a plausible means of deploying mRNA synthetically, although they had not yet decided on the best application for this technology. Scepticism surrounding this research was easing. Their findings were set out in a series of academic papers in 2005. Karikó filed patents and in 2006 established a very small company, RNARx, serving as Chief Executive.

It cannot be said that the entirety of the scientific community instantly scrambled in her direction. But two people recognised the implications of this work.

One was Derrick Rossi, an assistant professor at Harvard Medical School. He first considered Karikó's work as a postdoctoral fellow in stem cell biology at Stanford University. Rossi was focused on using embryonic stem cells to treat disease but frustrated by US restrictions on working with human embryos. He saw that mRNA might be a way that let him make stem cells without entering ethical, legal and political quicksand. By 2009, he thought he had managed to do this – triggering a series of events from which the company Moderna would be born.

The other interested party was Uğur Şahin, who was about to launch BioNTech and could envisage how the findings that Karikó–Weissman had outlined might be used against cancer. Although the full intellectual property licence was held by the University of Pennsylvania, Karikó's faith in mRNA was now vindicated.

Moderna and BioNTech were destined to become household names by the end of 2020. They had very different approaches to how they conducted business. In the early months of that year, it was definitely Moderna that took the centre stage, with a highly political strategy.

The Moderna story

Moderna was founded in 2010 to commercialise the research of Derrick Rossi and his approach of modifying mRNA via transfection into human cells. Its original name was ModeRNATherapeutics because it was a mixture of 'modified' and 'RNA'.

Moderna swiftly raised substantial investment from a wide range of backers including rich private individuals. There was apparently some tension between Rossi and his investors over the direction of the business. In 2011, Stéphane Bancel, very much a businessman, and like me a graduate of Harvard Business School, was brought in as the Chief Executive.

A year later, Moderna had achieved unicorn status with a valuation exceeding $1 billion. This was despite not having any product with convincing clinical data, let alone approved and on the market. Its worth was predicated on the assumption that mRNA would eventually become seen as gold dust.

Before the pandemic started, Moderna was developing an impressive list of twenty-four vaccine and drug candidates for conditions as varied as HIV and influenza, but until its Covid-19 vaccine was developed, no products had been approved by any regulator for commercial use. In 2013 it had reached a five-year deal with AstraZeneca for an exclusive option agreement to discover, develop and commercialise mRNA for a wide range of treatments. AstraZeneca paid Moderna $240 million up front as part of this option deal. This collaboration helped the company raise $110 million in additional equity finance. A year later, Alexion Pharmaceuticals paid Moderna $100 million for product options for the treatment of rare diseases but the partnership was abandoned in 2017 when animal trials raised major safety fears. This did not impede Moderna (as it had now been rebranded) from becoming a public company through one of the largest biotech initial public offerings in history, raising a cool $621 million on Nasdaq.

A lot was at stake when Covid-19 appeared out of nowhere. At the end of 2019, Moderna had accumulated losses of $1.5 billion since inception, with a loss of $514 million in the previous year, but had raised over $3 billion since it started life almost a decade earlier. It had brushed off periodic accusations of an 'obsession with secrecy', according to STAT and in particular a perceived reluctance to provide peer-reviewed papers.

Even by the standards of the pharmaceutical industry, where fortunes can be made and lost on a single product receiving regulatory approval or conceding failure in clinical trials, it was an outlier. Either its mRNA platform would come good (as it did) or there would eventually be a large crash.

What Moderna and its leadership certainly did not lack was confidence in itself and the mRNA thesis. It also had a well-developed flair for public relations and an understanding of political lobbying.

Moderna was first out of the gate in making the case that mass vaccination was possible for Covid. The vaccine codenamed MRNA-1273 was designed within two days of the release of the SARS-CoV-2 sequence. Moderna manufactured the first clinical batch of mRNA-1273 twenty-five days after the sequence design, which is quite remarkable. This achievement was trumpeted across the US media, moving its stock price sharply upwards. The high command at Moderna were convinced that their mRNA moment had finally come.

They needed to raise funding for Covid-19 vaccines. This would be an expensive exercise. In March 2020, Stéphane Bancel told Donald Trump that with the right backing his company could have a Covid-19 vaccine ready to hand over by September 2020. For an embattled president with a re-election bid due in November this must have seemed like divine intervention. The FDA approved clinical trials and Moderna received an investment of $483 million from Operation Warp Speed.

Moncef Slaoui, Patrick's old GSK colleague, stood down from his non-executive role at Moderna to become Chief Scientist for the entire Operation Warp Speed operation. Moncef and I spoke very regularly during my time at the VTF and he could not have been more helpful or more thoughtful. I would usually speak to him at 6 a.m. US time when he started his day in Washington.

It was really valuable to me that Moncef was such a vaccine expert as I learned a lot from him and always listened to his sage advice. He was highly confident in the Moderna technology and its ability to scale, and this confidence counted for a lot in my eyes. We always saw ourselves as partners and not rivals.

By the end of 2020, in what would prove a successful investment, Moderna had received more than $950 million of backing from the US federal government, virtually the entire cost of bringing the vaccine from initial concept to FDA approval. A brilliant outcome for a company that intended to sell its final product, at home and abroad, at a very healthy profit.

Moderna was clearly not shy of the limelight; it appeared to invite it. The first volunteer to get a shot in their Phase 3 trial was a television anchor at a CNN affiliate in Savannah, Georgia, live on air.

Moderna crosses the Atlantic

The American president, the UK VTF was soon to discover, was not the only political leader whom Moderna was lobbying. Its Chief Executive had little compunction about approaching Boris Johnson and Matt Hancock directly with his irresistible sales pitch. If the UK committed to meet the whole cost of a Moderna allocation straight away then the UK could be the first country outside of the United States to receive Moderna vaccines. The message rang loud in many ears.

But this funding would be 'at risk', so that if the vaccine failed then the entire sum spent would be lost. My approach in venture capital has always been to provide tranched funding against staged milestones. One hundred per cent upfront cash seemed risky to me. But how risky would of course depend on the data.

When Clive, Nick and I found ourselves installed at the VTF there was a strong expectation that, while we would press ahead with the two 'home-grown' contenders – Oxford University/ AstraZeneca and Imperial College, London – we would also place an order with Moderna. This was seen as the 'cover-our-backs' option. It was not a done deal but there was a strong belief that striking an early deal with Moderna was critical.

The VTF leadership did not want to compromise our work for the sake of expediency. I was not willing to sign up to any vaccine, home-grown or otherwise, without doing full, robust due diligence. I didn't care how good the sales pitch was but wanted to understand whether Moderna's vaccine would work and could be scaled-up, manufactured and rapidly delivered to the UK.

In a comparatively short period, our preliminary due diligence raised red flags relating to Moderna's ability to scale and deliver vaccines to Europe quickly. The company's prime focus was clearly on delivering vaccines to the US rather than Europe. We articulated these concerns. Although some in Whitehall referred to the multi-million-pound Moderna contract as 'chump change', I was not prepared to meekly hand over the money when there might be a better alternative available.

Clive, especially, was not convinced that he was being offered the chance to participate in the deal of the century. His crack team of experts could see that there was enormous potential in the Moderna vaccine, which had strong data in preclinical animal models. But Clive found it very hard to extract detailed answers to questions around scale-up and manufacturing generally, but also the specific scale-up plans in the Swiss factory in Visp from which our vaccines would come.

This was not seen in other due diligence processes we were running. Oxford/AstraZeneca were strikingly transparent, and so too were the other vaccine companies based outside the UK who appeared happy to engage with the open, industrially experienced team from the UK.

In our interactions with the team from Moderna, we were struck by their extreme hardball tactics and an element of 'take it or leave it'. Moderna suggested that 'there will be plenty of others willing to take our terms.' In venture capital at SV, we turn over every rock so we can understand exactly the risks we are taking on. Once we understand the risks, we can work with management to mitigate them and maximise the chance of success. But that wasn't on the table here, which made me uncomfortable.

One fun part about being in government was that UK officials were able to speak to their counterparts in other countries to establish which governments, if any, were willing to sign with Moderna on these terms, accepting their apparent lack of openness. It turned out in these private conversations with European counterparts that other countries were not exactly rushing to sign up.

Playing hardball on price and other terms mattered less than *when* and *how many* vaccine doses would be available to the UK. Clive became increasingly convinced that Moderna's vaccine would not be ready for administering into UK arms in late 2020 or even early 2021. Moderna had never brought any product to market before. They had no wish to co-operate with a pharmaceutical firm. The VTF team's conclusion was that the UK would not receive meaningful supplies of the Moderna vaccine until the middle of 2021 at best.

There were other matters of concern. Politicians around the Western world were getting more vocal and strident in their comments. I was worried about 'vaccine nationalism'.

The US Defense Act and US Prep Act

The US Defense Act had real teeth. President Donald Trump said he would invoke it if needed to ensure Americans were first in line for US-produced vaccines. The law enabled the US government to secure any supplies it wanted from US companies, including Moderna. This meant the UK would be exposed to the volatile and unpredictable Trump administration. It would be perfectly within its rights to secure all the Moderna vaccines, no matter where they were made. The UK would be relying on goodwill and, in the heat of an American presidential election, this was not the best place to find oneself.

Our fears about Trump's willingness to use the Defense Act were well founded. I heard that the White House called the CEO of Roche, Severin Schwan, to tell him they were seizing all Roche's Covid-19 diagnostics supplies, which were manufactured in the US. Thinking quickly on his feet, Schwan called Germany to tell them of this threat and agreed a counter-measure: were the US to carry out the seizure, then Germany in turn would not supply Roche's US site with reagents (crucial for diagnostic tests). The White House backed down.

The VTF team, both its outside experts and senior civil servants, found Moderna very intense to negotiate with, on contractual terms, price and matters of law. The company was keen that the UK should pass legislation equivalent to the US Prep Act, which would give them statutory immunity against any liability whatsoever. The US legislation protected all Covid-19 vaccine companies so that they could not be sued over side effects, even if the failure was a result of poor trial design. Moderna and others requested the same statutory protection from the UK. This was a non-starter for the government. Negotiating with Moderna to provide full warranties was difficult.

With decades of experience in highly complex and challenging deals, Maddy kept her composure, but even so Moderna would be one of the most difficult companies that she had ever had to cope with.

Tortuous decision-making in government

The whole early episode with Moderna provided me with my first exposure to government decision-making. We were free to get on with our work – subject to telling everyone what we were doing – and ministers made decisions only when public money was being committed. Moderna had demanded a deadline for a binding Memorandum of Understanding purchase order on Sunday 24 May 2020, yet our diligence team would only have access to critical information on Friday 22 May.

In order to give as much notice as possible, we had sent a draft memorandum to the Business Secretary (with many others copied in) earlier that week summarising the situation, with all the data that we had at that moment and financial terms 'to note'. We did not make a recommendation one way or the other at that point, since we did not yet have the due diligence conclusions from Clive that would come once his team had reviewed the new data.

However, our memorandum 'to note' was apparently understood by a Cabinet Office team as the VTF's formal recommendation to purchase the vaccine. They sent a long list of apparently sensible but not well-informed questions, which completely misunderstood the urgency and nature of the procurement process, the VTF strategy, and the risks that we would need to take to purchase any vaccines at all.

I had to pinch myself not to scream in frustration when I first read the Cabinet Office email with its laundry list of questions. I was still getting to grips with how government functioned, and so was amazed that a briefing note to the Business Secretary triggered a response from the Cabinet Office. It was annoying to have homework marked by people completely unrelated to the VTF with no apparent knowledge of what we were doing.

This saga reinforced my belief that we needed a single streamlined decision-making panel so that we did not have to jump through sequential hoops caused by people who were not engaged in what we were doing, but nonetheless felt qualified to intervene. And thanks to Nick, this is how we arrived at the single Ministerial Investment Committee. It was, therefore, one of the most important and difficult decisions for the VTF *not* to commit to a several-hundred-million-dollar contract with Moderna in the summer of 2020. Clive felt that his neck was on the block and his reputation would be broken if Moderna's vaccine became available in Europe at scale in September, but by now we were pretty sure that wasn't going to happen.

As an insurance policy, after Moderna softened a little, we bought five million of its doses to be deployed in the UK from late spring 2021. This was the maximum that Moderna said they could offer, although this order was later increased when availability improved for delivery to the UK later in 2021. It was not, however, to be the principal vaccine acquired from outside of the United Kingdom. The VTF had determined that there was another option out there.

The Uğur Şahin and Özlem Türeci story

Uğur Şahin read a January 2020 article about the coronavirus in China that had been published in *The Lancet*. He was instantly convinced that a global pandemic was imminent and that he had a moral responsibility to do something about it. He told his team that they needed to drop everything and to focus on investigating an mRNA vaccine as soon as possible.

Şahin and his firm had an atypical backstory. He had come to Germany from Turkey at the age of four, when his father joined many compatriots in the car factories around Cologne. A diligent and intelligent child, he studied hard and moved into medicine. Şahin was primarily an academic medical researcher at first, but by the time he met and married Özlem Türeci (also of Turkish descent but born in Germany) he had acquired a more commercial set of ambitions.

In 2001, the husband-and-wife team co-founded Ganymed Pharmaceuticals, a cancer antibody company. They developed a drug that increased the survival rates of those suffering from gastric cancer in clinical trials. Türeci proved to be a successful biotech

entrepreneur and, as CEO, sold Ganymed to Astellas Pharma for
€422 million in 2016.

Once Şahin ascertained that the difficulties with deploying
mRNA techniques might have been solved, he started to think
about a wide range of potential applications. He was particularly
intrigued to see whether he could develop mRNA 'therapeutic
vaccines' to treat cancer. Şahin co-founded BioNTech, which is
short for Biopharmaceutical New Technologies, alongside his wife
and Christopher Huber, a long-standing mentor, in 2008. He raised
a whopping initial investment of €150 million from billionaire
twins Thomas and Andreas Strüngmann, among others. In 2013, he
recruited Katalin Karikó as a Vice President and then a Senior Vice
President at the firm.

BioNTech was a hive of activity. It churned out papers on its
research. It sought to collaborate with a host of other companies. It
kept the patent offices busy with multiple applications. BioNTech
acquired a reputation as a real player in the mRNA sphere.

★

BioNTech's patent filings and academic publications were noticed
by Pfizer's senior team in New York. In August 2018, the two businesses entered into a multi-year research and development agreement to develop mRNA vaccines for influenza. Playing to their
mutual strengths, BioNTech would do the exploratory research and
design a potential vaccine, while Pfizer would be solely responsible
for the clinical development and the commercialisation of any
product thereafter. A year later, in 2019, BioNTech raised $150
million through a US IPO held on Nasdaq that valued the company
at $3.4 billion.

Influenza was no longer the first priority once the coronavirus
crisis loomed on the horizon. The BioNTech team designed five
possible Covid-19 vaccines that they felt had enough potential to
test in clinical trials. Then they would select the best vaccine

candidate for larger pivotal clinical trials. As a small company, they knew it would be very difficult for them to achieve what they wanted without a much larger partner. They asked the senior Pfizer leadership whether they would be willing to work together to develop a Covid-19 vaccine.

Pfizer had been founded in 1849 in New York by two German immigrants who had arrived a year earlier. It grew rapidly with a whirlwind series of mergers and acquisitions in the decade before the coronavirus. It was now led by Albert Bourla, born in Greece to Jewish parents who nearly perished in the Holocaust. Bourla had started working for Pfizer in Athens, before relocating to the United States, where he had been for the last twenty years.

Bourla was more than willing to co-operate. He was close to fanatical about the subject. What would be known as Project Lightspeed became his mission. He immediately made a commitment to BioNTech and vowed that Pfizer would spend whatever it took to find a vaccine, even though that meant a huge amount of money might be lost. When it was put to him that the aim should be a vaccine ready for deployment by mid-2021, he simply overruled this and insisted that it had to be done in 2020.

At the BioNTech end, with money no object courtesy of their relationship with Pfizer, the pace of progress accelerated. Phase 1 and 2 trials were launched in Germany in late April 2020 and in the United States two weeks later. By July, a leading contender – BNT162b2 – looked very promising.

This was not, by now, news to the UK's Vaccine Taskforce. The day after my appointment as VTF Chair had been made public, Ben Osborn, Head of Pfizer UK, read about it in a newspaper, tracked down my email address, and sent me a message of congratulations and an offer to be of whatever help that he could. I replied in minutes and we first spoke that weekend.

★

It helped that I had an array of contacts with Pfizer in New York too. I had sold businesses to them, my companies had partnered with them, we had co-invested together and of course I had hired great people from Pfizer. So this was a company I knew well and respected highly.

Yet in many ways the most critical actor as far as I was concerned was Sean Marett, Chief Business and Commercial Officer at BioNTech. I had backed Sean in a UK biotech company twenty years previously and we had stayed in touch as his career path took him to BioNTech. I had seen him most recently in London to discuss how we could work together on cancer vaccines.

Sean and I spoke immediately after I became VTF Chair and very regularly after that, discussing the nature of BioNTech's partnership with Pfizer and the progress of their vaccine development. As BioNTech was the Marketing Authorisation Holder for the vaccine, I felt that getting close to BioNTech would be critical. Nothing could happen without its consent.

Working with Pfizer/BioNTech had several other advantages. Pfizer was low-key but highly effective. Its Phase 3 trial, which started two hours after the FDA had awarded its approval, involved volunteer students at the University of Rochester – with no television presence. They had refused to take funding from Operation Warp Speed and hence were not in debt to the Trump administration. Pfizer intended to supply everywhere outside of the US from their plant in Belgium, which gave us some confidence that the White House would not commandeer ex-US supplies. They had immense experience with vaccines and they would need little external assistance.

I wanted to seal the deal. After several friendly calls and texts with Sean over a series of weeks in which he insisted that he could not sign anything until BioNTech had selected which of their four possible types of mRNA vaccines would be adopted, I was getting worried. Worried that we were not being taken seriously and that we would miss this opportunity. I would have failed at the first hurdle. Not good.

The issue for the VTF was speed. We were worried that the Trump White House would buy up the entire supply – not only in the US but also in the EU by employing the US Defense Act to intimidate other countries.

After discussing the problem with Jesse, I changed tack and told Sean that we would have no choice but to sign with Moderna if we had to wait any longer. Sean instantly relented and sent a term sheet overnight outlining how the vaccine could be supplied.

It was practically a case of love at first sight. Our due diligence team found both BioNTech and Pfizer incredibly accessible and candid. From early on, there was an open discussion about what a UK deal for this vaccine would look like, particularly as it might well be the first one signed so might have to serve as a template for others. We discussed the headline terms for a deal, namely doses, delivery dates and price. The terms had to be very flexible until the exact vaccine candidate was established since they had taken four initial vaccine candidates into the clinic for preliminary safety and efficacy testing. Clive's experts were convinced that their approach was credible.

We agreed the first non-binding heads of terms with Pfizer/ BioNTech in July 2020, including price, volume and delivery dates. The US Operation Warp Speed team seemed to be about a week behind us. The White House appeared, nonetheless, willing to seize the entire supply of the vaccine if it could legally do so.

The UK government can move quickly if it wants to

Kate, we have just had a long discussion with the CEO of Pfizer and his senior leadership team. Things are hotting up. We'll need to sign a deal tomorrow. I can explain what's happening on the phone: can you give me a call when you get a moment. Sean.

Eek. I called Sean and he warned us of Trump's plans to take all their available vaccine. Sean told me that if we wanted to secure our position in law then we would have to agree binding indemnity language and do so in twenty-four hours.

Fortunately, over several weeks in June and July, Nick and Maddy had worked incredibly effectively to get ministers and officials to understand that indemnities were necessary if we wanted to secure any vaccine from anyone. If we didn't offer indemnities against future liabilities then we wouldn't get any vaccines. Period.

I had attended meetings with the PM, Alok and ministers, explaining the need to be ready to sign indemnity language in our supply contracts. Officials had refined their calculations estimating the total potential liability over the last few weeks, so the necessary preparatory work had been done.

Thanks to all their recent work, Nick and Maddy were able both to mobilise Whitehall and to nail down the legal indemnity terms within twenty-four hours. As a result, protocol was thrown to the winds as the UK beat the US to sign the first contract in the world with Pfizer/BioNTech for thirty million doses, with an option for ten million more if necessary.

Whitehall approved Project Ambush. We made a potential commitment of over $800 million securing a material portion of the initial supply. It was a massive risk but the likelihood of getting millions of vaccine doses delivered quickly to the UK, together with a range of other terms, made it substantially better than the Moderna offer. This was the VTF's first vaccine contract outside the UK.

It was a time to celebrate at home. We decided to have a family picnic on the mountain. Noah and I rode on horseback and Nell and Jesse biked up the hill. We cooked sausages in a battered old frying pan which we ate in buttered buns with mustard and boiled a kettle for tea. The horses dozed by the side of the dew pond. Rarely have sausages and tea tasted better.

We announced our agreement with Pfizer/BioNTech on Monday 20 July with the US in hot pursuit with their contract out forty-eight hours later, but without the capacity to seize our supply. It was one of the most pivotal moments in my entire time as VTF Chair. It was a vital achievement.

At that time it was still thought that the Oxford/AstraZeneca vaccine would be first approved, but the delays to UK trials caused by the low levels of virus transmission in mid-2020 in the UK meant that assessment had changed by October 2020. Pfizer/BioNTech quietly nosed ahead and became the new favourite.

9

PICKING THE REST
OF THE PORTFOLIO

Winding back the clock to May 2020, we knew then that we needed more than two vaccines to have any realistic chance of success. We needed to review all the other possible candidates being developed around the world to select the most promising for the VTF portfolio, alongside Oxford/AstraZeneca and BioNTech/Pfizer. We had no choice but to spin an awful lot of plates at the same time.

'The average vaccine, taken from the preclinical phase, requires a development timeline of 10.71 years and has a market entry probability of 6%.'

The stats were bleak. I stared at the academic papers describing vaccine development success rates.

We always knew the odds were against us. But rereading the expert statistics and seeing these numbers in black and white was sobering.

We needed to build a portfolio to maximise our chance of success. While we had secured the AZ/Oxford and Pfizer/BioNTech vaccines, two unproven vaccines would not be enough to counteract the high chances of failure. We needed to secure other promising vaccines.

This was basic common sense. My venture capital brain jumped in action. The VTF would embark on a sophisticated exercise in smart investing.

The biggest challenge faced was that the well-understood and widely used vaccine formats were slow to scale-up and manufacture. They would take at least six months longer to make than the unproven adeno and mRNA formats. But the likelihood of these new formats failing was very high. We needed to balance the need for vaccines rapidly with the likelihood of success.

Not a straightforward balancing act.

Picking the portfolio was complex and Clive did not have the luxury of being able to spend months on end mulling it over. We wanted vaccines for the winter of 2020/2021 – speed was vital.

So where to start?

One report estimated that over two hundred vaccine candidates were being developed around the world. Another listed 167 possibilities, of which seven were in early clinical testing. Having decided to remove the consultants appointed to survey the horizon, I allowed our own experts to separate the wheat from the chaff. Which they proceeded to do with vigour.

Immediate favourites were identified. By the end of May, we had discussions ongoing with Janssen Vaccines (part of Johnson & Johnson), GSK/Sanofi, Pfizer/BioNTech, Moderna and Novavax. By early June we added nine more to the longlist from the UK, US, Canada and China. We didn't consider Russia.

In a fortnight or so, Clive and the team had chopped an opening set of around 190 options down to 30, then 23 and then 15. A critical factor in the triage of possible vaccines was whether they would enter clinical trials in 2020. If not, we did not think they could form part of the first generation of vaccines to control the pandemic. Rather more vaccine companies claimed that they would be ready for this than Clive deemed plausible.

As well as clinical trial timing, we set other key criteria to select the most promising vaccines. We reviewed the robustness and credibility of manufacturing scale-up plans and capabilities, the likelihood of early delivery of doses to the UK, the track record of the vaccine format and of the senior management teams, the preclinical and clinical safety and efficacy data, and the level of understanding of the MHRA approval process.

We picked these different vaccine candidates apart. We needed to identify the holes and decide whether they were dealbreakers or whether the VTF could lean in to support areas of weakness. Price was not a driver.

We had initially thought we would need up to twelve vaccines to build a balanced portfolio to maximise the chances of picking one that would work. That's what we had suggested in the Business Case submitted to the Treasury. But having done this due diligence it was clear that we could achieve the diversity we wanted with a portfolio of just seven vaccines.

So, while we were getting close to our final shortlist, I was thinking about what would make the UK an attractive customer so we could secure sufficient supplies.

Expanding the viral-vaccine footprint

We looked for viral platforms complementary to the AstraZeneca/ Oxford vaccine which could trigger very strong and durable immune responses. Our options included vaccines based on adeno-viruses such as Ad5, one of many viruses responsible for causing the common cold. In the USA, approximately forty per cent of the population has antibodies to Ad5, whereas in sub-Saharan Africa and West Africa, as many as eighty to ninety per cent of people do. But a vaccine based on an Ad5 format is likely to encounter pre-existing antibodies to the virus and the immune system may destroy the vaccine before it delivers its payload – meaning the vaccine may not work. So, we deprioritised the Ad5-based vaccines, including the one being developed by the Chinese company Cansino Biologics. (Russia's Sputnik vaccine also contained Ad5.)

I was particularly interested in the two viral platforms being developed by Merck, based on harmless versions of the measles virus and vesicular stomatitis virus. I held calls with the President of Merck Research Laboratories, the formidable Roger Perlmutter, to discuss how the UK could help them accelerate the development of their vaccines in return for supply. Merck is one of the world's finest pharmaceutical companies, with a great track record of launching innovative drugs and vaccines. Merck had partnered early with COVAX, the global vaccine facility for low- and middle-income countries and was not willing to entertain bilateral discussions with individual countries. We kept talking but kept looking. (As it turned out in 2021, alas, both vaccines failed.)

Another novel adenoviral vaccine was being developed by Janssen Vaccines based in Leiden, a subsidiary of the American giant Johnson & Johnson (J&J). Janssen had been founded in 1953 by the visionary Paul Janssen but acquired by J&J eight years later. Janssen's adenoviral vector vaccine was based on a rare human adenovirus called Ad26, modified to contain the Covid-19 spike protein gene.

I was keen to explore the Janssen vaccine because of my long-standing admiration for Paul Stoffels, then the Deputy Chairman and Chief Scientific Officer of J&J. He was a highly respected figure in our industry, not least for his strong ethical stance, immense integrity and commitment to global health. Despite all his titles and successes, Paul was very modest and is found on Sundays playing the organ in his local church in Belgium.

Paul had successfully persuaded Janssen to develop vaccines for Zika and Ebola, normally found in the poorest countries. His vision for their coronavirus vaccine was for truly global deployment. And if anyone could develop a vaccine for the world, then it would be Paul and his team.

I have known Paul for more than ten years, having first sold a respiratory biotech company, Respivert, to him in 2010. Paul was also an early champion of the Dementia Discovery Fund and secured J&J's commitment to investing in it. His Janssen neuroscience team provided valuable support to our SV work in developing new drugs for dementia. Just before the pandemic, we hosted Paul in our SV London office as we discussed how to develop new drugs based on exciting recent ground-breaking science in cancer and neuroscience.

Paul spends his time in the US and Belgium, so early in May I texted both his mobile numbers asking to speak. He immediately responded and we talked about what we were each trying to achieve. It was early days for us both and we continued to speak, mostly at weekends. Paul introduced me to his charming colleague Jaak Peeters, who had come out of retirement to spearhead the Janssen vaccine work.

Janssen had taken a couple of extra months to optimise the spike gene sequence to maximise its immunogenicity, and this proved a striking difference in preclinical experimental models. In these models, the Oxford/AstraZeneca vaccine didn't stop the infection but did reduce the severity of the disease, although the viral doses given were different, so the data cannot be directly compared. The Janssen vaccine, by contrast, actually *prevented* infection in all animals. This remarkable result was subsequently published in *Nature* in July 2020.

Janssen's Ad26 vaccine was distinctive enough from the Oxford/AstraZeneca platform that Clive believed it would add something extra to the VTF portfolio, even though at that point no Ad26 vaccine had yet been approved. (In July 2020, the EU granted Marketing Authorization for Janssen's Ebola vaccine, making it the first approved vaccine to be developed using Janssen's vaccine technologies.)

But we had confidence in this vaccine. Janssen had trialled its vaccine Ad26 platform for Ebola, HIV, Malaria, Filovirus, HPV and Zika in over 67,000 people, so had built a very substantial safety and efficacy package. Our due diligence with Janssen was impressive and thorough. Like AZ, Janssen was working without a profit motive. Janssen's vaccine was low cost, if not quite as low as Oxford/AstraZeneca.

With Janssen's focus on reaching low- and middle-income countries, Paul Stoffels felt strongly that a single-shot vaccine, without a complex cold chain, was the only practical solution to protecting hard-to-reach communities, including villages in many African countries. So Janssen ran two trials, one with a single dose and the second with two doses fifty-four days apart. Volunteers from the UK participated in the two-doses trial.

Right from the start, it was clear that Paul and his team were facing challenges in securing scale-up and bulk manufacturing capacity around the world. I've still not figured out why this was the case since they were an established vaccine player, yet AZ, who came into this field cold, were able to rapidly secure huge manufacturing supply contracts on several continents. We put our manufacturing team on the case to help. I introduced them to John Dawson, the CEO of Oxford Biomedica, who had spare capacity in their new Oxbox site. We also offered to share our excess vial-filling capacity with Janssen.

Janssen's focus on providing vaccines to the wider world on its own terms was important since this was the second goal given to me by the Prime Minister. In August 2020, we signed heads of terms that would allow for thirty million doses to be purchased by the UK Government with the option for twenty-two million more such doses if necessary.

Phase 3 clinical trials of Janssen's single-shot started in June 2020. They involved 43,000 people in the US, where viral transmission was high. On 29 January 2021, Janssen declared that twenty-eight days after only a single vaccination, their vaccine was 66% effective in preventing symptomatic Covid-19 with a robust 85% efficacy in preventing disease and almost total protection against death. Later they showed their two-dose version provided 94% protection against symptomatic infection, making a two-dose regimen of J&J's Janssen vaccine comparable to a two-dose regimen of Moderna's or Pfizer's. This equivalent efficacy is not a fact that is widely known.

On 28 May 2021, the Janssen vaccine received its conditional approval for use in the UK, becoming the fourth such vaccine approved by the MHRA. Like Oxford/AstraZeneca, Janssen's vaccine had very rare clotting side effects which were magnified by the media. Janssen's vaccine was not in the end used in the UK, because other vaccines were already being deployed and poorer nations needed it most.

Considering other mRNA vaccines

The next set of activity involved the mRNA sector. Moderna had shown its colours to the VTF team but we had determined that Pfizer would arrive first and be less exposed to supply chain drama. It was logical, however, to have a stock of the Moderna vaccine on order just in case, even if the early volumes were likely to be small. Moderna was the last contract signed while I was still the VTF Chair.

My successors would also embrace CureVac, which was developing a next gen mRNA vaccine. CureVac was willing for the UK to manufacture this vaccine, so this brought additional strategic value. As of 2021, the UK was still an importer of mRNA vaccines.

CureVac, a German company, had a unique mRNA technology which meant that their vaccine was stable at room temperature. This was a huge breakthrough. Clive and his team felt that, given the much lower dose than Moderna or Pfizer/BioNTech, and the unmodified RNA, CureVac would prove to be safer, less prone to side effects and easier to handle.

Others obviously reached a similar conclusion. In an extraordinary turn of events, the German newspaper *Welt am Sonntag* reported that the Trump administration had offered CureVac millions of dollars to move its vaccine R&D to the United States. The German government immediately made a counter-offer to keep it at home. Even by the standards of shameless vaccine nationalism this was astonishing.

CureVac entered clinical trials when a sea of variants had arrived in many of the countries where its vaccine was tested. Their initial vaccine fell short of the fifty per cent efficacy standard that had become widely accepted as the entry requirement for a valid vaccine. In October 2021, CureVac announced that its Covid-19 vaccine efforts would now be redirected towards the development of a second-generation programme in collaboration with GSK. This is one to watch.

Bookending the VTF portfolio with dependable protein-based vaccines

There were a lot of adjuvanted protein vaccines to consider. We ultimately selected two of them for the VTF portfolio, from a combined GSK/Sanofi effort and Novavax. These two choices could not have been more different.

Glaxo traced its roots back to a general trading company in New Zealand in 1873 but more recently had focused on pharmaceuticals. It had undergone a series of mega mergers, first with Wellcome in 1995, and then SmithKline Beecham to create GlaxoSmithKline (GSK) in 2000. (The proceeds of the sale of Wellcome helped supercharge the Wellcome Trust into one of the world's largest charities.) In 2015, GSK acquired Novartis's global vaccines business, paying over $5 billion in cash. Now the debate continues about whether to split GSK once again.

GSK had developed a very effective adjuvant called AS03, which was proven to help stimulate immune responses in the elderly. Adjuvants are added to some vaccines to enhance the immune response – a bit like a cup of coffee to get the immune system up in the morning. They are used to create a stronger and longer-lasting immunity against infections than the vaccine alone.

GSK's Covid-19 strategy was to provide its adjuvant to a range of different vaccine companies through partnerships, for example with SK Bioscience in South Korea, Medicago in Canada, Clover in China and Sanofi in France. The fact that GSK had chosen to part-ner with these companies gave us a leg up in prioritising which vaccines to consider. GSK's expert team, led by Roger Connor, President, and Thomas Bruer, Chief Medical Officer of GSK Vaccines in Belgium, provided valuable advice. And it turned out that Clive already knew and lived close to Sue Middleton who worked in Government Affairs, Vaccines and Global Health.

The fact that GSK had chosen to offer its AS03 adjuvant to arch-rival and vaccine giant Sanofi was quite surprising. It was a much younger but heavyweight partner. Sanofi had been founded in 1973, merged with Synthélabo in 1999 and then again in 2004 with Aventis to become Sanofi-Aventis. It then swung back full circle in 2011 and changed its name to Sanofi once more. Sanofi was responsible for designing and manufacturing the spike protein component of the vaccine.

Sanofi and GSK were the number one and two vaccine companies in the world. I had strong pre-existing relationships with GSK and got to know the Sanofi CEO Paul Hudson too. We discovered we shared a love for a fabulous Greek restaurant close to where I live in London. I felt confident that together they should produce a serious vaccine.

Like AstraZeneca and Janssen, GSK and Sanofi had committed to provide their vaccine on a non-profit basis. Even though they were behind the adeno and mRNA vaccine leaders, we felt that this was a strong and reliable bookend for the VTF portfolio.

We signed a heads of terms purchase order for sixty million doses in July 2020 for delivery in the second half of 2021. We hoped that if the adeno and mRNA vaccines failed, we could depend on these two vaccine giants to deliver.

However, there were delays in moving the project ahead and, in December 2020, GSK and Sanofi announced that based on initial clinical data, the original vaccine candidate needed to be redesigned and the earliest approval date was 2022. So, what we had thought of as our 'slow and steady wins the race' vaccine safety net did not work out. We were surprised and disappointed with how this option progressed.

In December 2021, GSK/Sanofi announced positive preliminary booster data. By February 2022, they announced that their fridge-temperature vaccine provided 100% protection against severe disease and hospitalisation, at a time when Omicron was dominant.

I do not know what, if any, role this vaccine would play in the UK pandemic management.

Novavax: the dark horse

Novavax was a completely different proposition as a company, even if its vaccine was also a protein subunit-based one like GSK/Sanofi. The business had been founded to develop a novel vaccine delivery technology, but as of early 2021 had not yet successfully launched a single product.

Novavax's vaccines against RSV and Ebola had failed and another for influenza was still being tested. Novavax almost went bust when the RSV trials collapsed and was forced to lay off staff. A headline in February 2019: 'Another Phase 3 RSV failure thumps belea-guered Novavax, but execs claim there's a way forward' suggested that Novavax was in the emergency room. It was about to be delisted from Nasdaq. This put a lot of people off it. But then the pandemic offered another chance to show how effective Novavax's vaccine format was in preventing infection from Covid-19.

Clive liked Novavax but, given the fragility of the company, I wanted more certainty about its credibility before we got too far. In late May, I called my friend and highly respected entrepreneur and investor David Mott for advice. He had just stepped back from leading healthcare in one of the most successful US venture capital groups NEA and knew the Novavax team well. David was enthusi-astic about the management and believed the technology was highly credible; shortly after our conversation he joined the board of Novavax, which gave me great comfort.

Clive was excited by Novavax's virus-like-peptide (VLP) based technology, since the viral spike protein assembles into a 3-D structure like the native virus. This meant it should generate a similar immune response to that seen with the Covid-19 virus itself. In preclinical models, Novavax's vaccine, together with their proprietary adjuvant Matrix M, showed particularly strong immune responses.

We held our first call with Novavax on a Thursday in May and followed up quickly with a more in-depth call that Saturday.

Another lovely day as I sat outside under a sunshade. My mind was wandering towards my youngest son Noah's upcoming twenty-first birthday, and we had just accepted a delivery of helium and a lot of balloons. I planned a celebratory outdoor lunch with Jesse and Nell. It did not exactly amount to the twenty-first birthday party of Noah's dreams, but given the pandemic restrictions I thought at least the balloons would lend some cheer.

I switched back to the task at hand. The Novavax team remarked that this wasn't the pace they typically experienced when working with government. It was an efficient meeting between two teams who both knew what they wanted to achieve.

Since Novavax's vaccines had already been tested in fifteen thousand subjects across their different trials we were satisfied that they were safe. The Novavax team had manufactured clinical-trial volumes of vaccines against coronaviruses before, including SARS-1 and MERS (although these didn't progress), so there was some pre-existing manufacturing data to review.

Our VTF SWAT team concluded that the most significant challenge for the company would be ensuring consistency in manufacturing the vaccine and adjuvant as production levels were scaled-up – and that turned out to be true.

The VTF experts were confident that this candidate vaccine had real potential and was worthy of consideration for the final cut but, unlike the GSK/Sanofi version, Novavax would need considerable assistance. This was the case even though Novavax had already acquired funding from the Coalition for Epidemic Preparedness Innovations (CEPI) and in July 2020 secured $1.6 billion US finance through Operation Warp Speed. Novavax requested help from us for manufacturing capacity and clinical trials, as will be described later.

It was a bold order to make for sixty million doses, which like GSK/Sanofi were not scheduled to be ready until the second half of 2021, but it would be a very UK-centric vaccine if it could be developed.

Discovering a Scottish route to vaccine success

All our VTF vaccines to date were solely focused on generating an immune response to the spike protein. This was a real weakness. There had been some very early candidates designed to include other SARS-CoV-2 proteins, but these remained miles away from prime time.

If there was anything that kept me awake, it was this vulnerability and dependence on the spike protein. For a truly balanced portfolio we needed to find vaccines which provoked a broader immune response to elements of the Covid virus beyond the spike protein alone – such as whole virus-based vaccines. These types of vaccines have been used for decades so are seen as old-fashioned.

But whole virus-based vaccines boasted a key advantage. If the virus mutated (as was to be expected) and existing vaccines didn't work against new variants, then the variant virus could be grown up to create updated vaccines. The VTF team thought it was essential to be able to cover this base.

As far as I knew, only the Chinese had containment facilities to grow up pandemic viruses to make vaccines. But Ian McCubbin knew of a small facility in Livingston, Scotland, that was owned by a French company called Valneva, which he believed could be adapted to suit the VTF's purposes.

Valneva's plant would need to be upgraded, so it would not be able to manufacture vaccines in bulk for a while. But it could be the back-up against mutant strains and a possible option for boosters, for younger children and for the vaccine-hesitant.

Valneva had been founded in 2013 following the merger of Austrian company Intercell and French company Vivalis SA. It had experience in the vaccines space, developing vaccines against Japanese encephalitis and cholera. The CEO Thomas Lingelbach and CFO David Lawrence were enthusiastic when we suggested we might be able to help them upgrade the containment facilities in their existing plant, as well as build a new bioprocessing plant on an adjacent site. There was an excellent working relationship between the VTF experts and the company's senior management team.

In many ways, this was the most important 'insurance' option for the VTF, even though we knew it would not be ready for production and distribution until later in 2021.

In July 2020, therefore, an initial heads of terms agreement was signed, which allowed the UK to acquire sixty million doses of the vaccine with the option of additional doses over the four years thereafter. In the event that frontrunner vaccines did not work out, or that the virus mutated so radically to escape the existing vaccines, the VTF had secured a state-of-the-art resource for the UK that could manufacture variant whole viral-based vaccines, or indeed any vaccine for that matter, since the plant had the flexibility to manufacture any biological-based product.

I regarded this as a huge win, even though it was a reserve effort not likely to come on-line before late 2021 at the earliest. If nothing else, if the whole inactivated virus vaccine turned out not to be needed in the UK, it could be diverted internationally. It would have real merit in terms of the overall portfolio in almost any conceivable circumstances. Added to which, the company was as keen as mustard for clinical trials to start in the UK before the end of 2020.

To add to this happy marriage, Prime Minister Boris Johnson visited the Livingston plant himself in early 2021.

Don't forget the immunocompromised

People who are immunocompromised, such as cancer, transplant and HIV patients, have immune systems that don't work well, or even at all. Certain medicines may themselves dampen the immune response and various diseases diminish the effectiveness of the immune system.

Such people would not be likely to respond to vaccines and would be very vulnerable if the virus struck. The Department of Health told us there were at least 500,000 such people in the UK, so we explored prophylactic options that could offer them protection, just as vaccination protected others.

Antibodies are a key component of immune protection, so the idea was to create a synthetic immune response using antibodies against the spike protein, for those people without a functioning immune system.

At least two antibodies would be required to protect against viral mutations and these would be combined into an 'antibody cocktail'. There were many antibody cocktail candidates in trials, and we were aware that this would be a lengthy and difficult process.

Any antibody cocktail would cost much more than our vaccines, possibly exceeding £1,000 per dose, as opposed to about £10 per dose for vaccines (taking a crude average between the cheaper AZ and the more expensive Pfizer/Moderna vaccines). Dosing with antibodies does not provide the immune memory that vaccination confers, so repeated treatments would be necessary. Furthermore, bulk antibody manufacturing capacity in the UK was non-existent. But these immunocompromised people were especially vulnerable and they needed protection.

Undeterred, Clive turned to the experts that the BIA had assembled to assist us identify the most promising approaches. They were led by Jane Osbourn, Chief Scientific Officer at Alchemab (one of SV's most recent companies, built to discover new antibodies for neurodegeneration and cancer). Joining Jane were Deirdre Flaherty at Abcam, Paul Varley (then at Kymab), and Paul Kellam, also at Kymab and Professor of Virus Genomics at Imperial College. This BIA group had created a consortium systematically to screen antibodies sourced from industry and academia in a robust panel of assays (a set of tests and experiments) to define which combinations provided most protection against the virus. Their knowledge was of incredible value to the VTF team.

We assessed the whole antibody field for long-acting prophylactic antibodies (as a substitute for vaccination in the immunocompromised) as well as therapeutic antibodies for those infected. These were all codenamed too, and I needed another page to remind myself which antibody product was which – Mercury, Sirius, Olympus, Ganymede, Apollo.

We drew our conclusions. We had to disappoint the BIA team: we couldn't continue to fund their consortium as their antibodies were too far behind the frontrunners, even though they might have been effective. We were excited by a long-acting engineered antibody cocktail (called AZD7442) that was being developed by AstraZeneca which suggested the protection could last at least six months. We signed a provisional agreement to buy a million doses.

Over the next few months, AstraZeneca became uneasy at the notion of making a million doses solely for the UK, since it would have been a very large proportion of all potential supply, so asked us to reduce our order.

But when I reverted back to the Department of Health to determine the minimum number of antibody cocktail doses they wanted, I was flabbergasted to be told that they didn't want any at all. New advice held that it would be easier to treat infected immunocompromised patients with drugs afterwards, rather than protect them before they got infected. This was the department, ironically, that at one stage had thought that antibodies rather than vaccines might be the 'silver bullet' to the coronavirus crisis, a pipedream rudely shat-tered when we pointed out the sheer impracticality of making population-scale doses of antibodies.

I think the concern was driven by fear of its likely cost. So, no contract for preventative antibody treatment was ever signed with AZ. I still think that was a mistake.

Clive and his colleagues had also decided that Ronapreve, created by Regeneron and Roche, was the most advanced and effective antibody cocktail for treatment. We recommended this for the RECOVERY trial being conducted by Oxford University, in return for early supply if successful.

The trial results in 2021 confirmed that we were right to conclude that both AZD7442 (now Evusheld) and Ronapreve would be highly effective for prophylaxis and therapeutic use respectively. When he contracted Covid-19 in late 2020, President Trump was treated with Ronapreve, which secured his rapid recovery.

These drugs were both approved by the regulators.

At the time of writing, Evusheld is the only approved long-acting antibody cocktail proven to protect against Omicron. In January 2022, the FDA revised their authorisations for Regeneron and Lilly's monoclonal antibody treatments saying 'data show these treatments are highly unlikely to be active against the Omicron variant.'

Planning for further variants beyond Omicron, AstraZeneca has back-up antibodies entering development to ensure they have spare antibodies if future variants evade neutralisation by one or the other of the current Evusheld antibodies.

In venture capital investing, we build portfolios of high potential but risky investments and double down on winners. We spend hours poring over timelines, budgets and the key milestones that generate value. And allocate resources and expertise to ensure we meet these milestones. Above all we try to help our companies succeed. I applied those same principles to the VTF.

10

MAKING IT HERE

Manufacturing does not just happen. Especially when manufacturing means growing mammalian cells. No vaccines can be made if the infrastructure does not exist.

The work of the VTF would not stop once we had identified a set of credible vaccine candidates. It was critical to have secure supply at scale, as well as early delivery. It would be unrealistic to expect that every one of the selected vaccines could and would be manufactured in the UK, but we would be running unacceptable risks if *none* of them could be.

The early stages of the Covid-19 crisis had seen an ugly international scramble to acquire supplies of personal protective equipment, especially by countries like the UK that did not have a strong manufacturing base in 'technical textiles'.

But unlike PPE, based on everything I had heard in the Vaccine Expert Advisory meetings, I felt cautiously positive that we had some of the skills and vaccine manufacturing capabilities needed right here in the UK. But it was inconceivable that the UK wouldn't rely on imports too. Vaccine nationalism was a risk if some countries decided to stop exports.

A very short history of UK manufacturing

Manufacturing for vaccines in the UK cannot be divorced from the wider fate of manufacturing in the whole economy. The reality in early 2020 was that it was not the force that it might have been.

The country that had the first Industrial Revolution and became 'the workshop of the world' in the nineteenth century, did not cherish that legacy. The UK manufacturing sector has slowly but consistently declined over the last few generations.

In 1950, manufacturing represented about 45% of both total output and employment; this had nearly halved by 1970. The UK was not particularly unusual, since many nations followed this same path. The recessions of the 1970s and 1980s hit low-value manufacturing in the UK hard, with customers moving to far cheaper competitors overseas.

The decline in manufacturing accelerated from 1990. In that year manufacturing had been responsible for over 17% of economic output and nearly 16% of employment. By 2015 those numbers were 10.4% and 7.8%. They would languish still lower in 2019 before Covid. Pharmaceuticals and chemicals represented a mere 7% of the UK's manufacturing footprint.

The UK was now an outlier in terms of its weak manufacturing. Not the best place to start in terms of being prepared to respond to a serious pandemic.

There was a sharp regional divide that almost certainly influenced political perceptions. Manufacturing in 2019 exceeded 10% of employment in the Midlands, Yorkshire and Humberside, but represented only about 7% in the South East of England. In London, seat of power for the UK, it was a mere 2%.

But as manufacturing became more 'boutique' it became more skilled. The perception that manufacturing was all about heavily-staffed unskilled assembly lines was a false one.

The public policy response was one of 'benign neglect'. The shift in UK manufacturing towards high-value but low-employment was viewed as inevitable, irreversible and not entirely unwelcome. Lord Sainsbury was a very well-regarded Science Minister under Tony Blair who had pushed the life sciences agenda. Paul Drayson was widely admired in a similar role under Gordon Brown, establishing the Office for Life Sciences.

The approach taken by the government between 2010 and 2015 built on this early energy. They looked for comparative niches of UK innovation and manufacturing strength, rather than just production at scale, and used public resources to build up those areas.

Many of these policy initiatives were important to the VTF. The Catapult technology and innovation centres, especially the Cell and Gene Therapy Catapult and the Centre for Process Innovation, were a huge benefit to us. These initiatives were started in 2011 after the eminent venture capitalist Dr Hermann Hauser had identified the need for much closer collaboration between the universities and industry. The Catapults were backed by Innovate UK, then led by Ruth McKernan. Their goal was to inject extra energy and more cash into applied R&D, rapidly moving academic ideas into industrial products.

Despite this, pharmaceutical industry spending on R&D in the UK kept declining, though in 2019, on the eve of the pandemic, the UK life sciences industry employed over 256,000 people in 6,300 businesses, generating a collective turnover of over £80 billion.

While the UK had some powerhouse pharmaceutical companies, such as GSK and AstraZeneca, most of their commercial production now took place outside the UK, in Belgium, Ireland and elsewhere. Governments in other countries offered better incentives to expand and grow.

Relaunch of the UK life sciences industrial strategy

Part of the problem was that the British government did not seem to have a clear sense of direction itself in relation to this vital industrial sector.

When Theresa May became Prime Minister in 2016, she created the Department for Business, Energy and Industrial Strategy. Some people thought it was surprising to include 'industrial strategy', believing that markets rather the government should determine industrial competitiveness. But many other countries had a national industrial strategy. Greg Clark as BEIS Secretary relaunched the government's industrial strategy review process to include a specific focus on life sciences.

Greg proved to be a friend and ally to the life sciences and biotechnology sectors. To support his industrial strategy review, Greg turned to Sir John Bell, the Regius Professor of Medicine at Oxford University, to refresh the UK's life sciences priorities and strategy. I joined John Bell's advisory group at that point.

The fresh look at a UK industrial strategy did not just aspire to fine-tune the interaction of academic discovery and industrial innovation, but also asked what areas the UK should double down on beyond pure research.

A consensus emerged that the UK needed to improve on its existing manufacturing base to provide the capacity to scale-up the production of vaccines. We focused on advanced therapeutics manufacturing as well as vaccine preparedness. Ian McCubbin leant in with his network and skills.

Anyone who meets John Bell will be struck by his straight-talking, no-nonsense approach. And as such a renowned medic, he was at the cutting edge of science and medicine. John led an Innovate UK workshop in 2017, one of many that were commissioned at this time as part of the industrial strategy deliberations. It evolved into the recommendation that the UK should establish and fund a new Vaccine Manufacturing and Innovation Centre (VMIC), in Harwell. Following this, £66 million was committed by the Government's Industrial Strategy Challenge Fund (ISCF) Medicines Manufacturing Challenge led by Andy Jones to create VMIC as a non-for-profit company, with the objective of innovation in vaccines.

Advanced medicines manufacturing capability in the UK

The immediate issue that had captured the attention of Sir Patrick Vallance at the start of the coronavirus crisis concerned manufacture and development of mRNA vaccines. He started to question Steve Bates, the head of the BioIndustry Association, as to whether the UK had the ability to manufacture this type of vaccine or possibly the adeno vaccines, which also represented a new and exciting category of discovery.

The BioIndustry Association has existed for more than twenty-five years, almost as long as the sector itself. It had a very diverse membership in early 2020, including about four hundred mostly small and medium-sized companies. It spent most of its time attempting to make ministers and officials understand and appreciate the importance of its sector.

The BIA had been calling for a life sciences strategy for some time before it became fashionable. It had banged the drum with even more force for investing in cell and gene therapy, since these new therapeutic approaches were widely recognised to have huge growth potential, in terms of economic opportunities as well as the development of new life-changing drugs.

Steve Bates told Patrick that the UK did not have any current dedicated mRNA manufacturing capability. As this was clearly a potentially disastrous situation, Steve mobilised Ian McCubbin to join him, his BIA colleague Netty England, and representatives of the Cell and Gene Therapy Catapult and Oxford Biomedica, to see what could be done to address this.

In early 2020, a Covid-19 BIA survey was prepared and circulated asking companies how they could help tackle the Covid-19 pandemic. It was even more urgent since the Oxford University vaccine team had asked the BIA for help too. Following the astonishing response from BIA members in terms of their speed and the willingness of the sector to drop everything to try to help, a volunteer 'Covid-19 manufacturing consortium' came together in February 2020.

Existing bulk vaccine manufacturing in the UK was admittedly light. Seqirus, a subsidiary of an Australian company with a plant based in Speke, Liverpool, made flu vaccine in chicken eggs but did not have the capability to pivot to produce Covid-19 vaccines at scale. And that was it.

But the picture was brighter than it initially seemed. Although the UK did not have any mRNA manufacturing capability as such, there were flexible, albeit small, bioprocessing manufacturing sites and we had many skilled people in the UK to build a specific UK mRNA capability. The building blocks for a broader manufacturing strategy for all vaccine types were there.

Primer on bioprocessing

There is a wealth of brilliant popular science books, articles and documentaries now, giving the public a grasp of the revolutionary theories and the geniuses behind scientific leaps forward; rarely, though, do they delve into the nitty gritty of the actual systems, how they look and are made. As the saying goes, genius is ten per cent inspiration, ninety per cent perspiration. Here I describe briefly the brilliant techniques and vital background technology we deployed, and how much this differs from PPE or equipment manufacturing.

Protein and adeno Covid-19 vaccines are grown in living cells using bioreactors that act like 'mini-factories' to create or 'culture' them quickly. Once cultured over several days, the cells are broken up and the drug substance is purified.

Living mammalian cell culture systems are widely used to produce biopharmaceuticals, including enzymes, antibodies and vaccine antigens. Most recombinant protein vaccines are expressed in mammalian cell culture-based expression systems, including many Covid-19 protein vaccines, Covid-19 adenovirus vaccines and Shingrix®, the shingles (herpes zoster) vaccine manufactured by GSK.

Other Covid-19 protein-based vaccine candidates, like those from Novavax and Sanofi, are produced in a different living system that uses a baculovirus vector and insect cells as hosts. It is possible to reach high densities of insect cells in culture more quickly than with mammalian cells, which makes this a cheaper process. But the resulting proteins are simpler than those produced in mammalian cells. This may or may not matter depending on the product.

I was obviously not effective at explaining the nuances and risks of bioprocess scale-up, as the level of government understanding of vaccine manufacturing remained pretty low during my tenure as Chair.

After the second meeting I attended in Downing Street, I was approached by several advisors asking me whether we could use antibodies as a substitute for vaccination. Again, it was a theoretically interesting question, but one that could be asked only by someone deeply unfamiliar with any of the issues involved; mentally preparing my response, I didn't really know where to start. I pointed out that even commandeering the entire world's antibody manufacturing capacity would not be enough for the UK population, and there was also the side effect that we'd bankrupt the country.

But what I tried to convey was that all living cell systems need to be scaled-up uber carefully, from the around 10-litre scale-up to commercial volumes of 1,000–2,000-litre-plus bioprocessors. Cells don't grow in a linear way – even if you sing to them – so scale-up is typically done in several steps, with quality, consistency and reproducibility assessments at each stage. Scale-up is a process that typically takes years.

Conventional bioreactors built of stainless steel or glass have historically been used to grow cells, which would be stirred and oxygenated in order to stimulate development. This is inherently time-consuming and facilities have to be totally sterilised after each use. More recently, it has become possible to speed up manufacturing by deploying new sensitive and sophisticated single-use and disposable three-layer plastic bags. These include within them an array of sensors to measure temperature, conductivity, glucose, oxygen or pressure. Like James Bond's martinis, the cells within can either be shaken or stirred.

With fewer parts involved and no need to clean and sterilise everything each time since the bags are delivered sterilised, this offers a less expensive and more efficient means of manufacturing. We focused our efforts on this more technologically advanced approach, but it had the disadvantage of requiring ongoing supplies of the disposable bags as well as ancillary products like connectors. These products were severely limited in 2020, and we couldn't get critical supplies shipped from the US.

In October 2020, Ian McCubbin – our 'Mr Manufacturing' – called me: 'Kate – our Novavax timelines may slip as key equipment we need is getting held up in the US. We can't move ahead without these essential parts.' When I asked why, he told me they were stuck in US customs. It seemed this may have been caused by the US Defense Act blocking exports of critical products. So I called Moncef Slaoui, the Warp Speed chief and asked him to help expedite essential equipment orders from the US. Moncef told me he would try to sort it. We sent him a list of what was stuck and miraculously it all arrived shortly thereafter.

In different circumstances, that glittering innovation, the Vaccine Manufacturing and Innovation Centre (VMIC) planned back in 2017 might have taken centre stage during the pandemic. In some ways it would, but indirectly to start with.

But VMIC was not yet built. Not even close.

The best case was that VMIC would open in late 2022, with construction of a 7,000-square-metre facility scheduled to begin in April 2020.

Even if it had been able to come on stream faster, the concept of VMIC was that it was primarily a place where academics and industry would collaborate around vaccine innovation and early scale-up. In its original spec, it had an emergency vaccine production capacity of only three million doses.

It seemed obvious to the VTF team that, given the global pandemic, the VMIC spec would need to be reconsidered; Ian was tasked to make recommendations in short order.

Our immediate and pressing need, however, was to work around the existing apparent absence of bulk vaccine manufacturing capability in the UK. We had to bring together a collection of companies who were willing to move mountains to make the Oxford vaccine.

'Virtual VMIC'

Ian put forward a brilliantly clear and thoughtful proposal that was simple as a concept but harder to implement swiftly. Oxford Biomedica would become, in effect, a virtual VMIC.

We had real stroke of fortune. Oxford Biomedica had just finished the first phase of a major new development called Oxbox. This involved a 4,000-square-metre building on a former Post Office sorting site that contained four state-of-the-art manufacturing and bottling units, with sophisticated air handling equipment and supporting warehouses, cold chain facilities and laboratories. The Oxbox facility had empty 'clean rooms' suitable for vaccine manufacturing.

Oxford Biomedica had been founded in 1995 as an Oxford University spin-out and had listed a year later. It was an early pioneer in cell and gene therapies. Over the last fourteen years, the high energy CEO John Dawson transformed the company into a global market leader in viral vector technologies for gene and cell therapy. It has six facilities spread over five sites in the Oxford area, around the corner from the Jenner Institute, and nearly seven hundred specialist staff.

One thing I discovered is that politicians love a good photoshoot. The new Oxbox facility offered the ultimate set. It was a brand-new manufacturing facility which was making the new Oxford/AstraZeneca vaccine. Politicians in hard hats and white coats are always good photo fodder. Perfect for capturing the role of government in its embrace of innovation.

The BEIS communications team got in touch and arranged for Alok Sharma to come and open the facility. Thrilled by this upcoming publicity, Oxford Biomedica commissioned a plaque to memorialise the occasion. They invited local dignitaries, press and photographers to mark this event.

Unfortunately, the day before the opening, Alok's office called to say he had been unexpectedly called away and was no longer able to come. They offered a new date. The Oxford Biomedica team felt a little dismayed, given all the preparation, but readily agreed the new date, rescheduled the photographers and guests and bravely commissioned a second plaque. As they told me, 'You can't use Tipp-Ex on a steel sign.'

New date, same story. The Secretary of State was again unable to travel up to Oxford. Eventually officials suggested that the Prime Minister would instead come and open the facility.

Undeterred, the Oxford Biomedica team returned again to the plaque-maker and commissioned yet another sign, this time with a new date and naming the PM. Guests were re-rescheduled.

Luckily, the PM showed up, so the third-generation plaque was not wasted.

Oxford Biomedica had become a crucial member of the emerging Oxford, soon to be Oxford/AstraZeneca, consortium, thanks to the efforts of the BIA and the Oxford University manufacturing team, and its own willingness to be flexible.

Ian's plan was that the money that would have been spent on equipment at VMIC, plus some more, would be diverted to Oxford Biomedica, which would acquire and commission the bioprocessing equipment in order to start manufacturing rapidly. This equipment would return to VMIC once it had been built.

Following its £66 million award, VMIC had recruited Matthew Duchars as CEO, an expert in vaccine innovation and scale-up. Matthew recruited an equally specialist skeleton team to oversee this new centre. Ian's plan was that some of the skilled scientists and experts who had already been appointed for VMIC would also temporarily move over to Oxford Biomedica to help them manufacture the Oxford/AstraZeneca adeno vaccine. This was agreed and £38 million additional funding was committed to create the virtual VMIC within Oxford Biomedica.

This was a very shrewd idea. But the Oxford vaccine relied on collaboration with others too.

Cobra Biologics, an expert in viral vector manufacturing, made Oxford's small-scale clinical trial material early on in its Keele Science Park location. Cobra was spun out of an early gene therapy company Therexsys in 1998 (which incidentally I had unsuccessfully backed at an early stage) and had recently been acquired by the giant US pharmaceutical services company Charles River.

Cobra, led by the excellent Peter Coleman, was involved with Oxford University from the outset and by June had reached a supply agreement with AstraZeneca to manufacture vaccines. In parallel, Symbiosis, based in Stirling, Scotland, a relatively small-scale operator, contributed to this manufacturing too.

Once the virtual VMIC was set up in Oxford Biomedica, we needed to consider the longer-term future for VMIC. We felt it would have to be able to manufacture vaccines on site at a far higher level than the three million doses that had been allowed for. This would require more money.

A further £150 million was provided in phases to accelerate the construction in Harwell to bring forward its opening date and to build its bulk manufacturing capability. When finished, VMIC would become one of the premier facilities for vaccine innovation and development, as had been its rationale when approved in late 2018. But based on this enlarged capability, it would now also have a surge capacity to manufacture up to seventy million vaccine doses, which would be enough for two doses for all the most vulnerable sections of the UK population in a matter of months.

This was the VTF's vision for it. It would be a transformation.

Fill and finish: turning drug substance into drug product by filling vials

This collaborative approach was incredibly impressive, but bulk manufacturing of vaccine was only the first step. The second part of the process, often vulnerable to delays, is where the vaccine is placed inside small bottles – 'fill and finish' (and enjoy the wordplay) could still be the *bottleneck*.

Ian was already driving the manufacturing work hard when I joined the Expert Advisory Committee. He would share detailed fill–finish charts showing capacity models and possible scenarios with different vaccines. These models weren't for the faint-hearted and Kevin Hall, Ian's right-hand man, gets the prize for simplifying such complexity into something I could understand.

Ian had hoped that there might be space at the GSK facility in Barnard Castle, but none was available immediately. There was some chance of limited support in the longer-term from the Thermo Fisher plant in Swindon but it was not an instant solution. The BIA's survey of the landscape had indicated that there might be another answer.

Salvation, again courtesy of some luck as well as insight, came from Wockhardt in Wrexham. This was a global pharmaceutical and biotechnology company based in Mumbai, India. It had recently invested in a new fill and finish facility in North Wales which could handle vaccines.

At this point, the VTF made an inspired decision. We would not only pay for fill and finish capacity for Oxford/AZ's and potentially Imperial's vaccines in the short-term, but we would reserve *everything* that Wockhardt could offer for at least two years. It was a deliberate choice to buy more than it was likely that the UK needed. Given we didn't know which if any vaccine would work, or how much bulk vaccine we would actually receive or need to be filled, Ian recommended we just reserve the full amount.

This excess capacity was a potentially enormous inducement in our discussions with our preferred vaccine companies overseas, since fill and finish resources were scarce worldwide. We could offer to receive bulk vaccine manufactured overseas and then bottle it in the UK. Our fill and finish capacity was part of the VTF's 'make the UK the most attractive customer' strategy.

To ensure that the Wockhardt production line would run smoothly, Ian and Andy Jones took a forensic interest in every aspect of the supply chain, such as whether there was enough sand used to make this specialist glass. No detail, however small or apparently obscure, would be disregarded.

Despite various media reports that there would be a shortage of vials, I was able to inform a Commons Select Committee meeting in November 2020 that:

I can say that we have got 150 million vials, stoppers and over-seals, and that we have the supply chain in place for future vials. We have gone back from saying how many future vials do we need? Do we have enough tubular glass to make the vials and do we have enough of the borate silicate sand to make tubular glass? The supply chain to the point of getting vaccines to the point of being able to deploy is under control.

UK industry altruism and foresight

The VTF and the UK as a whole benefited enormously from the proactive leadership of Steve Bates and the expertise of the BIA in the three months before I became Chair. If the BIA survey had not been sent out in February 2020 and not received a stunning response with offers of equipment, reagents and skilled capabilities, then it is hard to believe that Oxford and AstraZeneca would have been as well placed as they proved to be.

Nearly forty companies, charities and universities came together voluntarily to offer support to Sandy Douglas and his Oxford team in February 2020. They rapidly built the skeleton supply chain that was needed, working closely with different parts of government as well. They recognised the need for all-hands-on-deck and that paying for this would be sorted out later. As it turned out, all these organisations worked for free for six months, since contracts capturing the different contributions took time to complete.

We also took a pan-European approach to support the AstraZeneca vaccine manufacture. The Dutch vaccine manufacturer Halix B.V. struggled with scale-up of the Oxford vaccine. The European Medicines Agency information stated in December 2020 that Halix 'has been removed as a manufacturer from the dossier and will be added later in Q1 2021.' This suspension was likely because the plant wasn't ready to produce enough drug substance.

Before Christmas 2020, we sent a SWAT team of UK experts to Holland to spend weeks troubleshooting and training the Halix team. A few weeks later, Halix received EMA approval to start shipping vaccines. It was a further extraordinary irony, given all this cross-border work, that the EU subsequently blocked Halix from shipping contracted doses of AstraZeneca vaccine to the UK.

Despite all the frustrations that incidents such as these would engender, the overall feeling was still one of achievement. The UK's small but beautiful biotech industry had pulled together and was delivering incredible results for the country.

Fast forward to November 2021 and a great trip to Cardiff to speak at the 18th Annual bioProcessUK Conference. There, for the first time, I met in person many of the heroes who had bust a gut in 2020 to scale up and manufacture vaccines for the UK. Many of them were still working flat out on vaccines. They presented me with the Richard Wilson Impact Award, a very fancy blue and green glass sculpture now gracing the entrance of SV's offices. But we all had one night off and all celebrated in style at the Coal Exchange. The tipple of the evening was a well-known Welsh beer called Brains.

Repurposing a veterinary vaccine plan in Essex

Backing the Oxford vaccine by itself was not sufficient for a manufacturing masterplan. We needed to secure or build flexible capabilities to be able to manufacture multiple different types of vaccine, including mRNA, so that the UK had pandemic resilience in the years ahead as well as economic prosperity. That was Goal 3 from the PM, ever present in my thinking.

Patrick had mentioned the possibility of acquiring a veterinary vaccine plant when I was first appointed in May, and Andy Jones, the UKRI manufacturing mastermind, had been chasing that down. Shortly afterwards I received an email from Susan Searle, who I knew from her former role at Imperial innovations. Susan was on the board of Benchmark Vaccines and wanted to discuss the repurposing of one of their sites for Covid-19 vaccines.

Benchmark Vaccines is a public company with a business in the veterinary space focusing on aquaculture, including salmon and trout. It had opened this veterinary vaccine plant in Braintree, Essex, in 2017 which had advanced manufacturing facilities and a seventy-five-strong specialist workforce.

I spoke to Susan and the Benchmark CEO Peter George the following Saturday. They told me this plant had not proved a commercially effective investment and had come to the view that its interests would be served by closing it. Would the Government want to buy it?

I could see the advantages of such a transaction. We could upgrade the plant and retrain the staff for the bulk manufacture of a variety of human vaccines. But what did the VTF team think? Due diligence and legal negotiation would have to be done fast if the opportunity was to be seized. We went for it.

Ruth Todd put her most expert, impressive project managers on scoping and finalising the transaction. The process from formal interest to outright acquisition took less than two months. On 23 July 2020, the Braintree plant was sold to the Cell and Gene Therapy Catapult, led by Matthew Durdy, an experienced biotech professional.

We had acquired a bulk bioprocessing manufacturing capacity that could be used for a vast range of biological manufacturing. In normal times it could be deployed for cell and gene therapies, but in any future pandemic it could be switched speedily to whatever vaccine response might be needed.

Connecting Darlington and Braintree

Ian McCubbin was always one step ahead of us. What I love about him is that he had a masterplan. Ian recognised that the scale-up and process development work we were doing to support Imperial's saRNA vaccine with the Centre for Process Innovation, could feed directly into this new bulk manufacturing capability in Braintree.

The CPI had been established in 2004 and had later become the founding member of the High Value Manufacturing Catapult. As part of its remit, it had started exploring scale-up mRNA-based products, as well as DNA, protein, viral, microbial and nano medicines.

The Centre for Process Innovation's skills in biological process invention made it the logical choice to help develop any mRNA vaccine in the UK. The VTF wanted it to become a global centre of innovation offering a different set of opportunities to VMIC. In that light, CPI and National Horizons Centre together launched a new RNA National Training Academy to work alongside the CPI's RNA Centre of Excellence.

Ian's masterplan was that CPI would optimise the mRNA manu-facturing production process and then transfer this to the Braintree plant for bulk manufacture.

With CPI, Fujifilm Diosynth Biotechnologies and the GSK premises at Barnard Castle, which became available to the VTF team in spring 2021, the North East of England was becoming a really major hub of biological manufacturing activity. This was obviously music to the ears of Ben Houchen, the Tees Valley Mayor, with whom I had plenty of productive exchanges. Ben is the text-book example of why regions should have locally elected mayors.

The VTF acted as a bridge and broker between Novavax and the Fujifilm plant at Billingham, an old ICI herbicide facility that could start manufacturing the Novavax vaccine while it was still completing its clinical trials.

Steve Bagshaw became a critical player, recently retired as the CEO at Fujifilm Diosynth. Ian had brought Steve into the VTF manufacturing SWAT team in 2020 and Steve succeeded Ian as that team leader in the VTF in 2021. We once again pre-booked manufacturing slots without being quite certain what we would need and in what quantities (as we had done with Wockhardt) as extra ammunition in our arsenal.

Part of Ian's masterplan was to build a UK supply chain for Novavax, with the bulk vaccine being manufactured at Fujifilm, the Matrix M adjuvant being manufactured in Novavax's facilities in Denmark and the final fill and finish of vaccine and adjuvant together at Wockhardt.

To round off the Darlington hotspot plan, we invested about £5 million to support advanced therapies skills training in July 2020. Since this was under £10 million, Nick had the authority to approve this and sign it off, which made it pleasingly easy to complete. This funding was intended to train people within and outside the bioprocessing sector in the specialist skills required in the manufacture of advanced therapies and vaccines. Their success with apprenticeships has been impressive.

When I visited the National Horizons Centre on a rainy day in 2021, after I stepped down as Chair, they showed me round their state-of-the-art training facilities and their virtual learning platform. It was an amazing experience. The training of people in a bioprocessing clean room could be massively accelerated, and the costs reduced.

I regret to say that, based on my performance there, I won't be recruited into the bioprocessing industry any time soon. They gave

me a virtual reality headset to train me on basic clean room procedures and asked me to take a pH probe out of the bioprocessor. I
dropped it and out it flew into space. I ran around desperately trying
to catch this virtual probe, flailing about hopelessly in an empty
room while everyone laughed.

Valneva

Valneva, as set out in the preceding chapter, was something of a
personal project for Ian. He, rather than the company itself, had
spotted the chance of converting its site for pandemic whole-
virus vaccine production. As this was an area of vulnerability
given the likelihood of ongoing variants, the VTF wanted to back
it.

The investment in Valneva was not an act of charity or a wild
waving of the cheque book at a business. There was a model
whereby the VTF would pay the upfront costs of upgrading and
expanding the site to make Valneva's vaccine, but as a flexible state-
of-the-art capacity that could then be used to manufacture any
biological vaccine or drug as needed.

In return, the UK would receive a priority supply and discount
on the price of that vaccine in the future were it to be approved and
supplied. Hence, if the vaccine materialised, the Government benefited too. It was the sort of imaginative initiative that few other
countries had considered undertaking.

The bulk manufacturing saga

Stuart Speding, who led the antibody team, always improved the
mood of our Zoom calls with wonderfully flamboyant shirts.
Stuart had a complex job trying to juggle the various antibody
workstreams.

As part of our long-term preparedness planning, Stuart helped Ian lead the VTF initiative to establish bulk manufacturing capacity for antibodies. We felt strongly that not having this capability was a serious weakness in the UK's ability to respond not only to future pandemics but also more generally for long-term biotherapeutic supply.

We estimated that we needed up to twelve 2,000-litre flexible production bioreactors. These could be used to make Covid-19 antibodies, or any advanced biotherapeutic or vaccine. Building this manufacturing scale would require a substantial investment by government, but we knew there were several advanced manufacturing companies interested in partnering with the Government to help build and run a new manufacturing plant. Especially in the North East.

We held an Antibodies Supply Event in October 2020 to seek expressions of interest from specialist companies to work with government to build this bulk capacity. Government would provide funding for future orders and industry would manage and run the facility. Several companies duly threw their hats into the ring.

But there was zero interest from BEIS, even though the Treasury had explicitly indicated they wanted to support such an initiative. Sadly, we made no progress. Our drive to establish new bulk bioprocessing manufacturing capacity seems not to have progressed since I left.

The McCubbin magic

Ian and his team of manufacturing experts worked relentlessly behind the scenes to support the vaccine companies and manufacturers – identifying, foreseeing and troubleshooting all potential issues. They concentrated on everything needed to assist Oxford/AZ, Valneva and Novavax to manufacture in the UK, and to build mRNA vaccine manufacturing capability. This contribution of industrial skills and advice was what set the VTF apart from many other government-run bodies. We very badly wanted to succeed in producing vaccines early and in scale, both for the UK and for the world.

The net effect of this was that, very largely due to Ian – initially on behalf of the BIA and then the VTF – the UK had in the space of less than twelve months moved from having a minor vaccine manufacturing base to having one capable of providing flexible manufacturing capacity for all of the main types of vaccine at a population scale. We now enjoyed the capacity to supply repeat doses rapidly to the British people, as well as to export abroad.

It had been an intense exercise that had involved immense individual expertise, creativity, some opportunism and a little fortune. The future building blocks for making it here had been created. They would need to be sustained to make it here permanently.

Better still, a significant proportion of the vaccines (if not the antibodies) would be made in this country.

Between vaccine discovery and manufacturing capacity sat a further vital area: clinical trials. It was no good being able to make the vaccines if they were not proven to be safe and effective.

11

THE CLINICAL FINISH

Before the pandemic, I had never taken part in a clinical trial. I'm very happy that I can now say I've been a triallist for a Covid-19 vaccine.

One positive consequence of the Covid-19 crisis is that clinical trials have acquired a higher profile and become better understood. The blunt truth is that they are hard work. Bringing a trial together of altruistic volunteers is expensive, time-consuming and highly regulated. Safety is paramount. The risk of failure is strikingly high, in that only ten per cent of all drugs that start in human clinical trials will ever get approved. They are particularly difficult in the case of vaccines, in that the trials have to prove a counter-factual: they must show that the person concerned would have caught the disease had they *not* been vaccinated. This is a different sort of hurdle to that of showing, for example, that a new drug can impact the severity of a disease.

The history of medical experimentation on human beings is lengthy, tortuous, and – to put it in the mildest possible way – has involved some of the darkest moments of history (the most notorious being the treatment of Jews by Nazi 'doctors' in concentration camps). It has often been a literal case of trial and error.

The first record of a clinical trial came in 1747 when James Lind was investigating the cause of and possible prevention of scurvy, a particular menace on the high seas. Two months into a voyage, with scurvy already rampant on his ship, he took twelve affected seamen and divided them into six groups of two. All had the same basic diet, but the first pair had a quart of cider added, the second had twenty-five drops of an elixir of vitriol enriched with sulfuric acid, the third six spoons of vinegar, the fourth half a pint of seawater, the fifth two oranges and a lemon and the final pair a drink of barley water.

The exercise did not last long, as after six days the supply of fruit had been exhausted. Even so, one of the sailors in the citrus section was now fit for duty and the other close to full recovery. Of the other ten individuals, only those who had consumed the cider manifested any signs of improvement. The case for fruit at sea had been made. And the Brits have been known as *limeys* in the US ever since.

Running clinical trials in the UK

The National Institute for Health Research (NIHR) is effectively the research arm of the NHS. It is one of those institutions (and there are a number of them) with a very high standing among experts internationally, whilst being basically unknown to the public at large.

NIHR was founded in 2006 by Dame Sally Davies and funded by the Department of Health. A decade later it had a budget in excess of £1 billion and was the largest national clinical research funder in Europe. It had a network of fifteen Local Clinical Research Networks across England, while Scotland, Wales and Northern Ireland had their own equivalent arrangements. Its stated mission was 'improving the health and wealth of the nation through research'. It would come to play an absolutely seminal role in running clinical trials during the coronavirus outbreak.

Phase 1 tests are highly regulated and typically involve up to two hundred volunteers to determine whether a vaccine given at different doses is sufficiently safe, in terms of side effects, before assessing its clinical efficacy. A vaccine that was effective against Covid-19 but triggered other health difficulties would not be acceptable. The Covid-19 vaccines safety trials were no different to those performed on any other new untested drug or vaccine.

Once the safety was established, this would be followed by Phase 2 trials which would involve hundreds of participants to generate data as to what extent a proposed vaccine could elicit an immune response. It is important to recognise that generating an immune response does not tell you whether a proposed vaccine could provide protection against infection or severe disease, but just whether neutralising antibodies, as a proxy for the broader immune response, could be detected in all recipients.

In normal times, if the Phase 2 results were promising, the vaccine company would seek regulatory approval to move on to Phase 3 trials, which would involve several thousand human volunteers. However, given the urgency of the pandemic and the sudden availability of government funding, recruitment into the Phase 3 trials started once the safety data was available, before the Phase 2 immunogenicity readout.

The Phase 3 trials were specifically designed to include the elderly and those with underlying diseases, since they were most at risk from Covid-19 infection, and it was important to show that the vaccine was not just effective for fit young people.

Certain features of how the trials are conducted are defined by law. Each subject is randomly assigned either to the vaccine or the placebo alternative. The pivotal trials are 'double-blinded', meaning that the triallist would not know whether they had received placebo or vaccine – and nor would the clinical researcher. The data would be independently saved and only unblinded when the trial was completed, rather than there being a running scorecard.

In the context of Covid-19 vaccine trials, the volunteers would be split into two random groups, with one group receiving the vaccine and other either a placebo or another vaccine with similar reactogenicity. The effectiveness of the vaccine would be decided statistically based on who then contracted Covid-19 from the placebo and vaccinated cohorts.

Usually, after the pivotal Phase 3 data was collected, it would be assembled into a formal dossier of thousands of pages for submission to the regulators, which would typically take six to twelve months for review and response. In normal times, the regulator would start to evaluate all of the data only once the complete file had been submitted. This process was unacceptably slow for the pandemic. Too many people would die while the dossier was being reviewed.

The MHRA would take a new approach to Covid-19.

Even after a vaccine or drug was approved by the regulator, there would be ongoing monitoring or Phase 4 evaluation of the vaccine. This is a process also known as pharmacovigilance (a scientific term for inspecting it in action), which determines how well the vaccine was working in the real world and how resilient it would be if the virus radically altered.

Having NHS clinical records and data being recorded in real time for a national population in excess of sixty-five million was hugely advantageous to the UK; few countries had the size or quality of its medical records.

VTF clinical trials 'offer'

From our earliest discussions, Clive and I appreciated that clinical trials were a possible bargaining chip in negotiations with the companies developing promising vaccine candidates.

The UK offer was bound to be complex, not least because the clinical trials procedure itself is highly regulated and complicated.

The UK is a particularly good place to run trials as everyone has an NHS number with electronic medical records, which means that you can follow-up patients and clinical trial volunteers and build a rich data set on the effect and safety issues with vaccines. But to make this advantage a reality, we needed to act quickly and show we could recruit and run national scale clinical trials.

We seconded Divya Chadha Manek away from being a Deputy Director of the NIHR to the senior VTF team in May 2020, thanks to William van't Hoff who kindly allowed her to join us temporarily. She was well versed in the practicalities of how to make this difficult sphere work better and faster than it might do otherwise.

On day one as the VTF clinical trials lead, Divya asked me: 'What is the exam question here?' My answer was: 'What do we need to do to make it extremely attractive for companies to run their clinical trials in the UK?'

That meant we needed to either subsidise or wholly cover the cost of trials as upfront payment for future vaccine supply. We needed to demonstrate conclusively that such trials could be done at speed and with the utmost professionalism so that valuable time was not wasted. Divya pulled together an initial paper on what the 'offer' might be, drawing on her prior experience working with the MHRA. She liaised closely with Clive on what was most likely to be appealing to those companies and vaccines that were emerging on his shortlist, which itself was being compiled at an extraordinary pace.

Broadly speaking, the largest companies needed little support to run clinical trials, so when dealing with those Big Pharma we had to be a nimble, well-prepared and helpful customer. Pfizer had been clear from the outset that it didn't want government support. It declined to run trials in the UK starting in the summer of 2020 as it believed (correctly as it turned out) that the first UK lockdown would diminish the level of infection to such an extent that the trial readout would be materially delayed.

Moderna had been talking about running trials in the UK but that interest stopped once it became plain that ministers would not place a large early vaccine order, as the company had wanted. They may also have been put off by the reduced infection levels seen during the UK's initial lockdown.

To attract companies to run their clinical trials here, we had to convince them that we could very rapidly enrol a diverse set of volunteers to generate safety and efficacy data that met regulatory standards. But there was no large national pool of ready-made volunteers in the UK for the VTF to mobilise.

The NHS Registry

The solution would come as a bold innovation. We would create the world's first Covid-19 National Citizens Registry on the NHS website. This would allow any member of the public to express a willingness to take part in vaccine clinical trials.

It was what Divya had wanted to do for years. Jonathan Sheffield was equally positive. The NIHR as a whole was very keen on the idea of an NHS volunteer Registry, but it had never been able to secure the funding for the initiative. If a national Registry could be launched it would be an enormous asset in making the case for clinical trials in the UK.

I didn't doubt for a moment that setting up a Registry was the right thing to do, even though it was such a huge undertaking. The VTF wanted to leap from blueprint to delivery in a matter of weeks. We started discussing this in June 2020 and needed to be ready to launch the Registry publicly in July. If we left it any later, we would not have time to assemble enough people for the expected wave of trials starting in September and October. We knew it would take time and effort to recruit those people most vulnerable to the disease, such as the elderly and ethnic minorities. This would be a massive marketing challenge.

We had little practical choice but to collaborate with NHS Digital, which owned the patient data. NHS Digital was a relatively new and untested institution that had never done anything like this before. The danger of a technical malfunction was high, and the prospect of a very public meltdown scary: it could undermine the entire initiative at its outset. I would have preferred to work with a nimble tech company but this wasn't possible.

As we were launching the Registry, I sensed some disbelief in parts of government. I checked in with Divya: 'Do you really think it will be possible to get hundreds of thousands of people to sign up to our Registry?' Ever positive, she responded, 'We will give it a ****** good go. We can't afford to fail.'

It worked. An astonishing 360,000 people came forward before the end of 2020 and more than 500,000 public-spirited individuals by mid-2021. Even more amazingly, over 33% of the volunteers were over the age of sixty, far exceeding our original goals. By early 2022, about 50,000 had already taken part in eighteen different Covid-19 vaccine clinical trials.

★

The UK's clinical trial proposition was enticing. It seized the attention of Novavax who felt that running a Phase 3 trial in the UK, led by Professor Paul Heath, could be highly beneficial, since they thought that they could recruit rapidly and then generate compelling data within two to three months. The Phase 3 UK Novavax trial was initially scoped at 10,000 individuals, but once it became clear exactly how well recruitment was going nationwide, the company requested that the trial be expanded by fifty per cent to bring in 15,000 people.

This would be the largest double-blind, placebo-controlled Phase 3 vaccine trial that the UK had ever run. Yet despite this, the recruitment was completed at incredible speed within the planned six weeks, mostly due to Divya. Without being a nationalist, I was amazed that the Novavax Phase 3 trial in the UK commenced before its US equivalent.

The NHS Registry was also attractive to Janssen, who decided that, while the quickest way to deliver its single-dose trials was in the US where viral infection levels remained high, it would recruit patients in the UK for a double-dose trial led by Professor Saul Faust. Valneva also used the NHS Registry when heading to trials led by Professor Adam Finn, but with the difference that, because these trials were initiated *after* mass vaccination was underway in the UK, Valneva's vaccine would be compared not with a placebo but with Oxford/AstraZeneca. This meant that everyone taking part would receive a vaccine – they just wouldn't know which one.

Due to delays, GSK/Sanofi couldn't run large Phase 3 placebo-controlled vaccine trials, since the UK was starting its roll-out of licensed vaccines at that point. They chose instead to recruit 35,000 volunteers across sites in the US, Asia and Latin America where multiple variants were circulating, to show the breadth of their protective vaccine. They returned later to the UK to run booster trials.

★

There would, of course, be very difficult moments.

At the start, we had to secure approval from Chief Medical Officers not only in England but Scotland, Wales and Northern Ireland as well. I learnt more than I cared to about the workings of the 'devolved administrations' and had to send several pleading letters to different medical officers to secure their collaboration on the Registry initiative. While it did not particularly matter to me if they all signed up, I thought it would be a better pitch to the vaccine companies if we could state that we would reach the entire UK through the Registry.

I was really stunned at the recalcitrance of some of the individuals who withheld their assent literally until the eleventh hour, presumably to make a political point about not being pushed around by England.

The technical side of the NHS Registry did hit massive glitches. We insisted on expansive, robust beta testing in early July. We discussed our goals for sign-up. However, when I launched the Registry on national TV and radio on 20 July, over fifty thousand people visited the NHS website page, which was far beyond the scope of the system that NHS Digital had built.

I tore my hair out when I discovered that confirmatory emails that should have been sent instantly to over 150,000 potential registrants had been held in the ether for twenty-four hours. Only a small proportion of those individuals were, entirely understandably, patient enough to wait to sign up again on the following day. I have no idea how Divya kept her cool during this time.

Finally, the volunteers in the Covid-19 vaccine trials turned out to be substantially disadvantaged for their altruistic participation. Triallists' vaccine certificates were not recognised while their vaccines were not approved by the regulators, which complicated life for travel and some domestic events. Holidays had to be cancelled at the last minute. Astonishingly, people were being penalised for their personal generosity and public spirit.

I know from first-hand experience how disruptive it was to be part of the trial. It would have been much easier to have waited and just received a registered vaccine. But then we would not have had generated this world-changing data. So to all of you who participated in the trials, thank you.

In Scotland, the triallists were formally registered as unvaccinated. It took a lot of tree-shaking and personal emails from me before the Government stopped wringing its hands and recommended that triallists should be eligible to receive registered vaccines on top of their unregistered ones, and months longer before the NHS App was able to accommodate their unusual dosing schedules.

This has to be a lesson for next time, as I fear it may be much harder to recruit clinical trial volunteers again.

★

A wave of new clinical trials, with the advantage of the national Registry, started in 2021 after I left.

Their aim was to answer important policy, scientific and medical questions. One of the most significant was to explore the effect of a booster shot, studying the use of seven different Covid-19 vaccines when given as a third dose. This would be trialled on the most vulnerable groups.

The COV-BOOST trial was set up in the UK in June 2021, funded by the VTF, overseen by the NIHR and led by the University of Southampton. This was the first trial in the world to explore boosters. Almost three thousand people participated to determine the optimal combination of original vaccines and boosters.

The results, published in *The Lancet* in December 2021, but known to ministers well before then, led to the conclusion that a booster campaign was essential and that it should involve the Pfizer and Moderna vaccines.

Other issues were also addressed in this second wave of VTF-financed clinical trials for Covid-19. What happens if vaccines were mixed and matched? That too was the subject of trials. The first, COMCOV, looked at variations of using AstraZeneca first then Pfizer and the other way round and at different dose levels. Another trial, COMCOV2, introduced a range of options for the ordering of vaccines, adding in Moderna and Novavax as well.

The findings were revealed in December 2021 and included the discovery that an AstraZeneca injection followed by a Novavax jab was highly effective. This is a crucial result for those parts of the world where ultra-cold vaccines would be difficult to use and where having flexibility of vaccine selection based on availability would be extremely helpful.

By mid–2021 clinical trials using the registry were launched around the UK to generate data to inform further policy decisions. Was it safe for people to have one or more of the Covid vaccines alongside the annual flu jab, and if so, for whom? What was the effect of the vaccines on pregnant women or young children? These were vital questions, especially when schools and universities reopened after the summer break.

The NIHR had to pivot to ensure that clinical trials relating to virus vaccination were the top priority. Chris Whitty and Jonathan Van-Tam among others were pushing hard to drive all UK trials relating to Covid-19.

★

As we learnt from the Oxford University vaccine team, the immunogenicity tests performed by different companies to measure neutralising antibodies were wildly different. Antibodies generated as part of the immune response stick onto and eliminate the virus. Neutralisation assays measure the effectiveness of these antibodies in eliminating the virus. Professor Sarah Gilbert told me that:

> Neutralisation assays give vastly different results and there is a large difference in the data generated by NIHR and Public Health England given the same dose of the same vaccine at the same time-point but in different labs. The medians are 40 at NIHR and 290 at PHE. The only way to compare is to have assays run in the same lab. The same principle applies to the viral challenge studies. You can't compare data from Oxford and Janssen's vaccine studies because the challenge doses were different.

So, we recognised that we needed to create standardised assays so we could compare the effectiveness of the various vaccines, not just against each other but also with the emerging variants.

We turned to Porton Down. The facilities there, both the Ministry of Defence site and the Public Health England (PHE) section, are second to none. The secretive army base near Salisbury has, along with its satellite buildings elsewhere, enabled the UK to be a global leader in many areas including the experimental assessment of vaccine effectiveness.

Porton Down was ahead of the pack when it came to handling and working on new lethal pathogens. It was a high-priority, if perhaps a low-profile, aspect of the VTF's agenda. We hired a superb biotech entrepreneur, Kate Hilyard, to help lead on the work of developing industrial scale state-of-the-art assays, since she had experience from Roche, Cambridge Antibody and Charles River Labs.

In September 2020, the VTF received approval for £19.7 million for industrial-scale testing of variant samples to ensure that the vaccines chosen by the VTF would be effective against current and future vaccines of concern. The funding enabled these highly specialist tests to increase from 700 to 1,500 a week by January 2022.

The identification of the Delta strain by UK scientists reinforced their status internationally. In May 2021, ministers announced that a further £29 million would be spent to double that 1,500-a-week figure by the end of 2022.

The fact that we knew so quickly about the mutations and resulting variant strains was due to the extraordinary contribution of the UK. Whole genomic sequencing was a triumph for the COG-UK consortium led by the visionary Sharon Peacock. It analysed entire genomes and identified Covid-19 variants from samples taken from infected people. In October 2021, the UK had uploaded over one million SARS-CoV-2 genomic sequences into the Global Initiative on Sharing Avian Influenza Data (GISAID) database. This equated to almost a quarter of all samples held there. For much of 2020 the UK proportion was higher still, at almost forty-five per cent of the global total.

On a different tack, among the many unsung heroes in the public health arena were those who worked at public company Oxford

Immunotec on the study of T-cells. Clive rightly felt that we needed a much deeper understanding of the immunology response so we could define the measurable biological markers which correlate with protection against infection. To optimise the vaccines, we needed to know more about the cellular immune response, not just the antibody response. Antibodies were easier to measure than T-cells, which is why we did it, but Clive felt that the T-cell response was also critical for durable protection. So, we would need to gauge that too.

The UK worked with Peter Wrighton-Smith, CEO of Oxford Immunotec, to measure T-cell responses. This company generated critical data showing that high levels of SARS-CoV-2 responsive T-cells are associated with protection against symptomatic Covid-19 infection.

The understanding of SARS-CoV-2 infection and protection remains incomplete, but there is no doubt that the more that we learn about the detail of the protective immune response against the virus, the better prepared we will be to design vaccines and drugs to tackle it.

Participating in the Novavax trial

I participated in the Novavax trial. I had never been part of a trial before but thought I should practise what I was preaching. I immensely enjoyed it despite the aforementioned inconveniences. I signed up at the Royal Free Hospital with the wonderful Dr Fiona Burns, a specialist in HIV and clinical epidemiology.

The Royal Free was one of the standout hospital trusts in its response to the Covid-19 pandemic. I was honoured to be invited to give the annual Marsden lecture there in 2021. As part of my preparation, I was delighted to discover how this hospital was founded on 'firsts' and innovation. It was the first hospital to offer healthcare for free. It was the only London hospital that treated cholera victims in the epidemic ravaging London in 1832. It was the first to admit women for training as medical students. And it remains a global leader in clinical trials.

My second Novavax dose had to be in Cardiff not London. I particularly remember my trip to the CRO Synexus. It was a fabulous drive over the Brecon Beacons. I had shopped for Mum en route so that I could drop off her weekly bag of goodies, which supplemented all the vegetables and fruit she grew in her garden.

I was very pleased to see the waiting room full of Novavax trial-lists. The clinic was buzzing. But my Cardiff trip came on a morning of such intense hostile media coverage of me personally that my blood pressure boiled so high the clinic staff would not let me out until it had lowered. They kindly plied me with cups of tea and chocolate biscuits to calm me.

The long delay before Novavax submitted its application meant that I spent much of 2021 being regarded by the system as an unvaccinated person. There was a ministerial declaration in October 2021 claiming that this had all been fixed. But it didn't seem to work. I was nearly forced to quarantine for ten days after a trip to Switzerland because the NHS App and the Passenger Locator Form did not acknowledge that I had by then been vaccinated three times (Novavax twice, Pfizer once, with a second shot of Pfizer received a little later).

Yet despite all this hassle and the hurdles we encountered, the NHS Registry was undoubtedly a critical part of the UK success. We were able to execute clinical trials rapidly, and specifically recruit volunteers from those populations most vulnerable to the disease.

Human Challenge trials on a potentially lethal pandemic virus

After something of a tussle, where I felt that some parts of Whitehall consistently failed to understand their value, Clive and I secured approval to invest in developing a new controlled infection clinical trial capability, called a Human Challenge Programme. This is a trial in which healthy young adults, who opt in to such a scheme, receive a vaccine before being deliberately infected with the virus to test it.

As Sir Richard Sykes said in his report on the VTF in July 2020:

> Human challenge studies in flu revealed critical information and data about the infectivity of subjects prior to their showing symptoms and this was only discovered through the tightly controlled human challenge studies.
>
> I think it is a key priority for the VTF to get human challenge studies up and running for the controlled testing of new vaccines.

I spent a lot of time talking to my trusted friend and colleague Dr Garth Rapeport about Human Challenge studies. One of Garth's companies I had backed had performed them with a new respiratory drug. I would often bike to the subterranean Imperial College incubator to meet Garth before board meetings so he could explain in detail how these studies were progressing. We drank a lot of tea.

Garth knew the experts and facilities for running Human Challenge studies. He understood the ethics and regulatory issues too. One key point Garth impressed on me was that it is not ethical to run such studies without a *rescue medicine* to treat the infected individual and prevent them from serious disease. So Covid-19 Human Challenge studies could not start until there was a drug proven to work. We started with remdesivir.

Again, Clive and I turned to dependable entrepreneurial colleagues in the biotech sector to help support the VTF. We were fortunate to attract Priya Mande to lead the Human Challenge workstream. She brought thirty years' experience in the biotech and pharmaceutical space, including at PowderMed, led by Clive. Priya's current employer PsiOxus kindly agreed to second her part-time to the VTF in 2020. Despite, or maybe because of, doing two jobs in 2020, the board at PsiOxus promoted her to interim CEO on her return in 2021.

In October 2020, the VTF announced funding for the first phase of a Human Challenge Programme as a partnership between Imperial College, London, as the trial sponsor, BEIS, hVIVO and the Royal Free London NHS Foundation Trust. This unusually complicated £33 million initiative would require the co-ordination of multiple institutions to ensure that the necessary technical expertise materialised.

The objective was that once the SARS-CoV-2 Human Challenge model had been established in early 2021, the VTF would have secured the first three slots to run clinical trials on the most promising new vaccines ahead of everyone else. This would, hopefully, make the process of identifying a new wave of vaccines, fine-tuned in the light of experience and time, a faster proposition than wave one.

As I asserted in my end-of-term report for the VTF, published in December 2020:

> Building this world leading, ambitious capacity now will enable the UK to optimise and prioritise future pandemic vaccines, generating long-term value and pandemic preparedness for the UK for SARS-Cov-2 and beyond – a valuable legacy for the UK.

Not everyone in authority shared this vision, but we at least got the process started.

In February 2021 the Imperial College-headed consortium led by Professor Chris Chiu announced it had obtained regulatory approval to begin a Human Challenge trial involving ninety fit young people who had not had any previous exposure to Covid-19. In April 2021, Oxford University, supported by the Wellcome Trust, announced it would launch a Human Challenge of its own, to see whether those who had been infected by the virus were protected against reinfection.

In July 2021, Garth Rapeport was named first author alongside others from Imperial, Oxford and hVIVO in a seminal *New England Journal of Medicine* paper entitled 'SARS-COV-2 Human Challenge Studies — Establishing the model during an evolving pandemic'. In it he wrote:

> Our experience thus far indicates that a SARS-COV-2 human challenge research programme can be developed as part of the pandemic response. Its establishment has relied on broad collaboration that provided the varied expertise, broad consensus and funding required.

We have not yet taken the full value from this model and I remain convinced that this should be the start and not the finish of a Human Challenge exercise that has much to offer us.

The future of UK clinical trials

We realised that not every vaccine company would want to run clinical trials in the UK. The amount of support required varied enormously according both to the nature of the vaccine itself and, crucially, the previous experience of the company itself with vaccines. This was in part because we had a short timetable to run the trials in the UK before the first vaccines were approved by the MHRA. Once the UK population started getting licensed vaccines, it would be hard to conduct large placebo-controlled trials of any new ones.

However, my longer-term goal, shared with many in the NIHR and the Department of Health, was to expand the Registry beyond volunteers for coronavirus vaccine trials to include any patient with a poorly treated condition. These patients could be offered the opportunity to take part in any trials on experimental new drugs relevant to their disease.

To that end, we included in the NHS Registry questionnaire a specific question asking participants whether they would be willing to be contacted about other trials.

Amazingly, 94% of respondents said they would be willing to be approached for trials beyond the Covid-19 vaccine. The Registry could connect the patient to the trial. That would be a huge potential opportunity for the UK.

Several pharmaceutical companies have since asked me how they can work with the Registry to accelerate recruitment into their trials. I am convinced there is real interest in this national resource.

Expanding the NHS registry for use in therapeutics could improve the quality of clinical trials, since it could theoretically access large numbers of relevant patients. Jane Woodcock, acting Commissioner of the FDA, wrote in *Nature* in 2021 that only five per cent of the clinical trials run in the US on Covid-19 therapeutics actually generated actionable data. That's a massive waste of time, money and patients who unknowingly took part in pointless trials. I think with the NHS registry and professional leadership we could turn this into something very special to help rapidly develop new drugs.

It is up to Whitehall to capitalise on the fantastic digital start that we created for vaccines. They will need to explore how to work with patient charities such as Cancer Research UK, Alzheimer's Research UK and other disease-focused organisations to give patients access through clinical trials to innovative new treatments.

Real-world evidence

Following early reports of side effects in the vaccine trials, I received an email from Andy Pollard, who was running the Oxford vaccine trial:

Kate, I had a conversation with Ben Goldacre about safety monitoring and how we can get some good figures for expected rates of rare disease in the UK population to help with assessing observed safety events in the trials, and also to use as post licensure monitoring with vaccine linkage. Do you have a few minutes to hear from them?

Being able to distinguish between correlation and causation was fundamental to understanding the safety of the vaccines. To do this we needed to know the incidence of different diseases across the breadth of the population, so that we could determine the 'disease' baseline before vaccination. This data on the spontaneous incidence of rare disorders in Phase 3 clinical vaccine trials could then be used by regulators for informed decision-making about vaccine safety, rather than using broad population assumptions.

Ben is a Senior Clinical Research Fellow at the Centre for Evidence Based Medicine at Oxford. I was a bit hesitant as I wasn't a huge fan of Ben's book *Bad Pharma*. But I was impressed by his July 2020 publication in *Nature* on his analytics platform OpenSAFELY, which analysed the pseudonymised primary care records of twenty-four million people in near real-time. I wondered whether having access to this secure, state-of-the-art health analytics platform, which covered forty per cent of all patients in England, would be an attractive addition to the 'UK clinical offer'.

I really enjoyed Ben's get-up-and-go and enthusiasm for using the latest digital tools to help the VTF and the vaccines. Ben and I had several discussions about how to make this happen, as well as chats with some of our vaccine companies to explore the cost of doing this. Ultimately, I was told that the MHRA would do its own background safety assessments, so there was no point doing this additional work – even if it was rapid and at population scale. However, I do think this is a great opportunity and one that we should consider in the future.

Despite all the hiccups, my overall experience of running vaccine trials was so positive that I am now urging my companies to explore the option of running early clinical trials in the UK. With the flexibility of the MHRA, the trial infrastructure and capabilities, plus the momentum we have through the NHS Registry, the UK is well set up to really shine.

12

PREPARING FOR DEPLOYMENT

Deployment planning hadn't been high on my list back in May 2020. I was instead focused on getting my head round which vaccines might work and which we could buy. How we would then get these into arms was a second order problem. Planning for the Covid-19 vaccine deployment drive, however, started very early in Whitehall, well before the creation of the VTF itself.

I took a call one morning from the CEO of Boots, who had been a student at Oxford with me. I was putting out the recycling at the bottom of our lane when the call came through. I was surprised he remembered me. We had a good chat about how Boots could help with the Covid-19 vaccination roll-out as they do with flu, and I passed him straight onto the deployment team.

Whitehall had modelled the Covid-19 vaccination on the annual flu vaccination campaign, the largest of the NHS's seventeen different vaccination campaigns pre-Covid. It was not clear to me how the flu vaccination roll-out would work with the new virus, especially when from early on it looked like we would need two shots.

I was not confident that any vaccine would emerge and, in the happy event that it did, the chances that it would – conveniently – turn out to be just like the flu vaccine were minuscule. It was entirely possible that a large number of people, perhaps the entire population, might need to be vaccinated. That would involve a vastly bigger and potentially more complicated effort than anything that either PHE or the NHS had ever done before. Especially when combined with the annual flu jab campaign.

I hoped that a Covid-19 vaccine would prove more effective than that average flu shot, where generally only half of recipients are protected. And also hoped that the anti-vaxxers didn't spoil the show by spreading distrust. The average take-up of flu vaccines was between 70% and 75%, and we would need to reach higher than this to control the pandemic. But would the British people trust a new Covid-19 vaccine?

Yet it was vital to have a highly effective blueprint for deployment. It would be unbearable if one or more vaccines were to be identified swiftly and manufactured at scale, only for distribution then to fail, or find that too few people were willing to be vaccinated.

We were at the coalface of vaccine procurement and had intimate knowledge of the different vaccine stabilities and transport requirements. But the VTF had to work closely with other government departments and organisations to help shape a national deployment plan to make sure the precious vaccines could be delivered efficiently. And we had a secret weapon to lead this. Ruth Todd.

From submarines to vaccines

Ruth's actual role was much wider than co-ordinating deployment with the other departments, as she was the VTF Programme Director as a whole. She was involved in many of the decisions about manufacturing capacity for the vaccines in association with Ian McCubbin, aided by Steve Bagshaw. Her input was essential in numerous other aspects of the VTF's activities.

Like me, Ruth was a mum with a child in their last year at university doing their final exams. As well as keeping the show on the road at home, Ruth was a central linchpin in the VTF, building and managing a team of over a hundred. Her role in the vaccine deployment and roll-out was completely critical.

Such was the MS Teams-centred nature of the VTF's work that we did not meet in person until we rode in the hills together months after I had stood down as VTF Chair. During that six-month period, though, we would speak almost every day.

Ruth took on a large mandate. As Programme Director she had formal oversight of the Project Management Office, project management, supply chain management, intelligence and security. As we identified and secured a vaccine, Ruth would rapidly assemble a team beneath her, in what would be a race against time with the virus.

Building the VTF project management team

Ruth needed to find highly capable people to work with her, with skill sets involving understanding the realm of supply chains, and ability to navigate Whitehall. Only then would she be able to delegate enough to concentrate on vaccine deployment.

Ruth was fortunate in that she was able to swiftly appoint two highly experienced individuals, Jo Crowhurst and Andrew Jones, to become her chief aides. Jo had originally qualified as a chartered land surveyor, but when the recession of the early 1990s took its toll on opportunities in that sector, had turned herself into a real expert on change management.

Jo acted as a freelancer, taking on an enormous variety of problem-solving exercises over the years. In 2020 she was in a new position as Director of Operational Resilience in the Department for Environment, Food and Rural Affairs with a focus on what would need to be done in the event of a no-deal Brexit. While there she had made a profound impression on a career civil servant colleague, Emma Moir, who had subsequently moved on to BEIS and become part of the early VTF support staff there. She notified Ruth of Jo's ability to help her. A Saturday morning telephone call between the two led to Jo being reassigned to the VTF on Monday.

Jo would be the externally facing figure sat on top of the many bespoke projects – ultimately twenty-five projects when the VTF really hit full speed.

I first encountered Jo when she was leading the due diligence and upgrading of the veterinary factory in Braintree right at the beginning. I was hugely impressed and pleased to have someone of her calibre on the team. Jo dealt with the external partners that the operation would require to identify potential pitfalls in advance and get things done at speed.

Her counterpart would be Andrew Jones, a highly rated civil servant who had been acquired from the Home Office, who would act as the internally-facing individual, reporting back to the Whitehall machine, finding more civil servants to co-opt as time went on, navigating government departments and smoothing things over. It was the ideal combination.

The VTF Covid-19 Programme Board

Ruth created and chaired the VTF Programme Board, which co-ordinated the wider work of the VTF. Before this began, I kept a cheat sheet in Excel to forecast what vaccines we expected to have and when, plus of course the running-total of the costs we were incurring. But when Ruth joined, the Programme Board took this to a whole new level.

I was puzzled for a while as Ruth's numbers were so much higher than mine. But then, rather to my surprise, I was told that the government charged VAT on its own purchases, accounting for the difference.

Ruth was responsible for modelling various possibilities as to which vaccines might arrive and when, as well as the cold chain requirements for the very different vaccines in the VTF portfolio. Ruth was responsible for letting others know the state of the multiple series of negotiations on vaccine procurement and the progress of both clinical development and manufacturing scale-up. This by itself was an enormously important range of matters but it did not constitute institutional control over the vaccine deployment plan. Deployment was the responsibility of the Department of Health (in England) with all its various constituencies.

The Department of Health and Social Care had an extensive policy development role and was the dominant force in a host of legal and administrative questions. Separate from them was the JCVI, the independent entity advising the government on vaccine prioritisation.

It was up to the VTF to ensure that wherever any vaccines came from, they arrived at a central distribution point in the UK. From there it was PHE's responsibility to transfer the vaccines to regional centres as and when needed. PHE also had the critical mission of ensuring that there were enough people to administer the vaccine and that they were trained for specific vaccines. PHE was also, in a sense, working out its notice since ministers had announced in August 2020 that it would be phased out to be replaced by a new agency.

The chain of command did not end there. The last part of the roll-out process did not rest with PHE but with the National Health Service. This involved two further twists in the plot.

Healthcare was devolved and all distribution plans would have to be accepted by and influenced by Scotland, Wales and Northern Ireland, all of whom were sensitive to the fact that NHS England constituted eighty per cent of the NHS as a whole. Considerable diplomacy would be needed to keep everyone content. As the struggle over the NHS Registry outlined previously had shown, this was not straightforward.

Within England, the politics was further muddied by the strange institutional relationship between NHS England and an entity called NHS Improvement. The latter had been created in 2016 with overall responsibility for NHS trusts as well as independent bodies that provided NHS-funded care. This had proved something of a managerial nightmare. As of 2019, NHS Improvement had become more closely aligned with NHS England but not precisely fully merged. Who reported to whom about what was still not obvious to outsiders. Finally, there was the MHRA, without whose approval there would be no vaccine roll-out at all.

There was not much that anyone at the VTF could do but to accept all of this complexity. Despite this, between June and November 2020, a blueprint started to take shape.

★

Ruth's first priority was to build the programme management capability in the VTF to support scale-up, manufacturing and clinical development of each vaccine we had selected. The VTF created separate teams consisting of a blend of external experts and career civil servants to work with the high-priority vaccines in the summer of 2020. Some of these vaccines did not make the final shortlist for procurement; when each one dropped off, the relevant VTF staff were then redeployed elsewhere.

The threat to VTF security was very real and serious, so Ruth was in the hot seat to keep our vaccine work secure. I had a series of briefing calls where the types of hacking and interference were described in detail. It's amazing what hackers can do – even accessing networks through security cameras. Now I know what's possible, I am much more concerned about cybercrime.

The vaccine codenames taken from submarines provided a thin layer of security, but I was also keen to keep the vaccine companies anonymous, for fear of government leaks to the media that could undermine our negotiating approach. It turned out that there is a surprisingly long list of such vessels, starting with Ambush, Astute and Audacious and continuing onwards alphabetically.

Team Pfizer

Pfizer was spending its own money on its vaccine candidate and wanted neither government cash nor too much interference. Pfizer kept the VTF well informed on developments but largely ran its own affairs in terms of resources.

Oliver Excell (or OBE as he was known as his middle name was Benjamin) came in from PA Consulting to lead the VTF liaison team with Pfizer, and had the closest and most intensive dialogue planning the distribution of vaccines around the UK and anticipating the potential challenges of this ultra-cold chain. Ruth rated him very highly.

Pfizer's vaccines would have to be stored at exceptionally low temperatures and the company did not normally operate via large central distribution units, but took most of its products directly to customers. In terms of the day-to-day supply chain, however, Pfizer would need little in the way of assistance.

However, the stroke of genius, ensuring that this relationship would run smoothly, was that Pfizer were willing to embed their people into our team. This meant we were completely aligned, which made for efficient and transparent teamwork.

In our interactions with Pfizer, we were keen to prove that we were quick and competent. We wanted to impress upon Pfizer that the UK was likely to offer very early regulatory approval – a perfect location for launching its vaccine in 2020.

We had an excellent working relationship with the senior Pfizer team including Ben Osborn, Head of Pfizer UK; Darius Hughes, its vaccine lead; and Janine Small, who co-ordinated with and reported back to Pfizer HQ in New York. Building trust with this team was vital to convince the company that if MHRA regulatory approval were obtained then its vaccine should be launched early in the UK.

Janine proved a real star. She was joined at the hip with Sean Marett at BioNTech. This close relationship was massively valuable for us and she was rightly promoted within Pfizer thereafter. As for Sean, well, he couldn't be promoted any further.

Team Oxford/AstraZeneca

Unlike Pfizer, which had a global vaccine infrastructure and an established partnership with BioNTech, the VTF found itself offering substantial help to the Oxford/AstraZeneca vaccine team. It had the advantage of a supply chain largely based in the UK. A close bond was forged between the VTF deal lead, Anil Mistry, and AstraZeneca's Mark Proctor, who sorted out every problem every time. Mark was supported by Matt Doherty and David Hunt, who worked 24/7 to solve supply chain issues globally. Ian of course was omnipresent.

This would require an innovative approach at times. At one point, there was a problem with a production line for the fill and finish at Wockhardt in Wrexham, which apparently could not be repaired by anyone in the UK. So, we flew in a specialist from overseas to fix it.

In addition to Pfizer and AstraZeneca, there were project management teams supporting GSK/Sanofi, Imperial, Janssen, Moderna, Novavax and Valneva, as well as antibodies. While the team leaders for GSK/Sanofi and Janssen were not hugely overstretched, the teams supporting Imperial, Novavax and Valneva had a lot to do (as did the CureVac team in 2021).

Scenario planning, forward purchasing and anticipating the risks ahead

Much of Ruth's work involved troubleshooting, plus a microscopic examination of the vaccine supply chains. For her, among the many unsung heroes were the VTF risk analysis teams overseen by Morgan Di Rodi.

By late summer 2020, it was starting to look as if vaccines might be on the scene by the end of the year. Ruth alerted PHE as to the resources it would need to manage the unusually low temperature cold chain required. For some time, it was thought that Oxford/AstraZeneca might reach approval stage first. At the height of optimism, it was tentatively suggested that the earliest injections could start in October 2020, if infection rates in the UK rose to the level needed for robust Phase 3 trial results. By September it was clear that Pfizer's vaccine was the most likely to be first for roll-out, and that required much colder, more complex storage and transport.

This was when PHE ramped up its preparations. If Pfizer were to be the vaccine, then a substantial number of new freezers would have to be bought and sent to the right places. Gareth Thomas and Karen Powell at PHE took charge, amid a bonanza for super-freezer manufacturers.

They also took another critical decision. A mass vaccination campaign would require, among a lot of other resources, a far bigger number of syringes in stock and readily available than would be the case even for a flu vaccination exercise. There was a long-established industry standard specification for such syringes.

The PHE procurement high command instead decided to invest in a new type of syringe. These were so-called low dead space syringes which, as the name implies, involve less space between the needle and the plunger when it is fully pushed in compared to conventional units. They also have a detachable needle.

It was a risk to change the model on the eve of an unprecedented national campaign, but the decision proved a brilliant masterstroke: using these syringes meant a larger number of doses could be extracted from a multi-dose Pfizer vaccine vial. Low dead space syringes quickly became the first preference across the globe. In this, as in many other regards, the UK was willing to make bold choices and innovate on vaccines.

To force the pace further, it was decided to start training those who were likely to deliver the vaccines into patients *before* it was

certain which vaccines would be available. This switch alone probably saved six weeks, which would otherwise have been lost between
vaccine authorisation and deployment.

There still would be a host of supply chain matters to be addressed
in preparation for a vaccine coming on stream. That drive would
involve a vast amount of Ruth's time (not helped by having to deal
with four separate health administrations across the UK) and that of
three other women, Sue Williams and Tessa Walton from the VTF
team and Emily Lawson at the NHS.

VTF distribution planning

VTF had to ensure that any approved vaccine was delivered to the
main holding depot for England and Scotland at Haydock Green in
St Helens. From there the vaccines would be sent to the respective
centres for Wales and Northern Ireland.

Delivering a blueprint for this would mainly fall to Sue Williams.
Ruth had been her mentor since recruiting her to Land Rover in
1996. They had collaborated together on multiple supply chain
matters involving design and planning ever since. Almost the first
telephone call that Ruth placed upon becoming Programme
Director was to Sue, and it was of the 'your country needs you'
variety.

Sue was running her own consulting firm but agreed to join as
soon as she had completed an existing contract. She joined a fortnight later. She moved house on the Monday and by Tuesday was
working for the VTF, jump-starting off a kindly new neighbour's
Wi-Fi until her own broadband had been installed.

Sue fixed some immediate problems that Ruth had inherited.
She then dedicated herself to the in-bound planning for the arrival
of the vaccine. It fell to her to start developing operational plans for
the delivery of the vaccine. To start with, the required people and
skills were not in place.

Ruth would come to the rescue, via her extensive contacts with the Ministry of Defence. Squadron Leader Matt Skulskyj was an RAF expert on air traffic control who turned out to be a dab hand at logistics across multiple fields. These 'Two Amigos', as they dubbed themselves, would establish the strategy for receiving vaccines. The Squadron Leader was only one example of Ruth raiding the Ministry of Defence and Armed Forces for talent when she needed it. Steve Glass, who worked closely with her and eventually took on her role when Ruth left, came from the MoD. Ruth's chief of staff was Group Captain Sara Mackmin.

Ruth and her team needed more internal understanding of how to work with the NHS on the fine details of their plan. By good fortune Ruth was directed towards Tessa Walton. She had started the pandemic as an NHS Director and had crafted the blueprint for its vaccine deployment planning. She had left the NHS in September 2020, in part because she needed to recover from long Covid. Tessa arrived at the VTF in November 2020 in time to put the finishing touches to the deployment plan. Her knowledge of the NHS and who to go to in order to ensure the most effective outcome was crucial.

Leading NHS deployment

The NHS had taken time to settle on the right leader to drive through what was becoming a firm blueprint. Finding the ideal chief and team for a task of this magnitude was hard. In October 2020 the baton was passed to Emily Lawson, now Dame Emily, to ensure that any vaccines being delivered to the UK were rapidly deployed.

Emily had the background for this role. She is also one of life's great doers. Emily has both a doctorate in Molecular Genetics and an MBA, and worked for McKinsey for fifteen years where she rose to be the head of the Human Capital Practice. After spells with Morrisons as Chief People Officer and a similar turn at Kingfisher, she moved into the public sector and to the NHS as National

Director for Transformation and Corporate Operations and then as Chief Commercial Officer.

In the early days of the crisis, Emily had been instrumental in the invention of pop-up Nightingale hospitals. In her new role, she had been thrown in at the deep end, but seemed to have no trouble swimming through the treacherous waters. She took no prisoners and, in an organisation infamous for its many fiefdoms, would have little timidity in exercising her authority.

Meetings with Emily were not for the faint-hearted. In September 2021, she was promoted to Head of the Delivery Unit at 10 Downing Street before being sent back temporarily to the Department of Health and Social Care to oversee the booster vaccine drive. That later undertaking would prove to be vital and truly impressive by any international comparison.

Rehearsing with empty pizza boxes

By now, preparations for deployment were in full flow. Webinars were held all over the place to ensure that PHE and the NHS were up to speed with the plans. We were getting close to the likely date when we would have the final Phase 3 clinical trial data for the Pfizer vaccine, so Ruth insisted that the whole supply chain should be tested, in close co-operation with the Pfizer team, by performing dry runs involving pizza boxes, which were the size of the container for the Pfizer vaccine.

Ruth demanded this rehearsal to expose any gaps in deployment and then fix them before we started receiving real vaccines. Every single link in the various supply chains was scrutinised time and time again, with Ruth pressing to ensure that every conceivable hitch had been identified and accounted for. It had become the main preoccupation of the VTF steering committee. It was clear that Ruth had built a very credible plan and, equally importantly, had the right people in place to implement it.

I managed to slip out one afternoon while the pizza box practice was underway. It had just rained and now it was warming up. This was the ideal time for hunting for mushrooms. Thanks to my expert friend Dan Butler, I can now confidently identify over a dozen mushrooms and my favourites, like everyone's, are porcini. Fortunately, my timing was good. I was able to find over three kilos of porcini, parasol mushrooms and various boletes. I filled my basket and then stripped off to use my long-sleeved T-shirt as a mushroom-overflow bag. I listened to *Guys and Dolls* on my headphones and forgot about vaccines, briefly.

All we needed now was for Pfizer to seek MHRA approval for its vaccine. Once that occurred then it would be all systems go as the UK moved from preparation to an actual roll-out.

13

ROLLING IT OUT

The first hint that Pfizer might be on the verge of the final stage of seeking regulatory approval from the MHRA came privately and subtly on Friday 20 November 2020. 'We are almost there' read the cryptic but critical message.

By then we were having daily meetings with the company, PHE and, since the arrival of Emily Lawson at the helm of its vaccine deployment programme, the NHS. The result of each meeting was a 'to-do' list for immediate action. As the VTF had long hoped, it looked like Pfizer had decided that the UK would be the place to launch its vaccine.

The distinctions between the respective teams had all but disappeared. The emotional stakes were incredibly high. The prize was gigantic.

Process for vaccine approval

The Medicines and Healthcare products Regulatory Agency (MHRA), the UK's independent regulator, was the judge and jury of any vaccine that made it through trials. Medicine regulation has come on massively after the mistakes of the 1950s. Thalidomide was marketed for morning sickness without proper testing on pregnant women, with catastrophic effects on babies. Now the regulatory requirements around safety are draconian, including assessing teratogenicity, which is the formal name for the ability to cause foetal abnormalities.

The MHRA has always been an extremely well-regarded regulator internationally. It played a central role in the European Medicines Agency (EMA) when the EMA was based in the UK pre-Brexit, responsible for a large share of the regulation of European medicine.

In my day job at SV, I was very familiar with the complicated and highly regulated clinical trial process. Rightly, there are very strict rules about testing unknown substances on people.

While I knew the MHRA, I was a bit wary of them. I'd heard war stories about perfectly good-faith meetings with regulatory agencies which went wrong and set drug development programmes back by years. We needed our vaccine companies to work very well with the MHRA to get approval as fast as possible.

A formal regulatory application for a licence to market a vaccine or medicine typically comes right at the end of years of drug development. The regulator is required to approve each set of sequential trials, Phases 1, 2 and 3. A licence application may include tens of thousands of supporting pages of data. It would not be unusual for regulatory opinions to take months or even a year.

But in the face of the Covid pandemic, thousands of people could die while vaccines were waiting for regulatory review and approval on these usual timescales.

The brilliant CEO of the MHRA, June Raine, recognised the extreme urgency of the situation and the need to accelerate the timetable to assess new potentially life-saving vaccines and drugs. She pioneered a new 'close partnership' approach between the regulator and prospective vaccine companies, whereby the MHRA played a new role akin to an air traffic controller rather than a policeman. June wanted the MHRA to support innovative new medicines and get them to patients quickly. She rejected the past practices of accumulating and marking paperwork and aimed to drastically cut the time from development to deployment.

In March 2020, June attended a meeting with the heads of the different health bodies including NICE, NHS, Permanent Secretaries and officials. There was a discussion about how to handle the pandemic and June was invited to speak last. June told everyone that her goal was to get a vaccine approved in eighteen months. No one then thought this remotely possible. She did it in less than twelve.

June was a game changer. She was excellent on TV, and no one watching her could not be reassured that we had a real expert in control. I stopped feeling scared of the MHRA.

June devised a highly successful rolling review process. She encouraged the vaccine companies to share incomplete data as swiftly as it was generated. The MHRA would review the information as soon as it was received and advise on the next steps.

So when the final pivotal Phase 3 data was ready, or the final commercial batches manufactured, the MHRA had to review only this new data, the rest having already been assessed. This accelerated review process was massively important to the VTF's work and to the UK.

★

On Monday 23 November 2020, Pfizer officially confirmed that it would seek regulatory backing from both the FDA in the United States and the MHRA in the UK.

That morning I received a text from Sean Marett of BioNTech saying: 'Kate: We are getting a lot of people saying that the UK plan to approve the vaccine this week. Should we plan accordingly?'

To which I replied immediately: 'Yes I think the MHRA will be quick. We are expecting the final delivery schedule from Pfizer this week so target the vaccine [delivery] in the UK from the 30th.'

Sean instantly returned with 'Thanks Kate. We will plan accordingly.'

Both our teams were working flat out together, but I was pleased that we were each hearing the same thing. Ruth, as our project manager guru, was on the front line for this final deployment planning not me, and the same would have been true for Sean in his role as Chief Commercial Officer at BioNTech.

I was feeling super pumped up. I had gone mountain biking with Nell and the skies were blue and fresh. We had covered a lot of distance as the ground wasn't wet. We watched red kites soaring. Mum had been over for lunch and we had eaten outside. This was late November. And the VTF was humming. It was all feeling good.

Pfizer's announcement triggered a multi-stage process for the VTF and its allies in PHE and the NHS. We expected Pfizer to take a few days before submitting the final Phase 3 data to the regulator, which would give us time to intensify the preparations even more. I didn't know how long it would take the MHRA to complete its assessment, but all signs suggested it would come quickly. Knowing June, I was confident that the MHRA had done everything to prepare for a very speedy review.

Even if the MHRA accepted the safety and efficacy clinical data, the National Institute for Biological Standards and Control (NIBSC) had then to approve all aspects of the manufacturing process before Pfizer could be offered an emergency licence under something called rule 174. NIBSC would be required to inspect and endorse the actual initial batches that would be sent to the United Kingdom.

Ruth and Nick were keen to double-tick every box regarding NIBSC testing and approval, so I texted Sean, rather more formally than usual, to check that all was in hand from his perspective. Sean emailed back, cc-ing two of his regulatory colleagues:

So far the process is actually working well and further batches are already allocated and under test at NIBSC. BioNTech and Pfizer are working jointly on all fronts to ensure supply in UK. Constanze,

Ruben and myself would be delighted to speak on the phone with you and your colleagues if this would help: let us know.

It was all in hand.

Revised JCVI advice

The JCVI met on 30 November to consider for a final time which sections of the population should be vaccinated in which order. Two days later, the JCVI upended the NHS deployment planning by changing its prioritisation recommendation, based on the latest data.

Only weeks before, the JCVI had indicated that it expected to recommend that healthcare workers be vaccinated at the same time as the frail elderly in care homes, their carers and the over-eighties. This allowed the NHS deployment team to plan for mass deployment in hospitals, where there would be the facilities and infrastructure to vaccinate healthcare workers rapidly on site using the Pfizer vaccine.

The speed of vaccination was critical, given Pfizer's short shelf life and complex cold chain requirements and our laser focus on using every single vaccine dose. The NHS deployment plans envisaged that the Oxford/AstraZeneca vaccine, with its less tricky cold chain and shelf life, would then be used for the frail elderly and those outside of hospitals and in care homes.

But emerging epidemiological data on the impact of the Covid-19 pandemic forced the JCVI to change their recommendation to prioritising the frail elderly in care homes *ahead* of the healthcare workers. This was logical given that the death rate from the virus among the frail elderly was vastly higher than among younger care workers. Some estimates put it as much as one hundred times larger. But the late switch meant that a plan had to be devised at very short notice for vaccinating the most vulnerable members in the community with Pfizer, a simply monumental challenge.

I don't think the scale of this last-minute change has ever been properly appreciated. Emily Lawson predictably rose to the task and the deployment plans were changed.

★

We didn't know how much time the MHRA's innovative rolling review process might save. It might want more information from Pfizer, such as more monitoring of the volunteers. It might restrict who could receive the vaccine – or even reject the application outright.

We might not receive the vaccine doses we were expecting in the UK. I understood that Pfizer had manufactured only 1.5 million doses by September 2020. Delivering the vaccine through French strikes and UK traffic jams could prove a problem. The idea that a vaccine could be invented, approved, manufactured at scale and then be stuck in traffic on a motorway verged on the absurd if not the obscene. It was, though, a very tangible risk indeed.

Hotspot in Belgium

Despite all of the pre-planning and the practice runs, dealing with a product that had to be kept so cold for so long might be too much for the distribution system in the UK itself. A vaccination campaign launched with a fanfare could fall flat on its face in its early stages.

All of which made Puurs in Belgium the centre of the VTF's universe during these crucial days.

Puurs is not the most obvious place to find itself the pharmaceutical equivalent of Las Vegas. It is part of the municipality of Puurs-Sint-Amands within Antwerp, with a population of eighteen thousand. Its claims to fame before late 2020 were rather modest.

It had a widely admired church. It boasted a fine white asparagus which sold very well. Most of all, it was the centre of production for Duvel or 'devil beer'. This is a strikingly potent drink, and every August when a 100-kilometre-long foot march passes by the brewery, the participants and spectators alike are entitled to free samples.

Nonetheless, its comparative anonymity can be summed up by the fact that the 'Notable People' section of its Wikipedia entry consists of a sole individual, Dina Tersago, Miss Belgium in 2001.

Puurs was, though, to be the beneficiary of its geography – and of a strategic decision made elsewhere.

In the nineteenth and early twentieth centuries, Belgium had acquired a status in medicine well in excess of its size. It was seen as a national industrial specialism. As a consequence, the country decided to invest a large slice of its post-war Marshall Plan aid into becoming a global centre of excellence for the pharmaceutical sector. Over time, it would attract companies like Janssen, Biocartis, Novartis and GSK to build sites for both research and development and mass production.

Pfizer established a presence in Belgium as early as 1952. It came to Puurs in 1963 when it acquired a company, Upjohn, that had been based there. It would expand with the acquisition of Pharmacia in 2002. After a decision at a global level to focus on a smaller number of larger plants it became pivotal to Pfizer. Even before Covid-19 hit, it was producing about four hundred million doses of vaccines and medicines annually, employing over three thousand people, which made it by far the largest company in Puurs, exporting to 176 countries.

Puurs was so appealing to Pfizer and others because of its location. An expansion of the road network around it in the 1950s and 60s meant that it sat neatly between the port of Antwerp and Brussels Airport, and was thus ideal for the production and distribution of pharmaceutical products.

The site is extraordinary. It is over 200,000 square metres in size with a further 30,000 square metres of temperature-controlled rooms at Brussels Airport.

This allowed the Puurs site to respond to the emerging possibility that it would have to make, store and then send out millions and millions of doses of a vaccine that had to be kept very cold indeed.

The Puurs plant had the ability to deal with most of its supply chain itself, with one important exception, necessitating a commercial alliance with Croda. Based in Snaith in the East Riding of Yorkshire, Croda's expertise was on the formulation of the lipid nanoparticles which stabilise the mRNA.

I hope that Croda can continue to play a central role in helping to develop more stable formulations for mRNA vaccines. I expect there will be an increasing need for more stable nucleic acid products, whether for Covid-19 vaccines or new biotherapeutics using the latest gene editing or CRISPR technologies.

But despite all the work on stabilising the mRNA vaccine, we remained acutely focused on how to keep the vaccine cold enough for long enough.

Freezer farms and microchips

Pfizer's team at Puurs came up with very creative and rapid solutions to managing the cold chain challenge.

For Covid-19, Pfizer Global Supply created their own 'freezer farms', placing hundreds of new freezers in spaces the dimensions of a football field. They purchased almost a thousand freezers in the summer of 2020. In another stunning example of invention, the team then developed a thermal shipping box about the size of an airline hand luggage suitcase, which could keep the vaccine at the temperature required, packed with dry ice.

Within these 'shippers' were five 'pizza boxes' containing vials with 975 doses of the vaccine per tray, though the UK's decision to procure low dead space syringes meant that in practice we were able to extract more than this. Pfizer also constantly worked to optimise its processes, and so generated data continually to show how a less stringent cold chain might be needed.

Pfizer was required to provide monitoring data on the location and the condition of every single pizza box for the regulators. They had to prove that the ultra-low temperatures were maintained. If they could not prove this, the MHRA would suspend the product. Any increase in temperature might lead to the degradation of the vaccine, causing it to be ineffective, or worse still, trigger unexpected side effects.

So, every single pizza box not only had an individual GPS identification number but an individual temperature control unit as well. These would be kept under close scrutiny from a control tower staffed continuously. The upfront cost of all of this to Pfizer was huge, especially as there was no certainty that the vaccine would even be approved.

To ensure that it would clear that hurdle, there were ceaseless rehearsals to check that the system of temperature control would be reliable when brought into operation. By the time that the company had submitted its final dossier for regulatory approval in both the United States and United Kingdom, it had been determined that the temperature monitoring process was 99.998% effective.

Pfizer was now confident that, once the very last part of its Phase 3 findings was released, not only would the regulators allow it to proceed with the vaccine but it could then get said vaccine out of its plant.

It was widely expected that there would be at most a week before that critical data set could be dispatched to the regulator. In the meantime, all that the VTF steering committee could do was go over, again and again, every step of what Sue Williams called 'the journey of the jab' or 'the voyage of the vaccine'. Ruth had moved from daily meetings to an hour-by-hour implementation schedule.

Without wanting to celebrate too early, that week I joined the UK bioprocessing industry for a blind beer tasting online, since their sixteenth annual face-to-face conference had been cancelled.

My postman Steve duly delivered six beer bottles ahead of the event. Each one had a label with the logos of the main companies and institutes supporting the UK vaccines effort, namely Cobra Biologics, CPI, Cytiva, National Horizons Centre, Oxford Biomedica and VWR, and we had to guess what was inside. They gave some multiple-choice answers including Belgian blond, American IPA, stout and fruit beer. These were to be drunk with tasty snacks also provided.

Unsurprisingly I couldn't drink six bottles by myself. So, I jumped round the e-rooms meeting everyone in the conference as each team tasted and discussed the identities of the different beers. I got them all wrong but it was a really fun way to meet people, and to say thank you.

'America First'

We did not have to wait that long before Pfizer moved to the next stage of proceedings. The centre of action for this was not Puurs, but its global headquarters in downtown New York City. The date was Friday 27 November 2020, and it was a crucial turning point in the entire Covid-19 saga.

Under the terms of its contract with the US Government, Pfizer was obliged to send its final data to the US Food and Drug Administration first, but could then contact the MHRA a few hours later. I thought it was rather preposterous to have a race between the FDA and the MHRA as to who would approve the Pfizer vaccine first, but that's how it was set up. The US might, at a stretch, be considered to be at an advantage for the slight head start that it acquired.

In reality, any such premium was illusory. This was due to an almost comical turn of events. The Chief Operating Officer of Operation Warp Speed was General Gustave F. Perna, a formidable individual by all accounts. Concerned with maintaining the secrecy and security of the Pfizer data, he insisted that the information was downloaded on to three separate discs, which in turn would be transported by armed convoy between New York and the FDA's offices in Silver Spring, Maryland. Manifestly quite a time-consuming endeavour.

Assuming that the UK would follow the same highly secure path as the US, Pfizer indicated that it was ready to release its material to the UK only a few hours later. It had helped in this regard that the MHRA had, in its specific requests for information, mirrored as closely as it could the likely FDA enquiries, to avoid unnecessary additional bureaucratic detail.

When the call came from Pfizer, it offered to fly the final regulatory submission documents overnight for the MHRA to review in the morning. We answered that receipt by email was more than acceptable. *Just send us the data.*

Pragmatism and speed were always central to the VTF's ethos.

Pfizer had also agreed that it would send the key information to the JCVI so that it could make decisions about who should receive the vaccine in tandem with the MHRA determining if they would license it. The two organisations immediately started work and blocked off their weekend to come to their respective outcomes.

Success

On 9 November 2020, BioNTech and Pfizer announced that their vaccine was more than 95% effective. Forty-three thousand people in six countries had taken part in their Phase 3 trial so this was a stunning and unambiguous result. A breathtaking outcome. I leapt round the room dancing and shrieking with excitement. I phoned Jesse who was back in Westminster to tell him. Then called my mum.

It exceeded all expectations by a very long way and meant that the other vaccines we had backed were likely to be more effective than we had hoped. It confirmed that what once seemed the long-est of long shots – creating a protective immune response against this new respiratory virus – had indeed come to pass.

It took 266 days from the moment that the Pfizer CEO had taken on the task of finding the vaccine to the first approved injection of it.

This was a red-letter day for the VTF steering committee. The show was coming to town. It was even more memorable for Ruth Todd.

On that Friday she had been feeling unwell and, with terrible timing in the light of everything else that was going on, tested positive for Covid. She informed Nick, who tipped me off, her chief of staff, and her executive assistant but nobody else. Ruth was determined to see what she saw as her duties through, irrespective of a high temperature and feeling completely dreadful. With so much to manage she scarcely slept and kept herself going on a diet of analgesics. Ruth maintained the bluff effectively, and because she was working from home there was no risk to the rest of the team. But her refusal to rest meant she was then ill for weeks. Jonathan Van-Tam gently berated her for not taking her health more seriously.

The VTF team could not be sure how long it would take for the MHRA to send up the approval white smoke, if indeed they did, but could not wait for certainty about their deliberations. We were highly encouraged by the fact that the regulator was asking questions by the Sunday and that the JCVI had confirmed its revised priority recommendations. There was a ton of paperwork involved in moving towards the next stage of deployment.

And then came the political dimension. The increasing likelihood of success had not gone unnoticed. Although it was rarely obvious outside the VTF and Whitehall, the whole matter of credit, and the division of spoils when it came to the vaccine, were starting to become extremely sensitive.

The way the vaccine was divvied up between England, Scotland, Wales and Northern Ireland was essentially based on the Barnett formula for public expenditure. This was a mechanism designed in the seventies to determine the level of funding provided by the Treasury to the devolved administrations on an adjusted per capita basis.

Allocation of vaccines was an area which consumed Sue Williams' time as the VTF lead on the issue. It was smoothed by the warm relationship which Matt Hancock, the Health Secretary, had with his equivalents in Scotland, Wales and Northern Ireland. Michael Gove, the Chancellor of the Duchy of Lancaster, was also effective at diplomatic engagement across the nations.

The earliest that the VTF could credibly expect the MHRA to make its pronouncement was Tuesday 1 December 2020. That day came and went, which raised a little anxiety.

On the next morning – 2 December 2020 – in a carefully co-ordinated act, Pfizer informed the markets that it had obtained approval for the emergency use of its vaccine, which was further confirmed at a press conference during which the leading figures at the MHRA and the JCVI sought to reassure the public that they had not been bounced or rushed into their judgements.

Approval

The news broke while about thirty members of the VTF leadership team were engaged in yet another video call. The atmosphere at that moment was akin to the NASA control room in Houston during a successful Moon landing. While we all knew it was coming, it nevertheless was an amazing feeling. Approval was no longer an abstract concept. Lorries would soon be on their way to this country.

A by-now distinctly poorly Ruth was aware of all this but far too busy with the fine print of the delivery plan to follow it live on television. I didn't have access to a TV anyway, so would watch the news bulletins online. It would be 10 p.m. before Ruth saw any of it at all.

My celebration was to go for a run on the hill with my neighbour's wonderful sheepdog Gruff. Running with him makes me go faster, which is a good thing. We got to the top of the hill and Gruff darted around as I felt on top of the world in every way. What a team!

Military support for the final furlong

Moving the vaccine was not simple. It had to be kept at its very low temperature in a convoy of lorries designed for this sort of storage. The team felt it would be preferable to move it by road as the risk of a temperature malfunction was considered higher if it were flown to the UK.

The timing was not ideal. It was winter. There were strikes and blockades in France. The UK newspapers' front pages showed scenes of Kent and Calais with hundreds of lorries backing up, and the possibility of a no-deal Brexit getting closer and closer. There were significant security considerations to be managed.

Despite all this, the first lorries loaded with pizza boxes would depart from Puurs overnight on 2/3 December with the aim of arriving at their destination twenty-five to thirty hours later.

It was at this point that Squadron Leader Matt Skulskyj, assisted by a former Navy officer Tim Lee-Gallon, came into his own. He made the call that the VTF should stick with Plan A, which was to use the Channel Tunnel. Back-up Plans B and C had been developed to transport the vaccine by ferry and, failing that, use a dedicated plane to fly into East Midlands Airport if that remained the only feasible approach.

The Squadron Leader appeared not only to know but to inspire the faith of essential institutions everywhere. He liaised with various police forces in Belgium, France and the UK whose collaboration would be vital. The French constabulary, despite the political war of words raging between London and Paris at the time, could not have been more helpful. That was also true for the border forces of the two countries.

The staff at the Channel Tunnel were also magnificent. Almost as if the disruption occurring elsewhere did not exist, which it certainly did, the convoy and its precious super-cooled cargo made its way to be 'blue lighted' into the tunnel.

Which was an incredible event for a lot of people. Few involved wanted to or would have been able to obtain much sleep that night, such was the tension. Ruth, who by now had a roaring temperature, decided that as she was going to be awake anyway, she might as well spend most of the next forty-eight hours glued to the progress of the vaccines.

The same was true for Ben Osborn, Head of Pfizer UK, and his most senior colleagues who had put their reputations on the line within their company by insisting that the UK would be the first and best place to launch its most important product ever. If the vaccines had become stuck in a traffic jam several miles long, they would have looked foolish. Eyes were strained at the control tower at the security of supply and temperature of the boxes.

There were plenty of politicians and officials in Whitehall who were similarly transfixed, with hearts in mouths as the convoy reached Calais. The text message 'It's through', sent to 10 Downing Street, was received with as much relief as rapture.

Mitigation planning

Every aspect of the supply chain had been tested and challenged to the nth degree. Every possible risk had been identified and mitigations put in place.

We were well prepared when, inevitably, one of the lorries suddenly broke down on the M4. Our contingency plans had been developed in such detail that not only was the motorway swiftly closed, but there was another identical, but empty, lorry travelling just behind which had been included in the convoy to cover precisely such an eventuality.

The teams transferred the 'liquid gold' into the empty lorry and the journey continued.

Otherwise, for all the heartburn that it had caused for so many of those involved, the whole affair was a triumph for the VTF's set of logistical specialists.

The convoy made its way to Haydock Green in St Helens. It was a new facility that had been let by Industrial North West to Movianto UK, who operated it on behalf of PHE. It was, by the standards of the Pfizer site in Puurs, a relatively modest facility at 34,650 square metres. It sat just north of junction 23 of the M6, not far from Haydock Park racecourse.

It was a purpose-built facility that provided temperature-controlled storage for pharmaceuticals, medical devices and healthcare products. The success of the shipment was a blessing for Movianto as well, as it had endured embarrassment earlier in the year over a PPE storage blockage. It would house the supplies for England and Scotland. Wales and Northern Ireland had their own centres.

The single hardest element in that initial shipment had been completed. It was now a matter of moving the vaccines into regional centres, which would be at the behest of PHE.

That process started on 5 December with the provisional plan that vaccination would begin on Monday 7 December. There was strong pressure from government for vaccine injections to be given in all four nations on the same date, so to be safe the first vaccination was delayed until Tuesday 8 December.

The world's first Covid-19 vaccination starts in the UK

The powers that be outside of the VTF decided who would be the first person to receive an internationally recognised regulated vaccine outside of a clinical trial.

University Coventry Hospital, built on the site of the old Walsgrave Hospital that had operated from 1966 to its demolition in 2007, pulled the winning ticket. It is functional in appearance but sizeable in scope, with 1,250 beds and 27 operating theatres. One of the virtues of Coventry was that it was not a metropolitan site at the heart of the capital. It was provincial and more ordinary.

It seems that a similar logic led to Margaret Keenan, then ninety years of age and hence representative of the age group the JCVI most wanted to see vaccinated, being asked if she would go first.

Within forty-eight hours of the vaccinations commencing in the UK, more people had received Pfizer injections than the total number during the whole of the clinical trials process.

There remained the danger that people with rare medical conditions could suffer side effects that could not have been detected in the clinical trials. The publicity that this might receive could endanger the entire vaccination process, especially if it were whipped up out of all proportion by sections of the media.

Senior figures at the NHS had a torrid time when informed about two early instances of an allergic reaction to the Pfizer vaccine. The report on the first individual suggested that the reaction might have been unrelated to the vaccine, but the fact that there had been two reactions suggested something potentially more serious. The two individuals who suffered severe allergic reactions were already known to be hyper-sensitive and carried EpiPens.

The MHRA immediately changed the label to exclude the hyper-allergic and required a period of safety monitoring post-injection. This meant the deployment plan had to change again, and now everyone who had the vaccine was asked to wait, socially distanced, for fifteen minutes after injection to be monitored for side effects.

It sounds a small change, but the logistical switches meant that chairs and waiting space had to be found. Trained healthcare staff were needed to monitor and respond to any side effects. Emily took all this in her stride.

I was immensely relieved when this early bump did not put off the public. I was fearful of the anti-vaxxers mounting a fake news campaign and watched my Twitter feed relentlessly. The media largely repeated the message that the benefits of the vaccine outweighed any difficulties which might be linked to it. It was soon clear that take-up of the vaccine would be very high.

The initial logistics had worked, but that did not suppress VTF team instincts to fret about future deficiencies in the supply chain. Ruth became a virtual obsessive, haunting her own local vaccine centre. She looked at the barcodes to confirm the turnaround and shipping times by checking whether the stock of vaccines available was from the batches she had expected to arrive.

There were also distributional complexities: a whole shipment of vaccine might be too much for a certain smallish location, so that there were times when the vaccine would have to arrive in individual pizza boxes. In one instance this meant that an HGV ended up transporting a single box of 975 doses to one care home, but it was unavoidable. We also sorted out a system for returning the shippers and boxes to Puurs – they were an expensive commodity and hardly disposable.

In December 2020, Nadhim Zahawi was appointed as Minister for Covid-19 vaccine deployment. On 16 December, he reported that 138,000 people had been vaccinated in the UK in the first week. Nadhim tweeted 'A really good start to the vaccination programme… [this] number will increase as we have operationalised hundreds of primary care networks.'

Following a short manufacturing suspension in January 2021, breathing space to optimise production, Pfizer would eventually be able to deliver far more than the 1.2 billion doses of the vaccine that they had originally claimed for 2021, with manufacturing time now cut in half. Another extraordinary achievement.

On 8 December 2020, a voyage that had started with a woman originally from Hungary, championed by two Germans of Turkish extraction, and pushed through by a man born in Greece of Jewish heritage, would see the vaccine entering the arm of Margaret Keenan, aged ninety, originally from Fermanagh, Northern Ireland, receiving her dose in a hospital in Coventry.

AstraZeneca next

It felt like the Pfizer vaccine was a miracle, but if the UK roll-out were to achieve the scale and speed needed to protect the vulnerable as soon as possible, and a willing public was not to be disappointed or disillusioned by the date of their jab, more vaccine was needed.

We were confident that we would receive reinforcements. The day before the opening Pfizer jab was administered, AstraZeneca told us that they were not far from being able to seek MHRA approval themselves. Meetings that Jonathan Van-Tam and I attended with them had been highly co-operative and transparent. Daily meetings with AstraZeneca were now taking place alongside daily meetings with Pfizer.

On 20 December Oxford/AstraZeneca were indeed ready, but Christmas meant that their submission did not occur until 27 December. Both the VTF and the MHRA had been more closely involved with this vaccine than with the Pfizer one. We thought approval was, therefore, likely to come quite swiftly. MHRA gave it the thumbs-up three days later.

Which meant that there was a second exercise in terms of deployment for which the VTF would be responsible. The very beginning of it was, in a way, more straightforward because, for some technical reasons, the initial dozen or so batches from AstraZeneca were filled and finished in Germany and so much the same procedure as had by now been established for the Pfizer vaccine could be duplicated for the opening AstraZeneca operation. Its first vaccination would take place on 4 January 2021.

Some wrinkles emerged in managing two different vaccines at the same time. Pfizer's lengthy experience in vaccine manufacture and distribution meant that it was more certain of what it could deliver when.

The AstraZeneca vaccine depended on the speed at which the Wockhardt plant in Wrexham could undertake its fill and finish function. It largely did so well, but it had to deal with a bomb scare and the risk of floods in the early weeks of 2021. It tended to be a case of 'make and send' with the AstraZeneca vaccine, but this was compensated for by it being much easier to handle.

Oxford/AstraZeneca's vaccine: less than a year from start to finish

Yet despite all this, the critical point was that the set of VTF experts led by Clive had delivered. They had offered the right advice on safety, efficacy, the prospect of MHRA approval and manufacturing. EU approval for AstraZeneca followed shortly after the MHRA gave the green light on 30 December. Other regulators then confirmed that the vaccine was safe and good to go.

It was a moment of considerable relief. We had recommended a risky investment in a vaccine that proved to work well and that would save thousands of lives in the UK and literally millions internationally. This vaccine was cheap and straightforward to deploy.

We backed Oxford initially through what would be described in venture capital as a start-up, and continued with 'follow-on' funding for them to conduct trials and build manufacturing capacity.

This staged funding in the UK would allow the Oxford/ AstraZeneca alliance to make much faster progress than it had dared to hope for. As Sarah Gilbert and Catherine Green say in their book *Vaxxers*, they were now in a position to turn a brilliant concept into actual vaccines with critical support from others at the right moment:

> Then the cavalry arrived in the form of the Vaccine Taskforce. Combining technical expertise with a route to decision-making at the highest level of government, the Taskforce suddenly made what many had said was a crazy proposal in February a reality. Sandy [Douglas] was awarded funds to build a manufacturing consortium that could not only make lots of vaccine but also test it, store it, and get it into vials.

It would be further support from the VTF that made this result happen at the speed that it did. As Sarah Gilbert and Catherine Green again acknowledged:

> In 2020, there were three factors that enabled us to cut out the waiting and crunch ten years into one: first, the work we had already done; second, changes to the way funding was given out; and, third, doing in parallel things we would normally do in sequence.

Selling this vaccine without a profit was an extraordinary act of altruism, considering the sums involved and the rewards from which some of its rivals benefited. AstraZeneca has still not received the credit for this that it deserves. Pascal, Mene and their team have been selfless heroes.

All in all, Project Triumph *was* a triumph. It was Oxford's triumph. It was AstraZeneca's triumph as well.

By the end of 2021, AstraZeneca produced the most doses globally of any of vaccine, including Pfizer and SinoVac. It supplied two billion doses of its cheap Covid-19 vaccine to 178 countries across the world within a year of first approval.

It is likely that the AstraZeneca vaccine initially saved more lives worldwide than any other vaccine. The fact that it was being sold on a non-profit basis meant that it was given to those who needed it around the world rather than the worried well who could pay for it. This was in stark contrast to others who made a fortune.

A quite astonishing achievement from a standing start.

If I were the Queen, I would write their names in neon lights above Buckingham Palace for everyone to see.

'Champagne Supernova'

In January 2021, Novavax announced fabulous Phase 3 data from our UK trials, showing an overall efficacy of close to ninety per cent and strong immunity against what was then being called the 'Kent variant'. I was bombarded with calls from the media for comment. Since I was now back full time at SV, I no longer had the careful media preparation that I had got used to at the VTF.

The interviewer on the *Today* programme asked me how I felt, and I answered honestly that I was so happy that I had broken dry January to celebrate this phenomenal clinical result.

The *Daily Star* reported Novavax's data on 30 January 2021 with the headline 'Champagne Supernova'.

This was a momentous occasion, but those who know me might well have guessed that this wasn't the first time I had broken a dry January pledge.

I received lots of lovely congratulatory cards and letters following this from friends, neighbours and even strangers. Locals would drop off cards by hand. Steve, our postman, would deliver letters addressed 'Kate Bingham' with no actual address, and I was thrilled to receive these. I even received one from my grandmother's former neighbour who recognised my name and sent photos of my grandmother. The photos were new to me and showed her standing triumphant by the duck house she had built on an island in her local village pond. We clearly share the same genes.

In June 2021, the Phase 3 trials in the United States and Mexico reported very similar numbers to those in the UK trial – but five months later.

Manufacturing was much harder than we had anticipated. Securing regulatory approval for the vaccine and its adjuvant took six months longer than planned. We knew that scale-up to mass production was challenging for any company, even more so for one of Novavax's size and experience. And this vaccine required two components, the spike protein and the adjuvant. Each had to be scaled, quality controlled and approved.

Novavax finally sought formal approval from the MHRA in October 2021 and became the fifth vaccine to gain its approval in February 2022. The durability data continues to look good. I still don't know what medium-term role this vaccine will play in the UK's pandemic response.

Shouting from the rooftops

It rather goes against the grain to take a lap of honour, but although ministers would refer to vaccine supply as 'lumpy', the key point was that the vaccines were never going to run out. Based on the astonishing work by so many people, the UK was able to move at speed to vaccinate its opening target populations and then the wider public ahead of the anticipated schedule.

This meant that the UK was better protected than some other countries when Delta emerged in the spring of 2021. This new more infectious variant made deployment even harder. The country was able to make an early start on booster jabs. The UK's vaccine roll-out was – rightly – the envy of the world.

In March 2021, Vaccines Minister Nadhim Zahawi reported that the first thirty million people from the priority cohorts had all received their first vaccine dose, and by April 2021, 25% of all UK adults had received two doses. By June 82% of adults had received one dose and 60% two doses. The roll-out had been superb.

The Infrastructure Projects Authority team, sent by the Treasury and Cabinet Office to assess the work of the VTF, noted in their report of November 2020:

> The Review Team concludes that [the VTF] success has been founded on expertise and agility. This has put the UK ahead of the curve in its thinking, planning, delivery and creation of future resilience. The RT urges HMG to build on this through a lessons-learned exercise so that future programmes may benefit.

The end result was a very strong portfolio of vaccines assembled by the end of 2020. The ambitious targets that I had set six months earlier were achieved. All seven vaccines had entered the clinic in 2020. They would have the capacity to deliver more than sufficient doses to vaccinate high-priority populations in the first half of 2021, and then others. All of the first six approved vaccines in the UK were in the VTF portfolio. Even the 'stretch goal' of seeing Oxford/AstraZeneca approval in the year 2020 was met – with two days to spare.

The VTF had been at the very heart of what had happened. We had made it happen. We had identified what turned out to be the right vaccine candidates early. We had assisted in their manufacture and provided support to get the clinical trials recruited and delivered. We had persuaded Pfizer that the UK should be the country where they started business. None of that had been inevitable.

It also meant that, by the close of December 2020, I could look back with incredible pride in what the team which had come together so quickly had achieved.

14

GOVERNMENT (MIS) COMMUNICATIONS

When I started at the VTF I had no idea that working with government communications teams would be the hardest part of my job. Yet so it proved. By a long way.

I enjoyed telling people about the VTF strategy, how vaccines work, launching the NHS Registry and what we were doing, and found it all very straightforward, but I really struggled with the political side. There seemed to be an obsessive desire for political messaging and political angles, which massively got in the way of what we were actually trying to do: tell a simple story that would inform people, calm fears, enlist the support of business and attract volunteers.

'What has been the most challenging obstacle you had to overcome during your time to find a vaccine?'

This question was not posed by a politician or Whitehall official, but by an inquisitive A-level student from Rochdale Sixth Form College. Mr Harrison, her teacher, had invited me to give an after-school video talk about vaccines in November 2020. The quality of the questions from these budding biologists staggered me.

'If the coronavirus mutates, can the vaccine also be edited to provide immunity to the different strains?'

'Will there ever be enough vaccine produced to provide for the population or will we rely on herd immunity?'

'If a vaccine is found does that mean we can trust it enough to be safe in the long run?'

There I was, sitting in my son's bedroom in the cottage that had become my lockdown home. I had spent seven months running the Vaccine Taskforce. Seven months of working around the clock, building a team of experts, advising on the expenditure of hundreds of millions of pounds.

We hoped we had a workable vaccine that would be cleared for use, maybe more than one. But at that stage we didn't actually *know*. And as the students' questions showed, there was so much else we really didn't know for certain. I didn't know whether the vaccines would work against a mutated virus. I didn't know whether, if we had to design new vaccines against variants, we would have to start the clinical trials again from scratch – to say nothing of the massive work needed to manufacture these vaccines in bulk.

I described my career as a venture capitalist in biotechnology to these eager Rochdale students. I explained how I had spent the past thirty years helping scientists and entrepreneurs build small cure-for-cancer drug discovery companies. I told them how my previous work with Patrick Vallance had got me appointed to the VTF, which in turn led me to speak to this group of Rochdale Sixth Formers that day.

The Rochdale experience was, alas, something of an exception to the Whitehall rule. The communications ('comms' in the jargon) function there was invariably turned from what it should have been, a means by which to make policy more accessible and effective, to the overriding purpose of making the Government, and certain ministers in particular, look good. I was caught unprepared by the political side of communications and found working with government press offices to manage the media very challenging indeed.

At a crucial point I found myself caught in a media storm of hostile and abusive coverage which bore no relation to the facts. Even the timing of the attacks was bizarre, since they started six months after I was appointed, and even overlapped with the amazing Pfizer announcement that their vaccine provided greater than ninety per cent protection.

Given that the UK had been the first country to sign a contract to acquire this vaccine, it seemed not only inaccurate and unfair, but actively insane that both the government comms machine and press should be going after me quite so aggressively and with such hostility when the results of our work were so positive.

Government communications: partial, unfocused, semi-competent

When I first started as VTF Chair in May 2020, I had not appreciated quite how crucial the role of communications would prove to be. The PM had given me three very clear goals – to secure vaccines for the UK, to ensure effective vaccines were distributed internationally and to support plans to ensure we were better prepared for next time. But an overriding goal had also been set in order to make all this happen, namely to place the UK at the forefront of vaccine research, development and manufacturing.

Demonstrating the UK's leadership in vaccines was important for our pandemic planning as we wanted innovative companies to come to the UK to develop and manufacture their pioneering new vaccines. But if no one knew what was on offer in the UK, then why would they come?

I had not appreciated just how unfocused and patchily competent the many different government comms teams would prove to be, despite there reportedly being more than 120 people in BEIS comms alone. For example, on my appointment, I requested a press cuttings service so that I could be briefed on vaccine developments in the UK and around the world as well as on the general sentiment around vaccines themselves. I was told that the BEIS press office was not able to provide this. So, we instead relied on press cuttings from the BioIndustry Association – with a grand total of two comms people – to give that vital real-time feedback.

In early June I pre-recorded a speech at the GAVI vaccine summit where political leaders pledged funds and vaccines for distribution to low- and middle-income countries. However, I first realised how un-joined-up the press teams were, when some time after my GAVI speech had been pre-recorded under scrupulous supervision and direction, and subsequently broadcast at the GAVI summit, I was then sent an email by the BEIS press office confirming that they approved the content. Might have made more sense to do so *before* I gave the speech.

I was under some pressure in June 2020 to join one of the daily televised press briefings in Downing Street to discuss the overall strategy for the Vaccine Taskforce. I was reluctant to do this since it was too early for me to say anything of substance. The only key message I could have given was what an uphill struggle it was to find a vaccine for Covid-19 that could be proven to be safe and effective and manufactured at scale for roll-out by the end of the year.

I could have set out how no vaccine had ever been successfully developed against a human coronavirus and how we did not under-stand the pathology of this virus at all well. And these messages would have reinforced our strategy to build a portfolio so as to maximise the chances of securing at least one vaccine that could be protective. We were still in the process of doing due diligence so I was not in a position to talk about the specifics.

Eventually, after considerable persuasion, I agreed to join the briefing on 16 June and came up to London by train for it. But very luckily for me (and the world), Professors Martin Landray and Peter Horby announced their phenomenal dexamethasone data from the RECOVERY trial that day. They had proved that this cheap steroid had a significant benefit in treating severe patients. Alok and I were rightly dropped in favour of the Prime Minister who shared this news with the grateful nation and world. I was never asked to join another press briefing.

★

It was becoming clear that the new Vaccines Registry we were planning would require a different quality and quantity of comms support. We were hoping to recruit hundreds of thousands of volunteers to sign up to the Registry, but we also needed to send wider messages about the safety of any approved vaccines, and to flag UK technology leadership so that innovative companies, both large and small and around the world, would see the opportunity and use the Registry. This was a core part of our whole strategy.

In June I had a call with Jonathan Sheffield, together with individuals from the Department of Health and Lord Bethell, the minister in charge of clinical trials and my VTF team. We all agreed that a national communications campaign was needed to launch the new Registry.

I asked about our communication plans to support the launch and was told that the BEIS press office understandably did not have the capabilities to provide this type of specialist support.

I had not had any experience of running a big public campaign like this in my venture capital life, though I did have long-standing relationships with a few specialist health PR firms. So, I was interested when Jonathan Sheffield recommended a group called Admiral Associates, who had recently been seconded into NIHR to provide specialist communication support. It became clear that Admiral both understood clinical trials and were trusted by NIHR – trusted corporately as well as individually by the key NIHR people involved – so seemed a good resource to bring in to help us.

I spoke to the CEO Georgie Cameron. She was clearly experienced and shared our energy, with a laser-like focus on results, and had run national campaigns in the past. I then suggested she spoke to Nick too to scope out how they might be able to help us. Nick agreed this would be a key resource so he and his team then sorted out the contract and we got going. Given the storm that followed, it is important to be clear that I had had no previous relationship with Admiral or its team, and had no control over any comms budgets, or over the legal, procurement and contracting processes. All of these were handled by civil servants in the normal way.

Communications across Whitehall

Bringing in an outside agency applied both focus and specific expertise to our communications on the Vaccine Registry. Although I did not realise it at the time, navigating Whitehall comms was not for the faint-hearted. It turned out there were no fewer than seven different comms teams focused on vaccines across government, including Covid-19 teams in the Department of Health, PHE, NHSE/I as well as the Covid-19 international and domestic communications teams, the DCMS disinformation team tasked with tackling false propaganda and then, of course, the comms team supporting the vaccine taskforce in BEIS.

There appeared to be no coherent communications strategy in this area across government. In fact, only those working directly with me in the VTF actually knew the up-to-date facts about vaccines and what we were doing, and I am not aware that any of the other teams ever engaged with us. Goodness knows where they got their information from.

The internal impediments did not let up; indeed, they got worse. In mid-July we were preparing for our first press release, where we would announce the NHS Registry to support rapid enrolment into trials as well as announcing outline terms for the initial vaccines that we had prioritised, namely Pfizer/BioNTech and Valneva vaccines and AstraZeneca antibodies for the immunocompromised.

This was vital work, and so I was very surprised to be told that Chris Whitty was not willing to give a quote to endorse the launch of the NHS Registry. I mentioned this to Patrick.

Patrick joined the dots and it transpired that Whitty's officials had deemed – on the basis of what knowledge or expertise is unclear, in part since they never contacted the VTF team – that our work to support clinical trials was not of sufficient importance to bother Chris with and they had not even mentioned it to him. But once we figured this mad blockage out, I had a charming conversation with Chris, who immediately agreed to give a very warm endorsement for the press release.

I had a difficult time getting the tone of this first press release agreed with BEIS officials. The press office was focused on high-lighting the total number of vaccine doses that we planned to purchase, as if the more we purchased the better we were. However, this naïve 'numbers game' approach completely ignored the fact that we were building a portfolio of different vaccines and formats, since we expected many, if not all, of them to fail.

This was not *Supermarket Sweep* – it was not our goal to buy as many vaccines as possible regardless of need and thereby mop up the global supply; indeed, that was directly contrary to my instruction from the Prime Minister to support the international availability of vaccines.

In my judgement the BEIS press team line was irresponsible in the way it raised potentially false hopes. It also left the government massively open to the possibility that if one or more vaccines failed, as they were likely to, the headline numbers would fall, raising question marks about the whole programme.

The BEIS press office gave clear advice that if we tried to put too many announcements in our press release then these would get leaked ahead of time, so they suggested announcing things piece-meal. I did not like that idea; I wanted to come out with a bang, in order to give a coherent view of what we had been doing over the previous two and a half months to deliver the VTF strategy.

I had always been concerned about leaks, which is one of the reasons our vaccines were codenamed after submarines. But one of one of my funnier moments was when a radio interviewer commented on the brilliantly creative names of our vaccines, namely Ambush, Astronaut and Victorious. I realised that the draft press release had indeed been leaked, with the submarine codenames intact!

Calling in the PM; but vaccine work was apparently unimportant

It turned out that this lack of political interest in vaccines was more widespread than I thought.

Vaccines were not on the radar of the Number 10 press team either; they seemed to be regarded as politically irrelevant. Several days before our first 20 July release, the Number 10 press office told me they would not put forward the Prime Minister, or even a minister, to make this announcement, as it was not a priority for the government.

Not only that: they went further than this and banned me from speaking to any mainstream media such as the BBC, ITV, or Channel 4 on this announcement. They did, however, give me permission to speak to *Woman's Hour* and BBC Hereford and Worcester radio. Even if the announcement about the early vaccine agreements was genuinely not newsworthy, which I doubted, I have no idea how they thought we would be able to persuade potentially several hundred thousand people to sign up to NHS Registry to enrol into trials which could start as early as September with such a limited communications campaign. Try as we might, they simply did not get it.

What was so odd was that we were making very rapid progress. This indifference to the VTF and the wider vaccines story among advisers and officials was the first time I texted Boris to say the government was missing a trick. I thought we should be leaning in to ask the public to step forward and help with the trials. Simon Case, as Cabinet Secretary, subsequently removed my media restrictions, though the announcement was still made, incredibly, without ministerial support.

Gavin Williamson, the then Education Secretary, was predictably bombarded with questions about vaccines on that morning's news round and had nothing to say about them; maybe he would have done better if he had been briefed. It would almost have been comical – if the stakes had not been so high and the missed opportunity so great.

More official roadblocks

Political indifference had further serious consequences. We had planned a paid advertising campaign to support a large-scale push to drive people to sign up to the NHS Registry and these costs had been included and approved in our Business Case. We were particularly keen that our targeted campaign should reach those most at risk from infection, including the elderly, those with severe underlying diseases and frontline workers. We also especially wanted to attract people from black, Asian and minority ethnic backgrounds who were disproportionally affected by Covid-19 – and who the evidence suggested might be among the more vaccine-hesitant – to register.

We spoke to the Behavioural Insights team (sometimes known as the Nudge Unit, after a bestselling book on the topic) led by Dr David Halpern and Hannah Behrendt in order to explore generally how to increase vaccine uptake, and specifically how to bring these most vulnerable people into clinical trials in an effective, fair and transparent way. The NIHR teams were also helpful on advising on translation and advocates for different ethnic communities.

All this work was in vain. The Cabinet Office blocked expenditure from our budget for advertising the NHS Registry, even though these costs had already been approved. To this day I do not understand why that happened, and how one department of government can be allowed to derail the approved and already budgeted and signed-off activities of another department, let alone during a crisis of this magnitude. But I couldn't fight every battle.

This ban further complicated our work, as it meant that the VTF had to try to deliver a national message without the benefit of any targeted advertising support.

Our goal for the NHS Registry was to get hundreds of thousands of volunteers to sign up in time for possible clinical trials starting in September, and it was a core part of our overall strategy to woo the best vaccine developers around the world to the UK. For that purpose, we developed a media strategy that encompassed radio and TV interviews with me – and in some cases Divya for Asian radio – plus newspaper articles, podcasts and even longer quasi-academic articles. Time and scale were of the essence.

We recognised there was huge public uncertainty – and, apart it seemed from within the UK government, a massive thirst from all quarters for information – about how vaccines work, how they get developed and made, the risks of clinical trials and generally what to expect. It was hardly surprising that people were not willing to sign up to volunteer for clinical trials until they understood much more about why they *should* do this. So, I spent a lot of time on broadcast media explaining the background, outlining possible scenarios and answering questions, explicitly reassuring the public that safety testing had not been curtailed, even though the overall vaccine development had been dramatically accelerated.

I am the very opposite of a politician. With no interest in politics, I had no political agenda and no appetite to do media for the sake of it, nor did any member of the VTF. Yet from the start the team and I faced a continual problem with getting official approvals for each interview and article. The process required separate sign-offs from BEIS and the Number 10 press teams, a process which was laborious, time-consuming and completely not fit for purpose for a fast-paced media environment.

Frequently, by the time we received approval from BEIS and Number 10, the opportunity would have gone. This caused tensions between Admiral and the Whitehall press teams, which we tried to fix with regular briefings and invitations to join our Steering Group meetings; but this did not work, largely I suspect because of a lack of Whitehall understanding about or interest in what we were doing or why it mattered. And all of this was of course made worse by a measure of official hostility to the dedicated healthcare communications specialists which the VTF had had to bring in from outside government.

Describing the VTF strategy to experts

Our comms task did not only cover the general public, but academic and industry experts and life science entrepreneurs. These were both crucial opinion-leaders and also key recruiting agents for our wider strategy.

In this context, I seized on the opportunity to contribute an opinion piece to *Nature* – one of the top academic journals in the field – as well as to join a Q&A round table with its offshoot *Nature Biotech* on strategies for designing, testing and administering Covid-19 vaccines with a small group of leading experts in immunology, virology, epidemiology and vaccine development. This was intended to provide an authoritative overview of the critical issues facing governments and NGOs seeking to vaccinate a substantial propor-tion of the world's population.

I relied on a lot of help from the experts in the VTF as well as from my broader network to help with answers to these detailed science questions. My opinion piece, however, was focused on how we could operate more quickly next time if we could remove some of the key bottlenecks in vaccine manufacture and development.

I felt both the *Nature* publications could be helpful in showing how the UK was at the forefront of vaccine R&D and manufacturing, and by demonstrating its leadership in global co-operation to accelerate the distribution of vaccines to the most vulnerable and needy countries.

However, once again, the government press teams thought otherwise. The *Nature* opinion piece was held up for weeks thanks to not receiving approval from Number 10. Specifically, I was told 'Number 10 have fed back that they think there is more room to be positive in what we say' – as though *Nature* was the *Sun* and it was part of their job to take booster lines from the Government – and asked whether there was scope for *Nature* to extend their deadline (again!). I pointed out once more that this was not political but a thought-leader piece. Each iteration of the draft had been shared with BEIS and Number 10 over weeks, including the publication timeline, so the deadline was fixed. Alas, we could be certain that no one in Number 10 had the first idea about what the science involved, or the least interest in finding out.

The expert reaction to the *Nature* and *Nature Biotech* articles was extremely positive even so, and the same was true of our other comms. We received positive feedback on messaging and global reach from the PM's Strategic Communications Officer, who noted

> ... The high volume of pickup in the US, which is obviously a key market for the work we are doing on vaccines, and generally shows the UK to be a leader on global collaboration as well as our commitment to fair and equitable access for every country on vaccines... We are keen to see what can be done to increase our engagement in the US in light of how well the above story has fared.

The official handling of our third VTF press release on 17 August announcing preliminary heads of terms with Janssen (Johnson & Johnson), Novavax and GSK was more challenging. I found myself having to rewrite the release three times to correct the overreaching and inaccurate claims that were being added – apparently for political spin – by the BEIS press office. Eventually I had to spell out very clearly that I would not rewrite it a fourth time. After this completely unnecessary internal blockage, I spoke to one of the heads in the BEIS press team and requested that the obstructive individual be taken off the team, only to be told that 'That's not the way we do things here.'

We simply would not be able to function with that level of incompetence and obstruction in the private sector.

Following this, I suggested that I brief the broader BEIS comms team in detail so they knew what was coming and so we could work better together going forward. A call was duly scheduled with individuals from the VTF and the BEIS comms team. As well as the *Nature* articles, I was keen to outline the VTF strategy, what we had achieved so far and what we expected to achieve in more depth than could be included in a newspaper article or a short interview. We were in a pandemic where everyone was waiting for news of a vaccine, and this was creating huge uncertainty, and an environment in which false rumours and misinformation were likely to flourish.

I wanted to address that vaccine information vacuum, especially to reassure people who were vaccine-hesitant. Part of the purpose of including protein and whole virus-based vaccines in the VTF portfolio was to encourage those people who were worried about taking a 'new' vaccine. These old-style vaccines should provide reassurance and maximise take-up.

But I also wanted to show how the VTF could help deliver the UK's international leadership objectives to attract the best vaccine companies to work with us, to underline that the UK was open for collaboration both for trials and manufacturing, and to reassure potential clinical triallists that we were a genuinely expert team acting for the global public good.

So, we approached *The Lancet*, a leading medical weekly journal, who expressed strong interest at the beginning of September 2020 in publishing a wide-ranging article entitled 'The UK Government's Vaccine Taskforce: strategy for protecting the UK and the world'.

The fact that this approach had been discussed and agreed within BEIS seemed to be irrelevant. We faced continuous bureaucratic roadblocks. In one exasperated email to my private office on 7 October 2020, four weeks later, I wrote:

> We still don't have sign off yet for this report card piece for *The Lancet*! What is the hold up? Do I need to add this to my list of complaints about the BEIS/Number 10 press offices?
>
> What I don't understand is why a plain vanilla report card showing what we have done is in any way contentious. Soon this will be old and the opportunity wasted. There is no political angle other than to publicise internationally (without spin) what the UK has achieved. Bizarre and – continually disappointing.

The Lancet article was eventually published on 27 October and was widely read. The Cabinet Office then sent an enthusiastic email saying that in the first 24 hours there were 384 articles referring to it published in 38 countries with a combined total reach of over seven billion views. 'That's a really good outcome and really pleasing to see.' The irony was palpable.

Introducing Lee Cain

Despite all this positivity, I was not given approval to speak to the media about *The Lancet* article. When I pushed back against this decision, I was told that Lee Cain in Number 10 had blocked it. I did not know him at all but emailed him and we spoke shortly afterwards. I described the work we were doing in publicising the strategy of the VTF and how we were working to secure vaccines for the UK and the world. I asked Cain what he was concerned about.

He spoke to me in a manner that made me feel like I had been brought into the headmaster's office to be told off. He asked me whether I knew that most ministers only did one or possibly two media events per month? Of course, not being a political person, I did not know this. But it was irrelevant in any case because our goal was not to ration public awareness of vaccines but to increase it. He then told me that he had reviewed my media appearances and did not approve my doing any further media given my exposure over the last few months. And that was that.

It seemed to me that Lee Cain did not have even the barest understanding of the purpose or relevance of these media appearances. I tried to explain what I was up to: encouraging volunteers (especially those from ethnic minorities) to join clinical trials, and explaining how vaccines work and why they should be trusted, and persuading the most innovative vaccine companies that the UK was a great place to develop and manufacture their product – these arguments fell on deaf ears.

He did not give any further approvals for me to say anything publicly, and this proved to be the turning point in my relationship with the press officers in government. Suddenly the roof started to fall in, with a series of attacks in the media both on me and on the work of the VTF.

15

MUGGED BY THE MEDIA

It was shortly after my run-in with Lee Cain that the *Sunday Times* sent an extensive list of questions to BEIS. The email arrived on a Saturday morning, and they wanted immediate responses that day to claims that I had disclosed confidential information to US investors at an industry event, that I was conflicted and that I was not qualified to be Chair of the VTF.

None of these claims was in fact correct. The event in question was a US women's biotech networking event that included a range of professional women from different companies and disciplines. I thought this would be a good conference to speak about the UK's vaccine strategy since it included people from innovative biotech companies which were and are likely to be the source of new vaccines and technologies in the future. At SV, I routinely speak at these sorts of conferences and find the network and relationships invaluable to the creation and financing of new biotech companies and new technologies in the UK and US.

As with all my VTF media appearances, I had submitted a request to BEIS officials to take part in this event, shared the proposed presentation in advance and been given approval to go ahead. The event was not focused on vaccines as such but on women and leadership. I had no plans to invest in prophylactic vaccines at SV. The whole line of questions from the *Sunday Times* was a blind alley.

I had never experienced hostility from the press before. While I was shocked by the aggression and explicit accusations in the *Sunday Times's* questions, I also realised that I had made an error when I cut and pasted some slides into my presentation at that event; some sides had been marked 'confidential' in the footer, when in fact they were not confidential. I had not noticed the mislabelling before, and neither had BEIS officials when they reviewed my presentation ahead of time. I flagged the point to them and spent a day painstakingly writing down answers to each question in detail, which I sent back to the BEIS press office.

What would take me aback, however, was that BEIS would take it upon itself, without consultation with me, to decide how to respond to the *Sunday Times*. The BEIS press office and special advisers (spads) would choose what to say and when to say it. I had rather naively thought that spads were supposed to be a useful link between ministers and officials in the creation and delivery of public policy. I now discovered that spads report to ministers, and largely exist to promote their reputations and protect them from any flak. I seemed to be attracting incoming fire, and as a non-elected, non-Whitehall outsider, I was exposed, mute and dispensable.

The Whitehall approach seemed to be to respond with bland lines for publication without addressing the specific topic which could be used to fan the flames. In this case, their failure to contradict many of the specific allegations meant that these claims were allowed to build up into a fireball.

I was sent the *Sunday Times* questions at the last minute, outside working hours, on a Saturday morning with a demand for replies by 5 p.m. I was naïve to the political games here; it transpired that BEIS sent a response (which I did not see) after the 5 p.m. deadline and afterwards they told me they had somehow failed to mention the key point that I had received prior approval from civil servants both to attend the event and to give this presentation.

I was furious to hear they had held back this critical fact, which had the direct effect of blaming me. I complained to Nick who agreed that this omission was the government giving the *Sunday Times* a signal that they believed I had been out of line and that I was not acting with integrity.

The *Sunday Times* article appeared under the name of Gabriel Pogrund and unleashed a wave of hostile comments against me from every corner of the media. The BBC and *Independent* reported that Labour had called for a probe after UK vaccine tsar shares 'sensitive' documents.

All this was reinforced by the echo chamber of social media. One early example was from English 'actor, writer, comedian and presenter' Stephen Mangan, who picked up almost fifty-four thousand – *fifty-four thousand* – 'likes' for this tweet on 1 November 2020, echoing the presumption that my appointment was venal and that I was incompetent for the role:

> *Kate Bingham, heads Britain's vaccine task force. No experience in that area. She's a venture capitalist, Married to a Tory minister.*

David Schneider, who describes himself as an 'actor, writer, director, fool' with over half a million followers took these allegations further and tweeted (which has not been taken down):

> *Head of the vaccine taskforce*
> * *No relevant experience or expertise*
> * *Happy to share protected data with venture capitalists*
> * *Hides involvement with vaccine companies*
> * *Married to Tory MP*
> *CONCLUSION*
> *Perfect for the job*

Palliative care doctor Rachel Clarke weighed in with her – widely shared, also undeleted – tweet:

First @BorisJohnson appointed Kate Bingham his vaccine tsar (a venture
capitalist, no health experience, married to a Tory minister, schoolmate of
Rachel Johnson).
   Then her firm received a £49 million investment — funded by the UK govt.
Obscene cronyism.

As so often, this tweet set out a selection of facts which gave a wholly
distorted and untrue picture of me. My appointment did not lead to
any investment in SV, and there was no cronyism involved. Rather,
my status was that of an unpaid volunteer working as an adviser. I
stepped out of my job at SV at no notice to work on a six-month
secondment into government in order to contribute to the national
Covid-19 response. In any case, short term, unpaid secondments are
not normally subject to competitive recruitment — and in the desper-
ate crisis circumstances of a pandemic, the idea of a bureaucratic
selection process is a bit of a nonsense.

   I had not disclosed anything confidential. But, as I was to discover,
facts count for little in the face of ignorance and prejudice.

The PM intervenes again

Stuck at home in our cottage I felt impotent and powerless. I spoke to
the Permanent Secretary at BEIS, Sarah Munby, and requested that the
government publish a statement with three goals: to confirm that my
appearance and presentation at this conference had been pre-approved
as part of the VTF strategy; to lay out the VTF strategy and achievements; and to explain that I had the right experience to be Chair.

   Sarah empathised. She said that publishing a government statement was highly unusual but that she would ensure that the press
office responded to ongoing queries promptly. I knew Nick was
working the system behind the scenes on my behalf, but eventually he called and told me the spads were lying in the tracks
refusing to address the impression of my wrongdoing with a

published government statement. Nick recommended that I speak to Boris.

I did speak to the PM, and the statement 'regarding Kate Bingham and the Vaccine Taskforce' was finally published on the evening of 1 November. How much more effective would it have been if it had been produced, and the relevant facts put before the press, before the *Sunday Times* published their ugly allegations?

Once the allegations were out there, it seemed to me that the spads had done their level best to make me the target. But where had the allegations come from in the first place?

While it felt like the gloves were off with my relationship with the BEIS press team, the VTF private office remained upbeat and focused, circulating an email to the wider (now more than 100-strong) VTF team saying:

At the all-VTF team meeting on Wednesday, Kate spoke about everything that we have achieved in the last 175 days since she was appointed Chair of the VTF in May. It's really quite incredible that in that time we have nearly entered into agreements with six different vaccine suppliers, invested in vaccine manufacturing sites across the UK, helped to set up and join the COVAX facility, announced a Human Challenge Programme, encouraged over 300,000 people to sign up to the vaccine trials Registry, made a podcast series, and worked across government and industry to plan for vaccine deployment starting in a number of weeks. That amount of work is astonishing and could not have been achieved without the hard graft and unwavering determination of all of us in the VTF!

Even so, we found ourselves in the middle of a horrific press pile-on. Every journalist imaginable now tried to find a new hook to the story of incompetence, cronyism and corruption. The fact that the Test and Trace programme was not going well was used as additional evidence that wives of Tory MPs must be hopeless and corrupt. I was endlessly compared to Dido Harding (also married to a Conservative

MP), both of us being unfairly discredited. There were relentless conflict of interest allegations, some of which revealed a fundamental lack of scientific understanding, for example when the VTF's bulk antibody manufacturing initiatives were linked to SV's antibody discovery therapeutic companies. I had TV cameras and vans door-stepping my house in London, intimidating my neighbours.

On 4 November 2020, I appeared for a second time in front of the Science and Technology Select Committee. The hostile media coverage had created a huge amount of interest in whether I would be skewered in the cross-examination. Luckily, as it proved, comms officials and spads were unable to prevent my appearing before a Parliamentary Committee, and I was able to address the allegations head-on and state on-the-record that there was no truth to the claims that were being reported in the press. I told the Committee that there had been:

> a lot of nonsense reports and inaccurate and I'm afraid to say irre-
> sponsible reports... There was an error on the slide because there
> were footers that suggested they were confidential and that was my
> fault. I was working too fast. There was nothing confidential and
> those footers should not have been there.

Yes, there had been a clerical error, I said, but nothing improper had been done. And the wider picture was incredibly positive.

I hoped that would be an end to the matter. I was wrong.

Enter Cameron Brown

The following week, on Sunday 8 November, the *Sunday Times* head-lined another scoop, again under the byline of Gabriel Pogrund, which seemed designed to trash my reputation and work. They announced 'leaked' information that the VTF had spent £670,000 on the Admiral contract for PR, suggesting this was my personal vanity project.

I was bewildered by this claim. In an effort to get to the bottom of the issue, I spoke afterwards to Alok's spad at BEIS, Cameron

Brown; he told me that he had provided that figure to Pogrund of the *Sunday Times in* good faith, and that it was taken from a confidential memo that Nick had written to the Secretary of State. But, Brown said, he was acting in my interest since the *Sunday Times* was threatening to publish a higher number. I was left completely speechless that I had not been consulted before Brown proposed to turn over this information to the *Sunday Times*.

Again, the press had a field day. The *Guardian* trumpeted 'UK vaccine taskforce chief Kate Bingham expected to quit; Venture capitalist married to Treasury minister criticised over use of PR consultants' with the *Mirror* reporting 'Ministers under pressure to sack vaccine tsar amid "dodgy cronyism" claims'.

I have no idea what responses were actually given to the *Sunday Times* ahead of this second splash, given the shenanigans of official responses the week before. At no point had Pogrund spoken to me to check any of his claims from either article; nor, as far as I could tell, even attempted to contact me.

I did not see Nick's memo nor even to this day do I know the scope of the contract with Admiral, as that was handled by BEIS officials; spending decisions like this were nothing to do with me. As I understand it, the actual amount of money ultimately spent was far less than £670,000, though I do not know what it was. Needless to say, this point was omitted by the *Sunday Times* splash.

Again, it does not seem that BEIS officials managed to give the true picture, or to include a quote from me that would have helped to put the record straight.

My friends, however, all rallied. They sent me various lovely bottles, chocolates, flowers and endless messages encouraging me not to take these attacks to heart.

Dealing with Number 10

On Monday 9 November, literally the day after the second *Sunday Times* article, Pfizer announced its astonishing data showing that its vaccine was greater than ninety per cent protective against Covid-19 infection.

Thanks to the VTF, the UK was the first country in the world to sign a contract with Pfizer. We had secured forty million doses, which was proportionately higher than any other nation. So I felt that the tide of negative press should start turning. I knew we had done a great job at the VTF and felt it was only a matter of time before the world caught up with us.

Again, I was wrong.

Clearly, there was a stream of negative briefing against me with confidential data taken out of context being deliberately disclosed to the press, I was very disturbed to realise that much of this briefing had emerged from Number 10 itself.

I am quite clear in my own mind, and I have had it separately confirmed, that this hostility was not coming from the Prime Minister. But I now know from highly credible independent sources that it probably came from Lee Cain at the very top of the Number 10 press office and advisers.

On 9 November, *Politico* – a publication with an umbilical cord to Westminster – reported under a BAD-A-BING headline that 'Downing Street sounded less enthused noting Bingham's contract is up next month so she's off anyway.'

I still do not understand what could have been driving this negativity, though Reaction journalist Iain Martin tweeted 'Number 10 bashing Bingham to get Boris credit on vaccine'.

True, there were rare moments of humour such as a tweet from Tom Whipple, science correspondent at *The Times*: 'Well, Bingham's played a blinder, hasn't she?' followed by 'If Kate Bingham now wants to spend £675,000 hiring a team of strong men to carry her wherever she needs to be on a chaise longue while feeding her peeled grapes, that's fine by me.'

By the end of that day, I had had several confirmations that these hostile briefings were coming from Downing Street and that annoyed me mightily. Jesse was back in Westminster since it was a Monday and I was alone.

At about 9 p.m., I called the BBC Radio 4 *Today* programme
to ask whether they would like me to come on the show the
following morning to talk about what we had been doing at the
Vaccine Taskforce, and specifically to address the untrue allegations against me which were being repeated widely. I was angry
that I was being thrown under a bus by the government despite
all that we had done and were still doing. The government knew
what the VTF had achieved and yet they were not standing up
for me while I was trying to defend myself against such unpleas-
ant abuse. Indeed, spads were actively feeding the media witch
hunt.

The *Today* programme said that I was welcome to join any slot
that I would like in the following morning's edition. But before
I finally agreed I told them that I owed it to the Prime
Minister to give him an opportunity to step forward and offer his
unequivocal and visible support to me and the work the VTF was
doing.

And frankly I felt that if he did not want to provide this endorsement then that was fine; I would step down and return to my
normal work a couple of weeks before my six-month term was up.
We had in any case secured the Pfizer vaccine first, in large quantities and had confidence that vaccination would start in December;
and we still had a shot at securing the AstraZeneca vaccine approval
too by year end. Plus we had a much wider vaccine procurement
and long-term industrial strategy in place. I had discharged my
initial remit well.

I texted Boris and he called back later that evening.

Boris groaned when I told him what was going on. He asked
me where this was coming from and I replied that I believed it
was Lee Cain but certainly from Number 10. He groaned again.
I told him that I was happy to step back now or to extend
until the end of the year if he wanted me to. But I also said
that, if I stayed, the negative briefings had to stop, and I needed
immediate, unambiguous, visible and emphatic support both
from him and more broadly from the government. Boris gave me

that assurance and so I turned down the chance to appear on *Today*.

The following day, 10 November 2020, Matt Hancock appeared on the *Today* programme. He gave me the unequivocal support I had asked for:

> I will go out of my way to thank Kate Bingham for the service she has given this country, and the whole of the Vaccines Taskforce, because it will mean we are one of the best placed countries around the world for access to vaccines, not just the leading ones for AstraZeneca and Oxford that we have supported and developed here but also all the other ones…

He went on to say,

> And I think that sometimes, Michelle, if I may gently say let's look at the substance of what a group of people have achieved, and when they've given up six months of their life to come into government and do something bringing enormous commercial capability, which the government needs and for years people have said the government needs more commercial capability, we should say a massive thank you to the people who are prepared to step up in this national effort.

There was a positive briefing in Cabinet which was duly shared with the press and subsequently thanks to me at PMQs so I felt Boris had fully honoured his commitment to support me.

However, good news does not travel as quickly as bad news, least of all when there is political capital to be made. That same day, Darren Jones MP, the Labour Chair of the BEIS Select Committee, called for me to be sacked from my role as Chair of the VTF on the floor of the House of Commons. The Labour leader, Keir Starmer, declared 'the £670,000 PR bill of vaccine task force head Kate Bingham, cannot be justified at a time when people across the country are losing their incomes amid the coronavirus crisis.' Sir Ed Davey, the Liberal Democrat leader, said 'Kate Bingham must resign. Johnson's cronyism is a disgrace.'

It is important to record that, to his credit, Darren Jones wrote to me privately afterwards to apologise, saying:

> Now that further information has come to light it appears that it is in fact ministers who have questions to answer about public appointments, appropriate governance and oversight, the use of public funds and our civil service. I should have sought this information before raising the issue on the floor of the house and apologise for not doing so. I hope that my premature intervention won't discredit what has clearly been your excellent work at the UK vaccine task force. I'm sorry if I caused any distress and I hope that you will accept my apology.

That was a kind courtesy. He did not, however, withdraw this allegation in the Commons nor make his revised views known publicly, as far as I am aware.

On the evening of Thursday 12 November, I read press reports that Lee Cain would step down as director of communications. Following Cain's abrupt departure, Boris told me to work with Jack Doyle, who turned out to be professional, pragmatic and polite. How differently history might have been if all the VTF's government media interactions had been handled by Jack Doyle from the start.

Continued attacks

Needless to say, all this controversy meant that vast amounts of time were being spent by the VTF team dealing with responses to worried and angry government ministers, MPs, Select Committee Chairs, Opposition members and, of course, the press. It was hugely distracting and it slowed down our work on getting vaccines to the British public.

The change of tone from the Government had some effect. Even so, the *Guardian* in particular gleefully continued to run a torrent of what ended up being over twenty hostile articles repeating various abusive allegations, none of them true, and, with one exception, none of them checked with me. They claimed 'Bingham is not bound by transparency rules or the Parliamentary Code of Conduct on declaring interests' and that I appeared to 'circumvent standard rules of propriety governing public appointees', in direct contradiction to the BEIS statement, which had been on the gov.uk website for weeks.

The *Guardian* drew up detailed 'chumocracy' charts and even Dominic Cummings's parents-in-law were brought into their alleged web of cronyism. For example, 'For some within the department, Bingham appears to have been given free rein without the usual demands surrounding potential conflicts of interest because she was a Johnson appointee, and because her husband is Jesse Norman MP, the financial secretary to the Treasury.' In fact, the conflict of interest testing and evaluation before I was appointed was one of the most impressive and thorough aspects of all my government interactions.

These un-paywalled articles whipped up a storm and provided fertile fodder for anti-government critics on social media who assumed I was a Tory insider. Numerous hostile, inaccurate and needless to say unchecked comments from *Guardian* columnists Carol Cadwalladr and George Monbiot were widely shared and retweeted.

A lawyer named Jolyon Maugham published a series of untrue and denigrating tweets about me, and then launched a lawsuit naming me, which he then had to withdraw because he realised on further research that his criticism was ill-founded. Jesse made a tea towel out of Maugham's most offensive and inaccurate tweets for my birthday so we are reminded of them every time we dry up the dishes.

I found the unwillingness even of supposedly reputable media organisations and journalists to check their facts astonishing. On 11 November 2020, for example, in his programme *Thinking Allowed* on Radio 4, the veteran BBC broadcaster Lawrie Taylor led an episode on modern-day corruption by citing me as an exemplar of all that is wrong.

Taylor introduced corruption as a phenomenon involving 'casual arrogance', 'casual disregard' and 'sheer outright villainy' and discussed my role in leading the Vaccine Taskforce as such an example. To say I was appalled would be more than an understatement. I knew nothing about this defamation beforehand, until Jesse and various shocked friends of mine called to say they had heard the show.

Somehow, I was able to get a message quickly to BBC Director General Tim Davie pointing out 'this horrendous and abusive error'. The programme was immediately taken off air and was removed from iPlayer, reuploaded only once the offending language had been removed. I duly followed up with a very angry email.

The BBC removed the reference to me and agreed to publish a modest apology for not consulting with me before their broadcast, but interestingly did not feel any obligation to apologise for the claims made. At this point, I simply did not have the time or energy to pursue a legal battle to secure a proper apology and damages.

By the middle of November, as good news continued to pour in about the successes of our VTF work, the *Guardian* was in full flow. A huge spread was cleared for Jolyon Maugham to write:

> There is an England of my mind. And in it those who have made their fortunes offer their time and talents in service of the public good, modelling self-sacrifice and respect for good governance to ensure the nation thrives. But that England is no longer this England. Take the story of Kate Bingham…

The second sentence would have been true of me, if he had cut what followed. Maugham's 'Good Law' Project continued to attack others who had selflessly devoted enormous time and expertise during the pandemic.

And so it went on. I was especially struck by the media's unwillingness to see things except in terms of politics. The *Economist*, a supposedly reputable newspaper, repeated the same old canards without checking when it wrote '[Bingham's] taskforce spent £670,000 ($883,000) on public relations advisers, she was accused of divulging sensitive information to an investor conference—and, to cap it all, she is married to a Tory minister.'

Yes, I happened to be married to a Conservative MP and minister. Since when is that a crime or a bad thing? And what did that have to do with my own political views? Are wives still viewed as chattels?

The truth was that as Financial Secretary to the Treasury, Jesse was the minister responsible for HM Revenue & Customs, and through HMRC for management of the furlough scheme, supporting nearly twelve million jobs, as well as managing other fiscal measures such as the VAT cut, business rates reliefs and so forth. He too worked round the clock during lockdown, sharing our precious broadband for his endless Teams calls with the Treasury, and coming out of his converted bedroom-office at night to share a family dinner. These measures, and the Treasury's economic policy set by Chancellor Rishi Sunak during this period, are widely and rightly recognised as one of the highlights of the pandemic. So, it turned out that being married to *this* Tory minister was in fact a good thing.

It was a very odd time. As a member of the public, I was not used to being falsely accused by strangers repeating unfounded claims, and I found it deeply upsetting. It was also very damaging to the reputation of SV and my team who were smeared by association, and we worried that SV's investors, entrepreneurs and companies might be put off working with us.

For his part, Jesse was not going to sit by amid all this hostility. He rebutted many of these claims publicly on social media with the facts. And privately, although he did not want to add to my burdens by telling me at the time, he contacted dozens of press commentators and journalists to let them know what had actually happened, so that none of them could say they were not fully informed.

As the local MP, Jesse also wrote in the *Hereford Times* to set the record straight: 'My vaccines tsar wife deserves praise not slurs,' he said. 'Lots of people in Herefordshire know Kate, and know she is as straight as an arrow, and an incredibly warm and positive life force.' He went on to make clear that he had had no role in my appointment and added: 'Kate has been working around the clock leading the UK effort to source effective vaccines against Covid-19. She has earned nothing, and does not expect to earn anything, from her work as chair of the Vaccines Task Force.' All true.

Ferrets in reverse

The media tide was starting to turn. Even so, Moderna's positive Phase 3 trial data on 16 November triggered a mixed reaction, with critics questioning why the VTF had not acquired more doses: 'Did Kate Bingham drop the ball on the Moderna vaccine?'

The answer – if anyone had cared to ask – was quite clear: our due diligence suggested that they would not deliver a material number of doses before the middle of 2021, so we prioritised Pfizer, where we had greater confidence in earlier delivery. This turned out to be right. Yet again, however, checking to get the facts would have got in the way of a catchy headline.

I had extended my six-month role by a month to ensure that I did not leave until the vaccine roll-out had actually started. Rightly the press on 8 December was full of photos of Margaret Keenan and William Shakespeare, the first people to receive the vaccine, with outpourings of relief that the end to the pandemic might be in sight. Sir Richard Sykes had completed his positive assessment of my seven-month term as VTF Chair, and the government duly published our year-end report: *UK Vaccine Taskforce 2020:*

Achievements and Future Strategy which set out in detail what we had delivered, though the recommendations we made for future work had been removed.

I met Rachel Sylvester and Alice Thomson of *The Times* in my SV office on Thursday 10 December for the Saturday Interview, in an effort to give some perspective to my time in government. They wrote 'The vaccine programme has been one of the few success stories in the government response to the pandemic… This week Britain became the first country to start administering a vaccine.' They rightly recognised my thirty-year experience working in the biotech industry, and concluded by saying 'heading the task force has been a bruising experience.'

After Novavax and Janssen announced their positive Phase 3 data in late January, the press did a full collective U-turn. Instead of denouncing me, accusing me of self-enrichment and cronyism, they now published headlines saying: 'From zero to hero'; 'Vaccine chief Kate Bingham will rank with our greatest Britons'; 'Coronavirus: UK's nimble vaccine task force has left rivals trailing in its wake'; 'Three cheers for Kate Bingham'; 'Boris has made plenty of blunders during this pandemic but his vaccine strategy was pure genius'; 'Kate Bingham saved vaccines when Europe couldn't'; 'Champagne Super Nova'; and the simple headline from the *Sun*: 'Kate Did Great.'

It was exactly like something out of *Private Eye*. And all lovely to see when I took a bunch of newspapers over to read together with my mum that morning in front of the fire.

Back to the *Guardian*

However, the ironies were not over.

In late January Katharine Viner, editor of the *Guardian*, emailed me breathlessly, saying:

Dear Kate – Many congratulations on your continued vaccine success! I understand you're considering a proposal from our health

editor Sarah Boseley – she's excellent… and if you weren't interested in an interview then we'd love to run a piece written by you.
All the best, Katharine.

I was amazed at her hypocrisy. After reading months of hostile
and inaccurate commentary and over twenty aggressive headlines
and photos, there was no doubt in my mind that the *Guardian* had
been writing headlines to suit its political direction while deliberately ignoring the publicly available facts. The editor was in charge
of this exercise.

So, I wrote to Viner declining the interview, saying:

One might have imagined that the *Guardian* – of all newspapers –
might have been supportive, not dismissive and destructive, of
women who could act as female role models, especially in technology and science. But no. You did the exact opposite. You sought to
trash my reputation, apparently because you think you know my
political views, a subject on which I can say with certainty that you
and your journalists are ignorant. Do you really regard these as
consistent with your professed standards of journalism? Or consistent with your values?

This exchange led to a very slow and protracted process of the
Readers' Editor – their internal ombudsman handling complaints
– considering whether the *Guardian* should correct any of its copy.

In October 2021, after emails were 'lost' and meetings 'mis-sched-
uled', I replied to the Readers' Editor:

Based on your review of the coverage, you say that there are an
unusually large number of articles in contention. This is correct.
What it shows is that the *Guardian* repeatedly doubled down on its
negative comments and reporting on me. It became the house
position to state that I had spent money on personal PR, disclosed
unauthorised secrets, bypassed government integrity checks and
was incompetent to perform the job as Chair of the VTF – and to

keep repeating these claims even when they had been denied and rebutted by BEIS.

At no point did the *Guardian* make any effort to check again or reassess these claims, even when clear rebuttals had been published and other evidence had emerged to cast doubt upon them. Instead, it claims to have relied on the original checking it claims it had done with BEIS and 10 Downing Street.

This is a weak argument. Where a newspaper takes a decision to double down on insulting or defamatory content, as the *Guardian* did, it should make sure to cross-check its sources and seek further evidence before repeating the content.

But in any case, the *Guardian* has given no reason to believe that the original checking which it says it did with BEIS and No. 10 did in fact positively validate these negative claims. It is notable that the most you claim is that 'those articles were put to Downing Street or the department for business (BEIS) for a response', not that a response was forthcoming, nor that it positively confirmed the story. Since you cannot show this, the *Guardian*'s whole position falls to the ground.

But I was not finished yet.

It also casts doubt on the process of correction itself. The *Guardian*'s house position was (for reasons best known to you) to make false claims about me, but if the checking had been done properly, both originally and later, these checks would have undermined the claims. That being the case, the response should not only be on the detail from you, but it should include a proper overall apology from the Editor.

Eventually, the *Guardian* made a few minor tweaks justifying its position as reliant on reports from other newspapers as well as the government briefings. The whole experience was partial, grudging and focused on self-justification rather than truth. The *Guardian's* website has long proclaimed the words of its greatest editor, C. P. Scott, that 'Facts are sacred, but comment is free.' In fact, the *Guardian* showed a cavalier disregard for facts and sources. I very much doubt Scott would have been proud of the way this was handled.

I shared these email exchanges with my then 82-year-old mother, a lifelong *Guardian* reader who was as shocked as I was by their reporting and justifications. I enjoyed her reply: '*Pravda* always prints what the Govt tells it: ditto *Guardian*. Luv Muv.'

Across the Channel

Finally, the press's attention moved to continental Europe and one paper reported that 'Macron and Merkel publicly spread doubts about the Oxford-AstraZeneca vaccine. The former has since recanted while the latter, incredibly, is still saying she wouldn't take it.'

Macron and Merkel first claimed, falsely, that the AstraZeneca vaccine did not work in the elderly and then, without drawing breath, attacked AstraZeneca for not delivering the volumes of doses they had ordered. 'As a result, the vast majority of the six million potentially life-saving doses that the EU has managed to get hold of so far are sitting unused in stockpile.'

And AstraZeneca had, uniquely, offered their vaccine for an initial period at cost price.

It was during this continental media storm that I received a surprising call from Pascal Soriot, the CEO at AstraZeneca. I did not have much mobile signal indoors so I went outside to speak to him in the icy February rain.

Pascal described the challenges they were facing with the European Commission and asked if I would be willing to speak to the European press to share the UK's perspective on how we were working with AZ. I told him I was not keen to get into any debates about politics or Brexit, or how the EU Commission had handled their vaccine procurement programme, but that I was happy to discuss the strategy of the UK Vaccine Taskforce and how we had approached procurement, development and supply.

When I finished speaking to Pascal, I immediately called Jack Doyle in Number 10 as I was flatly unwilling to get involved in another media trashing. Jack's pragmatic advice was that if I could help AstraZeneca then I should. Jesse concurred. Having agreed very strict guardrails on content, I had a joint call with Stefanie Bolzen from *Die Welt* and Antonello Guerrera of *La Repubblica*, who published a transcript of the interview in English (albeit rather broken English since it was taken from a voice recognition transcript) alongside more detailed articles in their German and Italian newspapers.

I hope this interview was helpful for AZ, and for UK life sciences. It was in fact the first comprehensive and long-form media overview published anywhere of what we had achieved – surprising both in coming from Italy and Germany rather than the UK, and also in coming so late. It highlighted the benefits of the UK's decision to act early and independently and take risks. In particular, I explained how early engagement with AstraZeneca and Oxford, providing both experts and money, meant we were able to scale quickly, and that was why we got the AstraZeneca vaccine sooner than the continental Europeans.

The European press was more attuned to the importance of specific industrial and commercial experience than its UK counterparts. It published detailed articles comparing my background with that of Sandra Gallina, who was responsible for procuring vaccines for the EU. The *Corriere della Sera* reported the virologist Roberto Burioni's scathing tweets 'Gallina graduated from the interpreters' school [and] had to deal with health for the first time in July 2020, before [that] she dealt with agriculture and fisheries' while pointing out that 'in Bingham's CV there are various experiences of investments in biotechnology and drug development companies [over] 29 years.'

Changing tack, the European media then turned its collective attention to the vaccine contracts themselves and analysed the redacted AstraZeneca contracts signed with the UK and EU extensively. The contracts which Maddy McTernan negotiated for the VTF were recognised as much stronger and more practical.

As the German popular magazine *Bild* put it in late February 2021: 'Dear Brits, we envy you.' By 1 March 2021, the UK had already vaccinated 35% of its adults, including nearly all in the most vulnerable groups, while the EU was stuck on 7% and struggling for supplies because they had not placed orders in time.

Towards the end of 2020, Channel 4 commissioned David Dugan and Jamie Lochhead to make a factual documentary on the Vaccine Taskforce entitled *Jabbed*. Given most of the industry VTF team and Nick were stepping back at the end of the year, we were given permission to participate, but the civil servants in our team were blocked. I pushed very hard to include the senior Whitehall team of Ruth, Maddy and Tim since they were excellent and critical to our success, but it was no-go. I even called Matt Hancock late on a Friday night to get his advisors to change their mind – to no avail.

Fortunately, Sir Patrick Vallance and Jonathan Van-Tam bypassed the roadblocks and were interviewed, so at least we had a senior official government viewpoint. Jamie and David did a fabulous job and gave a very good account of our work. *Jabbed* was released in May 2021 to great acclaim and won a Scottish BAFTA.

Working with the media within the Government was a baptism of fire. I learnt a lot and made mistakes. I think lots of the flames of controversy could have been dampened if I had been allowed to give periodic factual updates on progress to the Opposition and other parties in the House of Commons as I had requested. I obeyed the government rules about not speaking to the press without permission, but in hindsight I was naive, and others exploited that naivete. I probably should have done what everyone else does: picked up the phone to the various journalists and discussed the position 'off the record', so at least their reporting could be accurate.

Unlike almost all the political journalists, I found the scientific journalists superb – even from the *Guardian* – thoughtful, careful and sticking to the facts. In particular, Fiona Fox, the founder and leader of the Science Media Centre, was an exemplar of robust, balanced reporting. A marvel to see: the *Sun*'s front page on 8 April 2021 drilled down into scientific statistics on reactions to the vaccine.

Next time I will insist on managing my own communications, and it will be run by an industrially-trained female scientist.

16

LOOKING BACK

The sheer intensity of the experience almost blinded me to what we had achieved. Within six weeks of my appointment, the VTF developed its strategy and built a team of industry and technical specialists alongside a team of Whitehall officials, expert in project management, contracting and diplomacy. We prioritised a shortlist of vaccines from over 190 candidates and signed contracts for seven vaccines across four different formats. And against incredible odds those vaccines turned out to be precisely the right calls. The government supported the VTF's work by making rapid and pragmatic decisions, especially about money.

Two of the VTF's chosen vaccines were approved by the MHRA in 2020, and that December the UK became the first country in the world to launch its Covid vaccination programme. Six of the seven vaccines selected have now been approved by the MHRA. (Valneva's approval came in April 2022; GSK/Sanofi is likely to be approved in 2022.) Data from UK clinical trials have supported regulatory approvals of vaccines in the UK, Europe and around the globe.

Given its in-depth knowledge of the challenges facing vaccine development and manufacturing, the VTF succeeded by creating a 'UK offer' to encourage vaccine companies to work with our government. We offered to act as partners and gave a commitment to work closely with them to help their vaccines succeed.

When I finished in December 2020, Ben Osborn, CEO of Pfizer UK, wrote to me:

> The collaboration has been outstanding and I have used this regularly with government as a best practice example of public/private partnership for a shared ambition. Beyond this though I would recognise the speed of decision making, 'can do mind set' and action that has led to the point where we are now vaccinating UK patients through the NHS. Indeed we are already sharing learnings internally so that the delivery and deployment approach across the globe builds on the experience in the UK.

And this was echoed with similar comments from Jaak Peeters, Johnson & Johnson Special Envoy for Covid-19 Vaccines:

> On behalf of the Janssen/J&J team and Paul [Stoffels], I would like to thank you for the very productive collaboration and partnership during this crisis period and congratulate you and your team for the outstanding results achieved during the 6 months of your leadership of the UK Vaccine Taskforce. The achievements are truly remarkable.

Novavax CEO Stan Erck's email was short and sweet. He had just received EMA approval based on clinical data from the UK trials: 'Kate and Clive, thank you very much. You two were instrumental in helping us get the data to support this vaccine. Away we go! Stan'.

We succeeded, and eighteen vaccine trials have run in the UK, attracting almost fifty thousand volunteers. The VTF provided funding and advice to supercharge existing UK capabilities in vaccine scale-up and bulk manufacturing across nine different industrial and public sector sites.

We created a national registry on the NHS website which accelerated recruitment into multiple clinical trials, including delivering the biggest Phase 3 vaccine trial ever run in the UK. But in August 2022, I received a disturbing email saying 'NHS Covid-19 Vaccine

Research Registry closing down'. We don't yet know how this will be resolved.

The key insight here was that this industrially networked, expert team was set up in such a way that we were able to pursue a deliberate industrial strategy to deliver the tasks set for the VTF.

And the overall verdict? Overwhelmingly positive on the Prime Minister's first Goal: to secure vaccines for the UK. No one ever imagined, and I certainly had no conviction, that we would be able to achieve what we did, let alone at the speed that we did. In July 2022, the *Economist* reported that, 'Covid vaccines saved around 20m lives in their first year... two had an outsized impact: those produced by AstraZeneca-Oxford and Pfizer-BioNTech. Each averted between 5m and 7m deaths; combined they accounted for more than half the lives saved by vaccines.' These were the first two contracts we signed for the UK.

In the UK context by the summer of 2022 the value of our vaccination strategy had been vindicated by three key events. First, despite initial fears to the contrary, the arrival of the Omicron variant starting in late 2021, did not render the vaccines ineffective. Second, when society was reopened in early 2022 and infection rates increased dramatically to heights never seen before, the number of deaths did not escalate similarly. Finally, the announcement that all adults over the age of 50 (and younger vulnerable people) will receive a further vaccine shot in late 2022/23 demonstrates that Covid vaccines work spectacularly well at averting serious illness and are here to stay in some form.

But we were less successful in achieving Goals 2 and 3 – namely to ensure that vaccines were distributed fairly around the world, and to ensure that the UK is better prepared for the next pandemic.

Regrets

So, despite all the accolades, I am disappointed that we failed to deliver some of the key detailed objectives set for the VTF.

The VTF 'largely' delivered Goal 1, but not completely. We were not able to protect those people whose immune systems do not respond adequately (or at all) to vaccination. That's about half a million people in the UK. And to my great regret we did not have government support to buy AstraZeneca's long-acting antibodies (Evusheld). This meant that many vulnerable individuals will have been needlessly infected or will have been forced to put their lives on hold by shielding. Unlike the UK, thirty countries are using Evusheld to protect their immunocompromised.

The Prime Minister's Goal 2 was for the VTF to ensure that vaccines were distributed fairly around the world but we made only modest progress on this. From our report card 'Achievements of the Vaccine Taskforce' published when I left in December 2020, it said:

> VTF has shaped new collaborative arrangements to ensure that successful vaccines will be distributed internationally.
>
> The Covid-19 Vaccines Global Access facility (COVAX), to which the UK has made up to £548 million available will provide access to vaccines for lower income countries – including one billion doses for developing countries worldwide. The UK through the VTF has helped to develop the COVAX facility and has shared its expertise and people with COVAX to support their global efforts.

The reality was that sharing vaccines internationally was a political decision rather than something the VTF could seriously influence. We provided lots of support to COVAX but decisions on what vaccines to share were made by the politicians.

Finally, we failed to meet Goal 3: to build permanent pandemic capabilities in the UK. In writing my six-month goals in June 2020, I set out comprehensive targets, namely to

> ensure the UK has the manufacturing surge capacity and supply chains to manufacture at least 70m doses of at least two different

vaccine modalities in addition to bulk antibody manufacture within four months during a pandemic at reasonable cost, which is able to operate commercially outside pandemics.

We did not achieve this.

We were not able to secure government backing for an industry partnership to build bulk antibody manufacturing capability in the UK, despite significant interest from several companies to build new facilities including in the North of England. This is serious: it means that the UK does not have a secure supply of bulk antibodies. Antibodies can be used as prophylactics and therapeutics during pandemics as well as treating cancer and inflammatory diseases in normal times. So not only are we vulnerable from a pandemic supply perspective, we have also lost an attractive economic opportunity. At a time when politicians are beginning to wake up to the challenges of energy and food security, pandemic security is no less important.

We failed to get the Vaccine Manufacturing and Innovation Centre on a secure footing before I left at the end of 2020. VMIC's remit was to support scale-up and development of new innovative vaccines, as well to manufacture population-scale vaccines. While the 'virtual VMIC' worked well for bulk manufacturing at Oxford Biomedica, the Government has now sold VMIC in Harwell to the US company Catalent. It is not clear what guarantees the acquiror has given to provide the range of scale-up manufacturing capabilities and development resources needed to explore novel vaccines in the future.

Finally, we were not able to build bulk mRNA manufacturing onshore, despite funding the Centre for Process Innovation and the Cell and Gene Therapy Catapult through its new Braintree site to create these capabilities. I don't believe that waiving patent rights is the correct way to boost global supply, as many commentators seem to think. In June 2022, I was pleased to see that the government signed a deal with Moderna to open a research and manufacturing center in the UK. This should provide the mRNA infrastructure and skills we need.

As a nation, we failed in other ways too. But these were the result of political decisions.

We bought a portfolio of vaccines before we knew which if any would work. As it turned out, the vaccines were vastly more effective than anyone could have predicted. This means the UK has a broad choice of different types of vaccine. The clinical data I have seen suggests that mixing and matching vaccines helps improve the durability and level of protection, and also that the vaccine-hesitant would be more willing to accept the more traditional vaccines.

But unfortunately, the protein-based and whole virus vaccines we bought have not yet been used either as boosters, or as primary vaccines for unvaccinated and perhaps vaccine-hesitant individuals. Only vaccines from Pfizer, Moderna and AstraZeneca have been deployed in the UK to date. Novavax's approved vaccine has not been used, J&J's approved vaccine has apparently been abandoned and Valneva's approved vaccine has been cancelled. GSK/Sanofi's vaccine has not yet been approved. This lack of diversity is a potential public health weakness, but it has also undermined the wider UK vaccines industrial strategy.

The ethos of the VTF team, originally with the approach of working *with* vaccine companies and manufacturers, seems now to have shifted from 'partner' to 'adversary', when the VTF moved from BEIS into the Department of Health on my departure. I've already flagged some of my views about this department. It seems that the VTF project teams are no longer led by industry experts working closely with vaccine companies to deliver shared goals. Now the teams seem to be led by generalists with an arm's-length, often adversarial approach – acting as policeman and marking homework, rather than offering valuable and expert support as a partner.

Once the first three vaccines were approved by the MHRA, it appears that the government lost interest and momentum in capitalising on the broader opportunities offered by Novavax and Valneva to provide both public health resilience and economic growth. In hindsight, I think we should have doubled down on experts to support Novavax and Valneva, especially in manufacturing; both were indeed successful clinically, but when compared to the original schedule, ended up with significant manufacturing delays.

Ineffectiveness of global response

I am particularly disappointed by the poor response to managing the pandemic internationally.

Despite the Government's generous early pledges to support the global pandemic response, the actual UK international vaccine contribution has been weak overall. By March 2022, the UK had donated only thirty-two million doses, fewer than Germany, France and Italy, all of which were much later into the game than we were.

To give some idea of scale, by this time, according to Airfinity, the US had donated 419 million vaccine doses globally.

The UK isn't even in the top ten of per capita donations world-wide, despite the success of its vaccine procurement. But the UK had a high share of the AstraZeneca vaccine, so the widespread disparaging international comments seems to have contributed to global unwillingness to use this vaccine. These statistics sit uneasily with the Prime Minister's instruction in my original mandate letter to secure and deliver vaccines quickly to the UK and abroad.

High-income countries acquired the vast majority of early vaccine supply without sharing their doses with those most at risk around the world. By January 2022, high-income countries had administered 1.8 vaccines per person. For low-income countries, only one in ten people had been vaccinated. At one point, the state of California had acquired more vaccines than the whole of Africa.

The WHO noted that the consequence of rich countries hoarding vaccines is that low-income countries are poorly vaccinated, creating 'the risk of more dangerous and vaccine resistant variants emerging'. This is precisely what has happened with the Delta and Omicron variants, causing yet more pandemic infections and deaths.

The Covid-19 pandemic highlighted the lack of investment in vaccine development and manufacturing capacity in low- and middle-income countries, specifically the African continent. This is where the UK and Western nations should be focusing their efforts. We need to build specialist manufacturing skills and infrastructure around the world.

The international vaccine consortium COVAX was slow to get going, and I saw a global community that was highly political in its approach – again often focused on process rather than outcome. COVAX's global facility did not always deliver the vaccines requested. Africa was forced to buy about forty per cent of its vaccines through direct bilateral deals with vaccine companies. The VTF's Tim Colley and his team, working with Andrew Witty and others, worked relentlessly to promote equitable vaccine distribution. Sadly, it hasn't been equitable.

Reflections on working with government

FOCUS ON PROCESS NOT OUTCOMES

Officials in Whitehall are not rewarded for specialist skills or finding innovative solutions to complex challenges, but for adhering to the correct procedures. I saw an almost obsessive desire to follow the proper process and in particular to avoid any suggestion of personal error or possible criticism.

Our VTF processes were robust rather than perfect, but they worked – and they delivered the outcome.

Official paranoia about how to handle the media and the media's possible reaction held back the pace of execution, as did hesitancy over risk. It's much safer for officials, who focus on political and presentational risk but generally know little or nothing about actual commercial or scientific risk, to drag their heels regarding complex decisions rather than risk career suicide by pushing ahead with an even vaguely controversial task.

This presents a paradox, since the desire to avoid risk often makes it worse. Not understanding or considering the longer-term implications of action or inaction frequently creates a much bigger unknown risk that falls on others, or on society as a whole. That is a completely perverse and potentially disastrous outcome. I do not think that the civil service understands this point.

LACK OF RELEVANT SKILLS

In my seven months at the VTF, I was disappointed by the nearly complete absence in the civil service of scientific, industrial, commercial and manufacturing skills. And if these skills are not in the BEIS, which also funds academic research, then where are they? The pressures to limit headcount in Whitehall meant that officials appeared to use strategic and operational consultants as an alternative. This had the added benefit, from their viewpoint, of providing a degree of official deniability. But such an expensive and short-term use of consultants does not help build this capability within Whitehall itself.

Very few Permanent Secretaries, the senior civil servants who are ultimately responsible for the commissioning of work, have STEM degrees. Less than ten per cent of graduates entering the Fast Track civil service scheme have STEM backgrounds. Instead, Whitehall is dominated by historians and economists, few of whom have ever worked outside the official and political worlds.

Politicians are no better. In general, MPs lack relevant skills and industrial, commercial or practical non-political experience. Ministers are not appointed based on skills and expertise and are rotated on average every eighteen months or so. This revolving door policy is too short to build up any pretention to expertise in even a single area. As Patrick Vallance has made clear, without any scientific expertise it is difficult even to frame the right question when considering policy options and making decisions.

There were, of course, exceptions. Nadhim Zahawi, as life sciences minister in BEIS, had a genuine interest in our sector, as well as lots of energy and an understanding of science and business. He trained as an engineer and so had a strong understanding of the operational aspects of our work and the commercial dynamics we faced.

The consequence of being surrounded by humanities and economics graduates meant that there were very few people in government with the experience to challenge our work, other than to object to the process we followed.

GOVERNMENT'S FRAGILE RELATIONSHIP WITH INDUSTRY

Even in BEIS, there seemed to be very few people who understood how our industry works, or who had any real relationships with the key companies and their leadership teams. This unfamiliarity was reinforced by an innate cultural hostility to business with deep suspicion about industry motives. Companies were seen and treated as money-grabbing fat-cats, whose only interest was to rip off the taxpayer.

I don't like being fleeced any more than the next person. But the Government appears to have no means of differentiating between rent seeking and rip-offs versus valuable corporate behaviour.

In November 2021 I was asked to give the prestigious Romanes Lecture at Oxford University, in which I highlighted, as an example, the government's inexplicable decision to cancel the Valneva contract three weeks before its Phase 3 trial results were received. This decision was apparently taken on the basis that ministers believed that the vaccine would never be approved, on what official advice remains unclear.

Whatever the reason, it was an amazingly foolish and short-term decision. After Ian McCubbin had identified this whole inactivated viral vaccine opportunity, we had, with the support of ministers, encouraged Valneva to upgrade and expand its manufacturing plant outside Glasgow. We thought that Valneva's traditional vaccine would be a safe choice for the VTF portfolio, with capacity to produce variant vaccines or vaccines against new pandemic viruses in the future. Even though it would come on line after the early vaccines were approved, we felt this was a very valuable option for boosters, for children and for export. It would have been especially useful for those worried about accepting a new vaccine format.

As it turned out, the Phase 3 data announced in November 2021 showed that the vaccine was highly effective and safe. The premature cancellation meant that the EU terminated their supply discussions and one hundred plus new jobs at Valneva were immediately lost.

When it cancelled the contract, I doubt the Government considered the needs of COVAX, which badly required stable vaccines which could be sent to low-income countries. Nor did it consider the need to build resilience in the UK's pandemic preparedness capability with a new flexible state-of-the art manufacturing plant. Nor the long-term economic opportunity in Scotland to build high-value advanced medical products for export.

The Government appeared to be solely focused on reducing its financial commitments. The UK contract allowed for 'at-will termination', subject to paying costs incurred up to that point. But by alleging breach, the Government sought to avoid even paying for the costs which Valneva had incurred in good faith.

As part of its contract with VTF, Valneva ran the clinical trials, scaled-up and manufactured the vaccine as well as upgrading and enlarging their facilities.

I spoke to people at highest level of Government who were shocked by what was happening. But there was to be no amicable wind-down with a company that had massively extended itself to help during the pandemic crisis. The Government instead continued with aggressive allegations of breach of contract, apparently driven by a desire – never denied – to avoid paying Valneva for the work it had done. These were costs incurred at the request and for the convenience of the Government.

Since then, Scottish Enterprise has pledged to make up some of the UK Government's funding shortfall, and the EU has signed a contract for the supply of sixty million doses. But, as I said in my Romanes Lecture, some might consider this behaviour by the

Government as acting in bad faith. It certainly sent the worst possible message to any future UK industrial investor or life sciences partner. Valneva was ultimately approved by the MHRA, which justified our confidence in the company – but only after the Government had controversially, and in my view improperly, cancelled the contract.

Recommendations for improvements in the future

I have often been asked about the lessons of the VTF, and what we can all do better next time. My immediate response is that we need better vaccines. The ones we are using now are excellent for stopping serious disease and hospitalisation. But we need next-gen vaccines that will be a lot better at protecting against infection and transmission, and last for longer. We need vaccines that will protect against all coronavirus variants (and ideally against flu and other respiratory viruses such as RSV too) and that are stable at room temperature. Even better, we need vaccines that are needle-free and can be self-administered – whether a pill, patch or spray with a single dose. Calling all innovators around the world to help!

My longer answer is that we need a fundamental reset that goes far beyond addressing individual symptoms. It will be very expensive not to address these issues now. While my experience working in government was on vaccines, what I saw was symptomatic of broader concerns across sciences more generally, so we need to act now to avoid being left behind globally.

Here, then, are five broad recommendations for the future:

I. REWARD OUTCOME NOT PROCESS

My first recommendation is to refocus Whitehall and government on outcomes not procedures. There are lots of easy wins here.

Professional development and promotions should focus not on rapid rotation between roles and departments as is the case now, but on contributing skills of demonstrable value. As part of professional development, I would reward specialist science skills as much as generalist skills, and explicitly reward tempo and focus on outcomes. I would also punish for failing to act.

I would change the current system to reflect the proven practices of organisational management in the private sector. This means promoting the outperformers rapidly and culling the deadwood. I would seek robust references on past performance of prospective candidates. I find it bizarre that the civil service presently recruits people from outside based on references but bars the use of references internally. How on earth can you tell if someone is any good unless you talk to the people they have previously worked with and for?

I would mandate that mid-level civil servants should not be able to climb the Whitehall ladder without at least two years of productive industrial or commercial secondments and public sector operational delivery experience. Unless they see how companies work from within, I don't see how officials can discharge their roles effectively.

I would also make changes to improve the effectiveness of government itself. I would train ministers in commissioning, business and financial skills and make such training mandatory for upward elevation to senior roles. Ministers should be chosen on the basis of skills and relevant experience rather than simply on perceived loyalty.

I would introduce serious relationship management with key sectors. I would assign Ministers to manage relationships with CEOs of the leading bioscience companies operating in the UK. Sir John Bell and Sir John Symonds have developed a robust life sciences strategy with government and this can help provide the roadmap. The role of ministers should be to build closer relationships with bioscience leaders and instil new confidence that the Government is serious about working with them and supporting their work for the long term.

Ours is a small industry, and fiascos like Valneva do not leave a good taste. Only by building trust with these critical organisations can we encourage them to invest in the UK, providing jobs, economic growth, and crucially resilience against future healthcare threats.

2. EMBED SCIENTIFIC THINKING AND SCIENCE IN POLICYMAKING, JUST LIKE ECONOMICS

When we wrote Business Cases at the VTF recommending the purchase of vaccines, the Whitehall template required multiple different areas of analysis including strategy, economics, commercial, finance, management and legal. But not, astonishingly, science.

In the VTF, our due diligence provided that scientific and technical underpinning, but I would require the science case to be made for all government decisions. The science case should be added to the Whitehall template. Scientific evidence should be central to policy and decision-making and should be just as important as economics. Creating a science case would also have the effect of stimulating wider and more in-depth understanding of science across Whitehall.

I would give the science advisers within each government department more authority and status to influence policy and decision-making based on scientific principles. I would appoint advisers based on their industry experience and problem-solving track record. I would incentivise departments to collaborate on relevant areas of science.

Finally, I would encourage the government to embrace the scientific method. This means enquiry, experimentation, observation and the accumulation of evidence and knowledge. Whitehall should be charged to challenge orthodoxy, but be flexible to pivot and change in response to new information, data and evidence. Using the scientific method can help deal with uncertainty and manage risk.

3. COMPLETELY OVERHAUL THE RECRUITMENT, PROFESSIONAL DEVELOPMENT AND INCENTIVES OF CIVIL SERVANTS

Science-related competencies, problem-solving and quantitative analysis should be essential skills for officials in today's data-based and innovation-driven economy.

I would set a target of recruiting fifty per cent STEM graduates at entry, prioritising those with research, analytical and statistical expertise. New STEM graduates should also have some training in economics so that they have a breadth of relevant skills. It is much easier to train scientists in economics than the other way round! Massachusetts Institute of Technology – MIT in Cambridge, Massachusetts – does this really well; they produce lots of brilliant PhDs trained in finance, accounting and economics.

I would take measures to slow down the turnover within the civil service, so as to build up specific, valuable expertise.

I would fire half the people dealing with public affairs communications across government, as I cannot see what the supposed 120 comms people in BEIS actually achieve. I would redeploy this talent to more productive ends. This would send a clear signal that the focus on government is on the delivery of outcomes rather than on spinning.

In the private sector, incentives are widely used to implement change. So, one suggestion would be to delay awards of honours to civil servants and politicians when they retire, so that a better judgement could be reached of their actual achievements and effectiveness while in post.

4. APPOINT A SENIOR AND PERMANENT PANDEMIC SECURITY CAPABILITY

The reason why the VTF was required in 2020 was that there was no one to advise on this work in government. Healthcare threats are just as serious as national security and defence and should be treated with at least the same importance. We invest in our conventional and special forces, we recognise the importance of developing our intelligence services, and we plan and train for a vast array of difference scenarios, yet we are neglecting the most likely and potentially most severe collective threat to the nation – the next pandemic.

I would appoint a permanent pandemic security expert from the private sector, perhaps as or alongside an experienced senior minister, with authority for building and maintaining a co-ordinated UK pandemic preparedness capability.

As it does with defence and security, this will involve close collaborations across Whitehall as well as with companies and governments globally. We will need to continue to invest in next generation vaccine and antiviral therapeutic formats, partnering with researchers and AI experts to predict future pandemic threats as well as to design new vaccines and therapeutics. The government will need to provide a budget for this work. I recommend that this individual reports to the Prime Minister, just like I did.

5. AGREE A STRONG INTERNATIONAL APPROACH FOR
THE FUTURE MANAGEMENT OF PANDEMICS

The Western countries were too slow to join together, and too self-interested. Of course, it is essential for democratically elected governments to protect and support their citizens, but the Covid-19 pandemic has been made worse – including for those citizens – by the West's instinct to hoard vaccines. While the UK fared well, as matters have turned out so far, global surveillance to identify pandemic threats and emerging variants could be considerably more thorough and more joined up.

It is essential that the UK, and maybe the G20 and other motivated countries, invest in building vaccine manufacturing facilities around the world, especially in Africa. These facilities should ideally be located in low-population countries, to mitigate the risks of their being swamped by domestic vaccine needs, and so the imposition of export bans. We need to build the skills, infrastructure and capabilities to make safe, approved vaccines, and to do so quickly in a pandemic. Such skills and facilities are relevant for all advanced medicine manufacturing, so an investment here will help build global health security as well as long-term economic growth in these countries.

I don't pretend to have all the solutions, and there are plenty of experts in global health, but we must agree a robust long-term basis for funding the provision of vaccines to low-income countries. Agreeing the scope of COVAX in 2020 was too slow. And this delay caused unnecessary deaths.

VC mindset

That leaves one final thought. As a lifelong venture capitalist (VC), I tend to see everything through that lens – 'If the only tool you have is a hammer, it is tempting to treat everything as if it were a nail.' Even given all my inherent bias, I think that the VC mindset was one of the drivers of the success of the VTF in 2020. This mindset could be applied across different sectors to address major social challenges, whether aging populations, national security or climate change.

The VC mindset means recruiting an expert team, empowered to act quickly. VCs are expert in managing uncertainty and risk and they recognise there will be losses as well as wins. Funding will be staged against achievement of milestones, and ventures which fail are cut quickly. But to maximise the chances of success, VCs work as partners with their companies, adding value where they can and supporting them in whatever ways can help them succeed. VCs also bring in specific experts, explore innovative solutions and lean on existing relationships to improve the chances of success. And incentives are aligned. If the company succeeds, then the VC succeeds too.

In wartime, both actual wartime and quasi-wartime scenarios such as the Covid-19 pandemic, government is the market, maker and buyer of critical services and products. In peacetime, we need to make changes to ensure that the UK has the competence and judgement to make policy and spending decisions, that as far as humanly possible will protect its citizens and the wider world.

Covid-19 has shone a spotlight on our country in many ways, and among them it has highlighted the effectiveness and collaborative nature of UK life sciences in times of crisis. Now, in more normal times, we need to improve the effectiveness of government in working with the life sciences sector, to ensure our domestic resilience and security, to create long-term economic prosperity and to protect the lives and freedoms not just of the vulnerable, but of us all.

ACKNOWLEDGEMENTS

I have tried to reconstruct the events of 2020 as carefully and accurately as I can. Inevitably there will be mistakes and things I have misremembered for which I apologise in advance. But the gist is right.

I am proud to have played a small part in the fight against the Sars-Cov-2 coronavirus when NHS workers have risked their health and their lives in fighting Covid and have been at the heart of the vaccine roll-out. But of course, without the brilliant Vaccine Taskforce team, the scientists, clinicians and our partners, we could not have succeeded.

A huge thank you to Sir Patrick Vallance who spearheaded the creation of the Vaccine Taskforce. Without everything Patrick did, we would have been in a much worse place. And thank you to Boris Johnson for listening to Patrick and trusting me as Chair.

I would like to thank my deputy Clive Dix for his brilliant partnership and wise judgements, and for giving me the confidence to lead. Massive thanks also to my Director General Nick Elliott who remained calm and shrewd throughout; and to all the VTF steering group: Steve Bates, Tim Colley, Divya Chadha Manek, Ian McCubbin, Maddy McTernan, Dan Osgood, Ruth Todd and Sir Jonathan Van-Tam for the long days, sleepless nights and immense hard work. And especially for putting up with my endless demands and quirks.

Without the expertise and advice of our due diligence teams, we might have made the wrong calls, so thank you to Steve Chatfield, Giovanni Della Cioppa (and to Rino Rappuoli for the introduction), Helen Horton, John Tite and David Watson. And thank you to Rasmus Bech Hansen and Caroline Casey from Airfinity for their incredibly helpful intelligence on the vaccine landscape.

Thank you for the brilliance, resilience and patience of the Oxford teams: to Sandy Douglas, Dame Sarah Gilbert, Catherine Green, Sir Adrian Hill, Sir Peter Horby, Teresa Lambe, Sir Martin Landray, Sir Andrew Pollard, Maheshi Ramasamy, Gavin Screaton, and to the indomitable Sir John Bell.

Without the expertise, speed and altruism of AstraZeneca, Oxford's academic vaccine may not have had the global success that it did. So, thank you to Per Alfredsson, Matt Doherty, Jennifer Eck, Andy Evans, David Hunt, Richard Marshall, Sir Mene Pangalos, Mark Proctor, Sir Pascal Soriot and Tonya Villafranca.

Thank you also for the innovation and ambition of the Imperial team led by Robin Shattock, Simon Hepworth and Sue Marlow. And thank you to the broader team at Imperial, Garth Rapeport, Chris Chiu and Peter Openshaw who played such critical roles.

Thanks also to the BioNTech and Pfizer teams for being such great partners and pioneers: Sean Marett, Janine Small, Ben Osborn, Darius Hughes, Stephen Lockhart and John Young.

Thank you to the uber professional Janssen team: Tobias Kamphuis, Jaak Peeters, Nerida Scott, Paul Stoffels and Johan Van Hoof.

I enjoyed working with the Novavax team a lot so thank you: Stan Erck, Greg Glenn, Brian Rosen, Silvia Taylor, Brian Webb and James F. Young.

GSK/Sanofi gave very helpful advice and support throughout so thank you: Thomas Breuer, Roger Connor, Sue Middleton, Thomas

Triomphe and to the Sanofi team: Roman Chicz, Ian Gray and Paul Hudson.

Congratulations to the Moderna team and thank you: Patrick Bergstedt, Said Francis, Thomas Kuhlman and Phil White.

Many thanks for the enormous contribution that Valneva has made: David Lawrence and Thomas Lingelbach.

And thank you to all the other vaccine and antibody companies even though we did not ultimately work together.

Without the BioIndustry Association (BIA) the UK would be nowhere. The manufacturing CDMOs and government bodies stepped up right at the start and without their heroic efforts the UK would have been much slower in scaling up vaccines. I don't have the space to name everyone involved in each team but this was a massive collective effort. Thank you: BIA (Netty England, Jack Fellows and Eric Johnsson), CGTC (Matthew Durdy and Stephen Ward), Cobra (Peter Coleman), CPI (Lucy Foley, Juliana Haggerty, Frank Millar, Dave Tudor), Fujifilm Diosynth (Martin Meeson and Steve Bagshaw), IBM (Kevin Hall), Innovate UK (Sarah Goulding, Andy Jones and Ian Muir), MHRA (Ian Rees), Oxford Biomedica (John Dawson), Oxford University (Sandy Douglas), PHE (Karen Powell), UCL (Pamela Tranter) and VMIC (Matthew Duchars). The 'BIA Antibody Taskforce' provided expert advice to us so thank you: Deirdre Flaherty, Paul Kellam, Jane Osbourn and Paul Varley. Bioprocessing training and skills were critical to our success so thank you to Kate Barclay and Laura Bennett.

We were quite forward in approaching good people we knew to be seconded into the VTF, so thank you to Priya Mande and to the board and shareholders of PsiOxus for sharing her with us. Thank you to Kate Hilyard for leading the immunology assays. Thanks to the Immunology Network led by Paul Moss and to Peter Wrighton-Smith from Oxford Immunotec.

The MHRA played a blinder. So, thank you to Dame June Raine from whom I have learnt so much and Kirsty Wydenbach.

Without the Principal Investigators and their clinical research teams we would not have had such great clinical data so quickly. Thank you to Saul Faust (Southampton), Adam Finn (Bristol), Paul Heath (St George's), Dinesh Saralaya (Bradford), Matthew Snape (Oxford), Andrew Ustianowski (Manchester) and to Fiona Burns, the PI on the Novavax trial at the Royal Free Hospital, for looking after me.

Thank you to the NIHR team and the leaders of the Registry: John Nother, Jonathan Sheffield, Imogen Shillito, William van't Hoff and Nicola Yallup.

Thank you to the experts whom I constantly leant on for advice and guidance: Seth Berkley from GAVI, Sir Jeremy Farrar from Wellcome Trust, Richard Hatchett from CEPI, Richard Mason from Military Intelligence, Trevor Mundel from the Gates Foundation, Moncef Slaoui from Warp Speed, Sir Mark Walport, former Chair of UKRI and Sir Andrew Witty, former WHO Vaccine Envoy. Special thanks to Sir Richard Sykes for auditing our work so deftly in June and December, and providing wise advice throughout.

Thank you to Georgie Cameron and her team at Admiral Associates for their expert advice in launching the Registry and their skills in handling the media even in the face of unnecessary attacks. Thank you to John Davidson, Sarah Hornby, Jo Taylor and Kate van Beek. Thank you too to Fiona Fox and her team at the Science Media Centre and to science journalists who reported so accurately and clearly.

Thank you to my friend Justin Rushbrooke for his advice and to the wise counsel and support of Nigel Tait and his team from Carter Ruck.

Thank you to Tim Palmer for sending me bottles of gin when the going got tough. To Sarah for her beautiful bowls, and to my friends and neighbours for their cakes, cards and unwavering encouragement. Thank you Gruff for keeping me fit.

And thank you to my teachers at St Paul's Girls' School for encouraging me to specialise in science, to my professors at Oxford and Harvard University. Something sank in.

Thank you to my team at SV who kept the ship firmly afloat while I was away doing vaccines. You (sadly) demonstrated that I was dispensable! So heartfelt thanks to my partner and co-conspirator Houman Ashrafian for managing SV, our companies, our investors and our partners to continue our goal to develop life changing medicines for patients. Thank you Alanya for infinite patience and dedication – my diary and I could not have managed without you. Also to Ruth McKernan for persuading me that working with government was doable.

Thank you to my brother Harry who gave me such important advice and really helped with the manuscript. Any budding authors would do well to look up Jerichowriters.com. And thank you to my other brother Kit, and Sarah and Nuala for warmth and wit.

Thank you to my mum Elizabeth Bingham for my robust genes, my seedlings and for not letting me believe everything I read.

Thank you to Jesse. There is no part of this book that hasn't been infinitely improved by Jesse's guidance and red pen. And thank you to our children Sam, Nell and Noah who kept my spirits up at all times. Not to mention singing, putting up pens, introducing me to rose harissa and night-time bike rides.

The development of vaccines was a triumph of scientific and industrial collaboration. Speed, skill and altruism shone through. I am thrilled that so many women have made such enormous contributions to science, healthcare, manufacturing and technology during the pandemic.

I hope this encourages more girls to pursue careers in these sectors.

★

Tim has a somewhat shorter list of individuals whom he would like to acknowledge. Above all else, this includes his wife Julia who has lived with this project throughout. He would also like to thank his son George Hames whose work on a previous (alas abandoned) book on the Covid-19 crisis proved to be immensely useful for this tome. Thanks to George's brothers Edward and Tom Hardman (and Edward's wife Frances). Tim would like to thank his parents (Fred and Daphne) for bringing him into this world. He would like to salute Patricia Simmonds, his mother-in-law, and Keith, his late father-in-law, who died either of or with Covid-19 on 23 March 2020 about fifteen minutes after the first national lockdown was announced and his brother-in-law Michael Simmonds and his husband Nick Gibb MP. Finally, he would like to appreciate the support of family friends, Michael Burke, Diane Rochford, Sebastian Rochford Burke, Robert and Christine Ironmonger and Abby Sinclair.

★

We would both like to thank our wonderful literary agent Caroline Michel, CEO of Peters Fraser and Dunlop, and her associate Kieron Fairweather. Thank you to our admirably dynamic publisher Sam Carter of Oneworld Publications who has made immeasurable improvements to the manuscript, ably assisted by Rida Vaquas and Holly Knox.

Finally, there is one person without whom this book would never have been written at all. He is Ian Armitage, a pioneering private equity professional who now spends much of his time as an astute philanthropist and investor. Tim, Kate and Ian worked together at the British Venture Capital Association in 2014–15 when Tim was Director General, and Ian and Kate were both board members. It was Ian's idea that the story of the Vaccine Taskforce should be set out in print and it was his backing for Tim that allowed it to happen. It also meant that the two of us could work together which has been incredibly stimulating and unexpectedly fun. It is, therefore, with enormous gratitude that this book is dedicated to Ian alongside Jesse (Norman) and Julia (Hames).

Kate Bingham and Tim Hames

UK VACCINE TASKFORCE
MEMBERS 2020

My original plan was to list everyone who had worked for the VTF in 2020. But to comply with GDPR, I can't do this without consent from anyone who is not already publicly associated with the VTF. If any 2020 member of the VTF would like to be listed, please email info@oneworld-publications.com and we will include your name in the next print run.

Steve Bagshaw	Nick Elliott
Devina Banerjee	Netty England
Steve Bates	Oliver Excell
Kate Bingham	Deirdre Flaherty
Alanya Calleja	Kevin Hall
Georgie Cameron	Kate Hilyard
Stuart Carroll	Sarah Hornby
Divya Chadha Manek	Helen Horton
Steve Chatfield	Andrew Jones
Chris Chiu	Paul Kellam
Giovanni Della Cioppa	Alistair Kirk
Timothy Colley	Sara Mackmin
Jo Crowhurst	Priya Mande
Clive Dix	Richard Mason

Ian McCubbin
Neil McNeil
Madelaine McTernan
Chris Minchell
Anil Mistry
Emma Moir
Jane Osbourn
Dan Osgood
Tara Raveendran
Matthew Skulskyj
Lynne Swinamer
Jo Taylor

Keith Thompson
John Tite
Ruth Todd
Dave Tudor
Paul Varley
Kate van Beek
Jonathan Van-Tam
Stephen Wallace
Tessa Walton
David Watson
Sue Williams

INDEX